ANCIENT ALIENS: CLOSE ENCOUNTERS WITH HUMAN HISTORY

ANCIENT ALIENS:
CLOSE ENCOUNTERS WITH
HUMAN HISTORY

· · · · · · · · · · ·

PHILIP COPPENS

ROSEN
PUBLISHING®

New York

This edition published in 2015 by:
The Rosen Publishing Group, Inc.
29 East 21st Street
New York, NY 10010

Library of Congress Cataloging-in-Publication Date

Coppens, Filip.
Ancient aliens: close encounters with human history/Philip Coppens.
    pages cm. — (Conspiracies and cover-ups)
Includes bibliographical references and index.
ISBN 978-1-4777-8157-9 (library bound)
1. Human-alien encounters. 2. Civilization, Ancient—Extraterrestrial influences.
3. Extraterrestrial beings. I. Title.
BF2050.C675 2014
001.942—dc23

2014028543

Manufactured in the United States

First published as *The Ancient Alien Question: A New Inquiry Into the Existence, Evidence, and Influence of Ancient Visitors* by New Page Books/Career Press, copyright ©2012 Philip Coppens

Acknowledgments

I have been posing the Ancient Alien Question for almost two decades now, and hundreds of people have joined me on my quest for an answer. I would particularly like to thank Erich von Däniken, Uli Dopatka, and Gene M. Phillips for inviting me, as a young man in my 20s, to air my side of the debate at a number of Ancient Astronaut Society World Conferences in the 1990s. Special thanks, of course, are due to Erich, as he is not only the pioneer in this subject, but also the man who kindly wrote the foreword for this book, which is truly a great honor and privilege. I thank Giorgio Tsoukalos for a friendship that began then, which has grown since, and especially for his unending devotion to the cause, however hard the going sometimes became.

My drive to answer the Ancient Alien Question was reignited by the wonderful team at Prometheus Pictures, the producers of *Ancient Aliens*. Your professionalism is equal to none and every minute of filming was a joy (yes, David Silver, that includes the eight-hour wait for a replacement camera in Rennes-le-Château). However, I need to single out Kevin Burns for his commitment and vision, as well as Evan Goldstein, with whom my part of the story began.

This book would not have come about without the vision of Michael Pye.

In my circle of friends, I would like to specifically thank: Paige Tucker; Jason Gossman; Sarah Symons; Mary Parent; Patrick Ruffino; Patrick Bernauw; Marc Borms; Chris Norman; Cris Winter; Gerard Lohan; Eileen, Cathy, and Janeth Hall; Debbie Nicastro; Herman Hegge; Dawn Molkenbur; Tobi and Gerda Dobler; Marianne Wilson; Theresa Byrne; Cynthia James and Carl Studna; Gail Heron Sterling; Geoff Potts; JoAnn Parks and MAX; Peter van Deursen and Anneke Koremans; Isobel Denham; Kelly Cole; Philippe Canal. Apart from being the best friends anyone could desire, you make life beautiful. By default, I will have forgotten some, and I sincerely apologize for that!

I thank the research and devotion of the following authors and often friends: Robert Bauval; Graham Hancock; Greg Taylor; Wim Zitman and Hendrine; Sam Osmanagic and Sabina; John Major Jenkins; Geoff Stray; Hartwig Hausdorf; Robert and Olivia Temple; Mark Pilkington; Howard Crowhurst; Hugh Newman; Andy Collins; David Hatcher Childress and Jennifer; Jeremy Narby; Antoine Gigal; Ralph Ellis; Jack Sarfatti; Uri Geller; Joseph Davidovits; John Ritchie; Duncan Lunan.

Special appreciation to the photographic skill of Rivelino, and the fantastic photo shoots in the streets and along the canals of Amsterdam.

I would like to thank my thousands of Facebook friends and followers, who allow me to have a great virtual banter on a daily basis!

Each and every member of the Coppens, Sonck, Harkey, and Smith family, though I need to specifically mention my parents; my brother, Tom, and his wife, Kathleen, and my nephews, Daan and Arne; Papa and Mama; as well as Patrick, Conor, and Shane.

Finally, I thank Kathleen. It is best summed up by Giorgio, who in December 2009, when he saw me again after many years, heard me speak about you and to you on the phone and concluded that there was absolutely no doubt that I was totally in love. You changed my life, made me into a new man, and were a constant source of inspiration throughout the writing of this book, and will remain so. As fate would have it, the final paragraph of this manuscript was written on our anniversary. Semper.

Contents

Foreword
By Erich von Däniken

Dear reader,

From 1953 until 1958, I was a student at the Collège St-Michel
in the small Swiss town of Fribourg. There, among other things, we
learned Old Greek and Latin. Time and again we had to translate
texts from the Bible, the Old Testament, from one language to the
other. I read in Genesis: "But when people started to multiply on
the earth, and daughters were born, the sons of God saw that the
daughters of men were beautiful, and they took as their wives any
they chose."

I was confused. What "sons of Gods"? My professor said that
this referred to "fallen angels." *What "fallen angels"*? I wondered.
Later, we translated the words of the biblical prophet Ezekiel as he

described seeing a vehicle come out of the clouds with a lot of noise. He described the wings of the vehicle, its wheels, and even its metal legs. My professor believed that this referred to a vision, and that Ezekiel had described "God in his chariot."

Doubts gnawed at my beliefs, and, as a 17-year-old, I wanted to know whether other cultures in ancient times had similar descriptions to those of the Christian-Jewish tradition. So while my classmates were playing soccer, I sat in the university library and read...and read...and read. Soon I understood that many ancient human traditions contained similar reports to the stories in the Bible, only with other words and other heroes. Could one believe the texts?

At that time I decided to take those texts that had been written in the first-person, as an eyewitness report, to be true. And there were many. Again and again I encountered descriptions of "gods" who drove around in the clouds, of beings who came down to earth with "smoke, fire, earthquakes, noise," and selected people who had the privilege of being taken to "heaven" by the "gods." There, these people experienced a training program. Even artificial insemination and changes in the genetic code were reported in the old books I read.

At some point I realized that all these actions were not compatible with the traditional idea of the "Beloved God." But when I replaced the word *god* with the word *extraterrestrial*, everything suddenly made sense.

In 1965, I had my manuscript for *Chariots of the Gods* finished—but found no publisher. From 24 publishing houses, I got the usual rejection: Sorry...not suitable for our program...too unprofessional...and so on.

At that time I was director of a first-class hotel in the Swiss ski resort of Davos. (I come from a restaurant family.) One of my guests, the chief editor of a German magazine, was friends with the head of the large German publishing house ECON, and he arranged a meeting for me. *Chariots of the Gods* thus found a publisher. In May 1968, the book was #1 on all German best-seller lists.

I gave up my hotel career and devoted myself entirely to my new profession: researcher of ancient texts and searcher for clues in archaeological ruins. *Chariots of the Gods* was a provocative book that had more than 230 question marks. I had written the book not in a scientific form of writing, but in a popular one. It contained some errors (unavoidable for a young author). In the scientific literature it is no different: There, too, one finds errors in books that are 30 or 40 years old. After all, science is a living thing, and not a religion, in which one must simply believe. After *Chariots of the Gods* there followed a further 28 nonfiction books. I corrected old errors and misunderstandings in the new books. Today there is for me not the slightest doubt: Millennia ago, extraterrestrials visited the Earth. These visits became myths, legends—and also religions.

We should set up new branches of science; for example, a "Central-American-Indology," in which the links between the cultures of Central America and India are examined. Or a "New-Age-Philology," in which old texts can be retranslated such that the religious "heaven of bliss" becomes "the universe" or—depending on the circumstances—"giant spaceship." Perhaps a science of the "Chronology of the gods," in which the unspeakably complicated information about the gods from antiquity would be investigated in the aim of finding a common denominator. The questions *when* and *how often* the aliens were here would also be a research objective of the "Chronology of the gods."

Our limited knowledge of reality is mostly based on the present—quite understandable, because we live in the "now" and not in "the day before yesterday." What happened today, what makes headlines today, concerns us. What happened yesterday no longer interests us. This fatal short-sightedness robs us of the sense of historical events. We feel the presence of knowledge as a culmination of all knowledge from the past. We claim to be the best-informed society, and accordingly, all our ancestors knew much less than we do. However, this attitude makes us proud; it makes us rather contemptuously overlook the past. This is dangerous, because those who do not know history are doomed to repeat its mistakes. This backward attitude has led historians and archaeologists to believe little about our ancestors. The astonishing thing is the smoothness with which this fallacy is implemented in practice: If an old historian such as the Greek Herodotus, 2,500 years ago, says something that fits into our current knowledge, then that statement is happily placed on record. But if the same historian, often on the same page, makes a remark that does not suit us, we label it false without batting an eyelash, calling him a liar, an exaggerator; degrading him to the level of an ignorant person who has not understood anything.

For example, the Egyptologists of our time copied from Herodotus that Pharaoh Menes (circa 2920 BCE) diverted the Nile above Memphis. With closed eyes and ears is suppressed what the same Herodotus, 18 lines later in Volume 2 of his *Histories*, notes: "After Menes followed 330 kings, whose names the priests read aloud from a book." The diversion of the Nile and the name "Menes" fit, but the 330 kings interfere. The same Herodotus, in chapters 141 and 142, also tells of his visit to Thebes (today's Luxor). There the priests showed him 341 statues, and the high priest said to each statue a few words. After the visit, the chief priest assured Herodotus that these 341 statues represented a period of 11,340 years. At that time the gods had been on Earth in human form. What did we do with those 11,340 years? They are dislodged, swept off the table, reinterpreted as a misunderstanding, or read as "lunar years," although in Egypt there never was a moon year and Herodotus nowhere used one.

Around 300 BCE, there lived in Egypt a high priest named Manetho. He was the "Scribe of the Holy Temple" and surfaces

Foreword

with the Greek historian Plutarch as a contemporary of the first Ptolemaic king (304–284 BCE). To Manetho are attributed eight works, including a book on the history of Egypt and the so-called Book of Sothis, which includes the names and years of the reigns of the prehistoric kings, dating back to the time of the gods. Manetho wrote that the first ruler of Egypt was Hephaistos. Then follow Chronos, Osiris, Typhon (a brother of Osiris), and then Oros (also Horus), the son of Osiris and Isis. Manetho: "After the gods the family of the offspring of the gods reigned 1,255 years, and in turn other kings reigned 1,817 years. After which are 30 kings, Memphite, 1,790 years. After which there are others, Thinite, 10 kings, 350 years. And then the kingdom of the offspring of the gods, 5,813 years."[1]

The original writings of Manetho are no longer available. But the historian Julius Africanus and the Church father Eusebius (died 339 CE), who, as Bishop of Caesarea and an early Christian chronicler, was received into the Church history, copied large parts of Manetho's work. Here Eusebius expressly noted that the dates of Manetho were probably lunar years—which, added together, *still* account for more than 14,000 solar years.[2]

Diodorus of Sicily, who lived in the first century BCE, was the author of a 40-volume historical library, in which he reported in the first book that the old gods "had in Egypt alone, established many cities" that from the gods descendants had emerged, of which "some of them became King of Egypt." People in that distant time were forerunners of Homo sapiens, or a primitive form that "only the gods had weaned...not to devour each other."[3] From the gods the people learned (according to Diodorus) the arts, mining, the manufacture of tools, the cultivation of the soil, and the production of wine. Also, language and writing came from these helpful celestial beings. Diodorus used sources that are not available to us anymore. He nevertheless knows exactly what he's talking about, as in the 44th chapter he compares the Egyptian dates with his own visit to Egypt: "Over

Egypt Gods and Heroes have ruled, not much less than 18,000 years, and the last divine king was Horus, son of Isis. Of human kings that have ruled the country by Moeris not much less than 5,000 years up to the 180th Olympiad, in which I came to Egypt myself."[4]

So goes the ancient literature. Worldwide. Always these "impossible numbers" are cited, which our historians and archaeologists do not want anything to do with. In a joint effort, we should go over the books and subject the knowledge of our primal ancestors to a new analysis. To that end, this work by Philip Coppens is an important and outstanding contribution.

What is it about the Ancient Alien Theory that is important for the human race? They were here, these aliens, thousands of years ago, and they promised to return. It is not only ancient cultures that knew the idea of a second coming, but also the modern, vibrant religions: Christians are waiting for Jesus, Muslims for the Mahadi, the Jewish community for the Messiah, and so on. Can every religion be correct? What if all of them are wrong?

This "Shock of God," as I call it, is preventable. We can prepare ourselves for the return of the extraterrestrials. All of this has nothing to do with a new religion. I will turn myself around in my grave if my ideas turn into a cult. It is not about belief—it is about testing. The facts are there.

Yours sincerely,
Erich von Däniken

Introduction

Have we been visited by extraterrestrial beings in the past? Did these "ancient aliens" contribute to the birth of human civilization? Do our ancient monuments contain evidence of their presence?

In 1968, Swiss hotelier Erich von Däniken posed these key questions in his book, *Chariots of the Gods*, which sold more than 63 million copies, proving that millions of people in the Western world were open to the notion that we might have been visited by extraterrestrial beings. Now, 35 years on, there is still tremendous popular interest in this "Ancient Alien Question." The television series *Ancient Aliens* is continuously rated as The History Channel's most watched documentary. What was originally conceived as a two-hour special grew into a phenomenon that saw more seasons added, each with more shows than it had before.

Ancient Aliens

But despite media and public interest, the phrase *ancient aliens* remains taboo within the scientific community. Whether or not we were alone in the human adventure that was early civilization is a question that is still not answered, or even addressed. The closest topic explored by science is the Search for Extraterrestrial Intelligence (SETI), executed by a handful of radio astronomers, each one of whom continuously sees his budget challenged and then removed because it is perceived to be a niche discipline. Even so, SETI merely investigates whether there are extraterrestrial civilizations somewhere out there, in the depths of the universe. It is far less controversial than the Ancient Alien Question, about which science states that it knows that there were no alien interventions in our past. Is science right?

In *Chariots of the Gods*, von Däniken posed more than 230 questions, each one of them challenging the scientific paradigm of the late 1960s. Demonstrating that science had not properly explained a given structure, artifact, or legend, he then queried whether they could be evidence of an alien visitation or intervention. He pointed at the pyramids of Giza in Egypt, and the phenomenally intricate walls at many of the Peruvian archaeological sites, such as Sacsayhuaman, where the most oddly shaped stones, some weighing more than 100 tons, fit perfectly together, as if first designed on a computer screen. Questions are also raised by quaint descriptions in the Bible, such as how Lot's wife could possibly have turned to salt when looking back at Sodom being destroyed by God. And what are we to make of Genesis 6, where there are references to giants and "the sons of God" coming down to mate with "the daughters of men"? The question of alien intervention in our planet's history has continued to be posed...and only in the rarest of occasions has science provided an answer.

"Science"—I use the term occasionally to encompass the entire scientific field and its members; similarly "archaeology"—feels it should not have to answer these questions, because, as scientists see it, they are posed by an idiot (though on occasion science will try to find a nicer word for it). When Erich von Däniken spoke at Northwestern University in Evanton, Illinois, on December 2, 1973, he invited the audience to look at the evidence with "today's Space-age eyes—not the eyes of yesterday." During the questions afterward, he was asked if he had received any academic degrees, to which he replied, "If a degree were offered in my subject, I would be the professor." On February 12, 1975, the University of Bolivia actually bestowed him with the degree of Honorary Doctor, for his valuable services toward the enrichment of the academic and scientific heritage of the university, as well as for bringing to the attention of the world the importance of the archaeological treasures that exist in the altiplano of the Andes.

What von Däniken wrote in 1968 is the underlying principle of the Ancient Alien Theory: that we need to re-examine all our archaeological records through the lens of the late 20th and early 21st century, as we might have failed to recognize that some ancient structures were built with highly technological means and/or by, or with the help of, nonhuman intelligences.

Though science as a whole has refused to accept this invitation, individual scientists have. Dr. Hermann Oberth, the father of modern rocketry, was once asked about the Ancient Alien Theory, and he replied that he was convinced that there were other intelligences in the universe, and that they had probably visited Earth in ancient times. He added, "Most conservative scientists are against everything that is new, just as they were against my plans to build rockets that could take man to the moon. Scientists who considered themselves to be very modern-thinking people announced that man might reach the moon, but not before many, many thousands of years."[1]

Skeptical scholars have claimed that they do not need to look at the Ancient Alien Question, because von Däniken has been proven wrong. They cite certain ancient sites, like Peru's famous Nazca lines, hundreds of lines drawn on the desert sands of Peru, somewhat resembling the layout of a modern airport, which were hardly explored by scientists at the time von Däniken brought them to global attention. *Could it be an ancient airport?*, von Däniken pondered. The suggestion has since become one of the most famous examples of the Ancient Alien Question. By posing it, von Däniken forced scientists to study the lines closely, after decades of neglect. He forced science to come up with an answer. Though the answer revealed that the Nazca lines were *not* the product of an alien civilization or intervention, the investigation did radically alter science's understanding of this region and the local civilization, discovering that it was far more advanced than previously assumed. There is even speculation that the people who created these geoglyphs between 450 and 600 CE possessed hot air balloons!

On rare occasions such as this, science has addressed the Ancient Alien Question, but still, at more than 40 years later, most of the 230 questions posed by von Däniken remain unanswered by science. Worse, science refuses to pose the question itself, and, almost half a century later, it therefore remains the task of people outside the scientific community to ask the question again.

Since 1968, many new archaeological discoveries have been made. Some, like the pyramid complex outside of the Bosnian capital of Sarajevo (discovered in 2005), have clearly illustrated the standoff between traditional historians and archaeologists when it comes to discoveries that challenge our accepted view of history. Western European and American archaeologists even declared a boycott of the site: They all agreed that they would not provide archaeological services for the project. I participated in a scientific conference on these pyramids in August 2008, which was attended by more than 50 academics, including 20 leading Egyptologists, among them the deans of archaeology of Ain Shams and Cairo University. During the debates, the audience

Introduction

was astonished to learn that these leading Egyptologists did not know that officially the oldest pyramid is now in Peru (dated to 3200 BCE, almost a millennium older than those of Egypt). Neither did they know that the world's largest pyramid is in Mexico (Cholula). When the leading archaeologists of our time do not even know—or can't accept—the latest scientific findings in their field, is there any hope that they will ever be willing to address the Ancient Alien Question?

The answer is a clear *no*, as can be seen in one of the most famous examples of the Ancient Alien Question: the Great Pyramid of Giza. Elements of the Giza Plateau continue to pose serious problems to established archaeologists: Egyptologists declare that the blocks of the Great Pyramid were hewn from a nearby quarry, but French scholar Joseph Davidovits strongly disagrees. Davidovits is internationally known and respected as the father of the new science of geopolymers. Geopolymerization is a chemical process through which artificial stone can be created that is almost indistinguishable from natural rock. This science is considered to be a revolution in the building industry. Applying this new science to old discoveries Davidovits has identified the blocks of the Great Pyramid as geopolymers, not natural rock—a conclusion he has reached through both chemical and observational analyses. However, leading Egyptologists, such as Dr. Zahi Hawass, misinterpret his conclusion by thinking that Davidovits is saying the blocks are "cement," and vociferously proclaim that the Great Pyramid is clearly not made of cement, and therefore Davidovits is wrong! Hawass's approach to new and radical conclusions is typical of science as a whole when confronted with new discoveries; rather than trying to respond to a most scientific theory supported by substantial evidence, Egyptologists prefer to ridicule and push aside this esteemed scholar. Of course, assuming that Davidovits is right—and he more than likely is—the next question to be asked is how the builders of the Great Pyramid were familiar with a chemical science that was only (re)discovered in the late 20th century. That is exactly the question Egyptologists do not want to hear asked, for it is automatically followed by the Ancient Alien Question.

Today, hundreds of sites across the world display signs that the history of these monuments is far more involved than mainstream archaeology would have us believe. One of the more intriguing locations is Puma Punku, a small archaeological site that is part of Tiahuanaco on the Bolivian altiplano near Lake Titicaca. The site comprises stones that are so perfectly assembled that a razor blade cannot be inserted between them, and some of them weigh more than 100 tons. Most critically, some stones are very oddly shaped: One block has a six-sided opening on one side that becomes, on the other side of the same stone, a five-sided opening. Why anyone wanted or needed a stone with an opening that goes from a hexagon to a pentagon is a question archaeology has not posed—maybe because, even in the 21st century, modern science has no need for such intricate designs. There is also one stone at Puma Punku that has a 6-millimeter-wide groove containing equidistant drilled holes, which is an incredibly detailed feature to accomplish even today, and which clearly had some purpose to the site's builders 1,500 years ago. Archaeology remains largely silent about Puma Punku.

The Ancient Alien Question is a worldwide problem. When we look at Cuzco (Peru), we see intricate walls, some having 12 angles to each stone, on top of which very basic stones have been piled. It is clear that the lower levels are of a technologically sophisticated society, predating the Inca civilization, which used it as a foundation for their own buildings. But which civilization that was is a question not posed by science.

There is also the gigantic standing stone in Carnac (France). The Grand Menhir, weighing 340 tons, was cut from a single piece of granite-like rock and transported "by a means we do not understand for certain," according to the site leaflet. Elsewhere, there are three 800-ton stones incorporated into the base of the

Introduction

Temple of Baalbek in the Lebanon, while one weighing more than 1,200 tons lies abandoned in a nearby quarry. At the end of the 20th century, we had equipment capable of lifting up to 2,000 tons, but were still unable to transport these blocks. This means that the engineers of Baalbek possessed a technology that surpassed modern capabilities. Archaeology has never been able to explain how our ancestors were able to accomplish this.

Because archaeology and history are such insular disciplines—always looking within a culture but never across cultures—a series of pertinent questions are never asked, let alone answered. For example, why is it that in 2500 BCE, the three pyramids of the Giza Complex in Egypt were laid out in the formation of Orion's Belt, and that about two millennia later, the three pyramids of Teotihuacán in Mexico, on the other side of the world, were constructed similarly? Clearly, there was a common understanding or an exchange of ideas, yet science dogmatically states that there was no such contact, and that the cultures of Egypt and Central America developed completely independently from each other until Columbus discovered the New World in 1492. Why is it that cultures that supposedly never met still held gold to be the metal of the gods, even though gold as such has little practical value or utility? Such evidence makes it clear that our ancestors communicated far more frequently than accepted history dictates. At the very least, a group of experts must have traveled around the world, sharing advanced knowledge among many ancient civilizations.

In 1968, von Däniken also identified a number of artifacts that in his opinion were evidence of advanced technology, such as the ancient Baghdad electric batteries, which have now been proven to indeed be able to hold electrical charges, and a small bee-like carving that he believed was a tiny representation of an airplane, which has since been reproduced and is shown to have perfect flying capabilities. Terra Preta, a type of soil, has recently been identified as being present across the Amazon basin. This soil type is incredibly fertile—and artificially engineered. The presence of this soil is evidence of a lost civilization that was once spread across the Amazon; as many as 20 million people lived there at one point. Indeed, in 1541, Spanish friar Gaspar de Carvajal chronicled the area's "cities that gleamed white," with "fine highways" and "fruitful lands."[2] But shortly afterward, none of these cities could be found, so scientists referred to de Carvajal and others reporting similar bustling cities as deluded. Today, this erroneous interpretation of history is slowly being rectified, as it has been archaeologically shown that these cities indeed existed. This lost Amazonian civilization shows how quickly traces of an advanced civilization can disappear, and demonstrates that our perspective on history needs to adapt and change on an almost daily basis. Alas, this happens all too seldom. By posing the Ancient Alien Question, it will become clear whether civilization (agriculture, organized religion, and so on), that great adventure our ancestors began several thousands of years ago, was a purely human enterprise or was aided by otherworldly intelligences. Indications are that the truth about our past is far more interesting than what we have believed, and this book will show that the evidence clearly suggests that we were not alone.

Indeed, what astronomy is discovering is that the building blocks of life did not originate on Earth, but came here from outer space. In the early 1970s, Francis Crick, the co-discoverer of the structure of DNA, argued that DNA was too complex and intricate to have been accidentally created in primordial ooze on planet Earth. Half a century later, he is being proven correct. Scientific juggernauts like the Lawrence Livermore National Laboratory are now proposing that comets brought amino acids to our planet. British astrophysicists Sir Fred Hoyle and Chandra Wickramasinghe have even shown that a number of viruses—including the common flu virus—come from outer space, arriving on our planet via passing comets whose dust settles in our upper

Introduction

atmosphere. In November 1999, the Leonids meteor train was found to contain signatures of organic material. All life on Earth is therefore likely to be of extraterrestrial origin, with the building blocks of DNA, according to the latest scientific research, even spontaneously being created in interstellar space. This suggests that DNA-based life is intrinsic to the very fabric of the universe; it means that somewhere out there, the odds are good that we could find life as it exists on our planet.

Our ancestors understood that they were not alone, and said as much. The legends of so many civilizations speak clearly of a time when "the gods" walked among us. The Egyptian civilization is but one of several that have such references. Science scoffs at these legends. But, as in the case of the Amazonian civilization, it is clear that the stories were finally found to have been true—we just chose to ignore or disbelieve them, until the evidence was so substantial and direct that it had to be accepted as factual. Hundreds of legends exist about deities that descended from the skies and interacted with humankind and taught them civilization. Almost every ancient civilization on this planet has written accounts that say as much. This is a cross-cultural phenomenon, occurring in civilizations that officially never had any contact with each other. The Ancient Alien Question is merely asking, if some legends are proving to be true, whether other legends could be true as well. And there is substantial evidence, from the Giza Plateau to the mountainous heights of Peru, that the answer to the question is *yes*—We Were Not Alone.

Chapter 1

One Small Question for Man, One Giant Question for Humankind

The term *First Contact* applies to the moment when we employ a means of communication with alien beings that also have a means of talking back to us. There are several ways First Contact could happen. The most popular idea, originating from the UFO phenomenon, is the image of ET landing on the lawn of the White House and greeting the president. However, scientists hope *they* are the first to establish communication with ET, via radio signals. In science fiction, First Contact was most famously envisioned in the television series *Star Trek*. It occurred—or should that read, *will occur?*—on April 5, 2063, when Zefram Cochrane made the first warp drive flight on a ship called the *Phoenix*. The flight was noticed by the Vulcans, who then landed on Earth to make contact with humankind, telling us that we were not alone in the universe. From there on, we boldly went where no one had gone before.

In real life, theoretical physicist Michio Kaku has said that First Contact would be an earth-changing event. After the discovery of fire, agriculture, writing, and mathematics, he says, "First Contact would top everything."[1] It would be the most giant step humankind had ever taken, or encountered. The question, of course, is whether First Contact has already been established, or is still a thing of the future. Proponents of the Ancient Alien Theory argue that First Contact has already happened, but that this momentous event has somehow been forgotten. Could that truly be the case?

Contact

In 1997, I attended the Ancient Astronaut Society's World Conference in Orlando, Florida, and visited the Kennedy Space Center while I was at it. That same week, I saw the enjoyable movie *Men in Black* and the deeply inspired *Contact*, the latter based on a Carl Sagan novel in which the Search for Extraterrestrial Intelligence project (SETI) makes contact with an alien civilization. What happens next is relevant to the Ancient Alien Question: The message humankind receives contains a blueprint of an extremely complex device, whose ultimate purpose is unknown, but is assumed to send a person to the aliens' home world. The construction of the device also requires the active cooperation—and finances—of several nations. Once it is built, someone is selected to occupy the "seat," which turns out to propel this person to another dimension, apparently light-years away, where the "only" thing that happens is a conversation with these alien beings—without leaving behind any material evidence that contact has been made between two intelligent species. When the human scientist asks the aliens whether they constructed a series of what seem to be stargates or interdimensional portals, the alien answers that they do not know who built this mechanism through which they and other species can hop through the universe; someone long ago built it, but the *who* is unknown.

The ensuing congressional hearings formally conclude that there is no evidence that contact was established, and that the device malfunctioned. Though the scientist swears it sent her into another dimension, none of the instruments there to monitor the device registered this event.

Let's take this outside of the realm of fiction. If this scenario had occurred in real life, the only physical remains of contact with aliens would be two devices: one blown up by a terrorist on Cape Canaveral and the other on an island near Japan. Fast-forward several hundred (if not thousand) years, and what would we see? What would we remember? Would anything survive? Let's be totally realistic, and ask what our ancestors a thousand years from now will find at Cape Canaveral. Will any of the metal launch platforms survive? Unlikely. Some of the ruins of the buildings might be found, but maybe not even that. If we are lucky, there might be accounts of how, for a brief period of time, humankind sent people into space, and that we once went to the moon. Today, there are several popular authors who hotly contest that we ever went to the moon, arguing that the landing was just American propaganda created to instill a sense of superiority over the Soviet Union at the height of the Cold War. Though I do not agree, let us assume that some of their writings also survive the test of time, and the future historians incorporate them in their accounts. Future history might then say that "There was a widely held belief that humans walked on the moon, but even in their own times, some thought otherwise." The historians might go on to say that they have found archaeological evidence at Cape Canaveral, but that the question of whether or not we ever went into space, or to the moon, cannot be proven.

I hear some thinking, *Hold on here. What about the hundreds of satellites orbiting our planet? Isn't there physical evidence of our presence on the moon? The photographs of Cape Canaveral and its numerous launches, the hours of footage shot onboard the various Space Shuttle missions?* Assuming it all survives the next millennium, it will indeed all add to the controversy, but if a historian wants to explain it all away, he can do so. That is precisely what those unwilling to believe we went to the moon are doing at this very moment.

Contact's main message is that *belief* and a willingness to explore are two vital ingredients required to establish and accept alien contact. It was the final message that Carl Sagan sent out to humankind, as he died during production of the movie. But his quest for extraterrestrial life began many decades before.

The Man Behind *Contact*

Sagan's youth was characterized by an interest in science fiction. The remainder of his life was spent in an effort to answer the question of whether or not there was life elsewhere in the universe, including how to contact it, if so, and whether it had already contacted us. In 1951, when he first set foot in the halls of academia, he predicted that humankind would set foot on the moon by 1970. It was not a scientific prediction; he just hoped that we would take this important step, just as his heroes in science fiction books had done. Sagan felt that the moon, then the rest of the solar system, and finally the entire universe had to be researched in an effort to find life. He wanted to be Captain Kirk.

His first scientific writings speculated on the possibility of life on Jupiter, Venus, or Mars. Even though science constantly gave a negative answer to every question he posed, Sagan would not stop asking. When it became likely that our entire solar system was devoid of any intelligence, he felt we had to set our sights on other such systems.

In retrospect, such enthusiasm might seem childish. But when Sagan started his quest, in the early 1960s, there really was little if anything known about the physical conditions on our neighboring planets. Many scientists were open to the possibility that our own solar system contained other life-forms. Various UFO sightings and stories, specifically during the previous decade, seemed to underline this possibility. Sagan was initially intrigued by these accounts, but his own research convinced him more and more that the methodology used by UFO researchers would never lead to a satisfactory answer. He also believed that the "evidence" they presented was not evidence at all. In later years, he would do his best to undermine the entire field of ufology, as he felt it was a powerful detraction from where the real quest for extraterrestrial intelligence should be directed.

Sagan spearheaded the Western scientific search for ET, and however scientific his approach was, it is a fact that most other scientists looked down on him and his attempts. They felt it was an endless game; the universe was simply too big to find out whether, somewhere, life might have originated, too, and could be flourishing, with alien intelligences trying to make contact with us.

Sagan understood the difficulty of his quest; when he discovered that life did not exist on Venus, it merely meant he had to look elsewhere. It is like the famous Edison statement that he had found 2,000 ways of *not* making a light bulb before he found a way to make one. Sagan was inspired by his science-fiction heroes from his youth, who always went farther, pushed boundaries, and, to paraphrase Gene Roddenberry, boldly went where no one had gone before.

Sagan was a scientist, and felt that it was his personal mission to educate the public about scientific methodology. He feared that the public wouldn't understand his scientific methods because they seemed more alien than the intelligence he was searching for. He was horrified when he noticed that the public adopted "pseudoscience" as a methodology—it provided them clear, unambiguous answers to the questions everyone had, but for which science did not have definitive answers. He was thus instrumental in the creation of CSICOP (The Committee for Skeptical Inquiry), a group of skeptics who can be seen as the modern-day Inquisition, and who battle what they call "pseudoscience," whether that is ufology, the Ancient Alien Theory, astrology, or parapsychology. But in the end, Sagan became disillusioned with their methods, arguing that they were just as unscientific.

When NASA began to send missions to Venus and Mars, in an effort to map those planets, Sagan was there to make sure the missions would educate and inform the general public. He felt that those missions had to have cameras, which most scientists felt was unimportant. *What could a camera possibly contribute to scientific research?* they wondered. At first, Sagan's proposal was not accepted, but soon enough a camera became a standard feature on missions, to show the general public on an accessible level what those alien planets looked like.

It wasn't until the early 1980s that Sagan became a household name. The American television channel PBS created a 13-part series produced by Sagan, called *Cosmos*, which became the realization of his dream: bringing a scientific topic into the general household, via the medium most suited for that purpose—television. Sagan became the host of the series, and it was the perfect excuse for his scientific colleagues, who had always seen him as being on the edge of science, to proclaim they felt he was more of a celebrity than a scientist. They felt scientists had to live in labs and ivory towers, never leaving them to give an opinion on any show whatsoever. Science, they felt, had no requirement to be accessible to the general public.

In 1986, Sagan finished *Contact*. The book was largely autobiographical, mapping a scientist's quest to find extraterrestrial life. From the early 1990s onwards, Sagan knew that his life might not be long-lasting. He suffered from an illness that only bone-marrow transplants would heal. It created in him a sense of urgency, and also gave his work a more religious framework. The opposition between religion, the irrational side of human-kind, and science, the rational opposite, was found everywhere, from the pages of *The Demon Haunted World* to the screens on which *Contact* would posthumously be projected.

Selling the movie itself was a difficult exercise, as its subject was science—never as popular as science *fiction* in Hollywood. The movie strove to convince the public of the importance of the search for extraterrestrial intelligence, but it starred a single female as the main character. She was furthermore without children, and an atheist—three characteristics that did not sit well in America, and Hollywood therefore had to be more force-fully persuaded that the project had a chance of box office suc-cess. Eleven years later, on July 11, 1997, the movie *Contact* was shown in American theaters; the following month I would see it in Orlando. Seven months earlier, Carl Sagan had died in Seattle, following a lung infection. He himself had made an interdimensional voyage, but unlike the scientist of *Contact*, he would not return to tell the tale.

Message in a Bottle

Sagan was responsible for three attempts to notify the uni-verse of our existence: In 1972–3, the *Pioneer* spacecraft was equipped with plaques of his design, detailing a diagram of a hydrogen atom; a pulsar map with the sun at the center, show-ing the relative distances of 14 pulsars and the binary code of their periods; figures of a nude man and woman set in front of a to-scale silhouette of *Pioneer*; and a sketch of our solar system. Then, in 1974, Sagan, together with Frank Drake, created the so-called Arecibo Message, in which a message was beamed into space, aimed at the M13 star cluster. The message consisted of 1,679 binary digits that, when collected, formed an image of our little blue planet. The message incorporated the numbers 1 through 10, as well as the atomic numbers of the elements found in DNA, the formula for DNA, a DNA helix, and much more information about life on planet Earth. In 1977, Sagan created the Voyager Golden Records, containing 116 images detailing life on Earth and methods of finding us, just in case something intelligent were to stumble upon the little probe.

In the five decades of humankind's space exploration, we have sent a small number of these and similar messages into the universe, some riding with our interplanetary probes, others specifically broadcast via radio to distant galaxies where we hope someone is listening. At the same time, we have used our telescopes to listen to anyone out there who might be broadcasting—so far, without any success. In fact, some scientists believe that an extra-terrestrial intelligence is unlikely to use radio waves to communicate their presence because radio signals have to compete with background noise and require a selection of radio frequencies, thus reducing the chances of being discovered.

Instead, it is thought by some, including American physicist Paul LaViolette, that beacons, sometimes referred to as "galactic lighthouses," would be built, announcing to anyone in the galaxy that they are not alone. John Learned of the University of Hawaii has proposed using the Cepheid variable stars (the brightest of the "variable" category of stars, which change luminosity through time) as a beacon, arguing that by manipulating their pulsation cycles, much like Morse code, the stars could be used to broadcast a message to the universe that would be far more likely to be received by alien civilizations. He has outlined a theoretical model as to how this could be accomplished, and though we currently lack the resources and some of the technology to accomplish this, future generations might advance as far—extraterrestrial civilizations might have advanced as far a long time ago.

The idea of galactic lighthouses was originally proposed by Thomas Gold in June 1968, but has been most popularly promoted in the last decade by Paul LaViolette. His book, *The Talk of the Galaxy: An ET Message For Us?*, argues that some of the pulsars that we have discovered *have* actually been modified by an extraterrestrial intelligence, and that our radio telescopes are therefore picking up an extraterrestrial message; we just refuse to accept it.

The idea that pulsars could be created by an extraterrestrial intelligence received widespread attention in 1974 with the discovery of PSR 1053+29. Its extraterrestrial origin was proposed because of its strangely constant pulsation rate. The pulsar also betrayed no sign of spinning down, which meant it was not behaving as "normal pulsars" did. Alas, observations of this specific pulsar throughout the following years showed that it was in fact slowing down, though at such a slow rate that it still begs the question of whether it might be an extraterrestrial signal. Since then, more than a dozen other such pulsars have been identified, and scientists continue to question whether these are indeed galactic lighthouses, though most scientists *believe* that, no matter how weird, we are confronted with a totally natural phenomenon.

The best candidate for a galactic lighthouse is PSR 1937+21, one of the fastest pulsars in the sky, flashing 642 times per second, with a very constant pulsation period. In fact, the beacon surpasses the best atomic clocks in its precision. The so-called Millisecond Pulsar is also unique in that it is one of two pulsars known to emit giant pulses, becoming the brightest pulsar in the sky and therefore making it easily identifiable. After all, we have identified it, and the only question we have is whether its period is artificially created or natural, with the usual division between the two camps.

LaViolette, in *The Talk of the Galaxy*, states that, "If extraterrestrial civilizations are attempting to communicate with us and are distinguishing their transmissions by doing 'something that can't be done in nature,' the pulsar signals certainly are the closest thing known to fit this criterion." But apart from communication, he also points out that the pulsars are ideal for space navigation, as they provide a means whereby a spacecraft can determine its position through triangulation. In short, pulsars could be the echoes of the imaginary network of space portals that Sagan concocted to allow for interdimensional travel in *Contact*.

Were We Not Alone?

The Ancient Alien Theory proposes that we should not merely be looking into the deep abyss of space, trying to find out whether contact *can* be established, but that contact might have already been established, in the ancient past, and that physical or other traces of this contact are still visible or present here on planet Earth.

The theory of evolution suggests that we are the pinnacle of creation, and science is quick to assume that we are at the pinnacle of civilization. We think of today's world as unique compared to previous ages, but our everyday existence is only partially so:

- The ancient Romans would create one-way traffic in certain streets to cope with peak-hour traffic.
- Pompeii had arm-waving traffic policemen to cope with congestion.
- Babylon had street signs 2,500 years ago.
- At Nineveh, there were "no parking" signs.
- Antioch had street lighting.
- The Aztecs used a permanent colored strip in the paved road to divide the two lanes of traffic.

By today's technological standards, the Apollo space capsules of the 1960s were pretty basic, and the computers NASA used to put a man on the moon are far inferior to your average modern laptop. In fact, what the moon landings showed was how relatively easy—provided we had the correct understanding of astronomy and astrophysics, and a means of escaping the Earth's gravity—a voyage to the moon was. Isn't it interesting that, whether we look at the Ancient Egyptian or Mayan civilizations, we always find that these ancient peoples possessed a body of astronomical knowledge far surpassing their requirements—in fact, far surpassing our own requirements?! Immediately we see one of the three basic ingredients of space travel fulfilled by what scientists until a few decades ago considered to be primitive societies.

That these societies were not primitive at all is precisely the message Erich von Däniken beamed into the world in 1968. His medium was not a radio telescope, but a book, *Chariots of the Gods*. Though he popularized the topic, von Däniken did not create the subject. Some of the pioneers of this could-be science were actually Russian. Nicholas Rynin (1877–1942) graduated from the Imperial Institute of Communications of St. Petersburg in 1901. After the Revolution, he wrote a three-volume book called *Interplanetary Contacts* (1928–1932), credited as the first encyclopedia on the history and theory of rocket technology and spaceflight. Less-well-known is that in it he analyzed ancient legends regarding air and space ships, from the Greek legend of Icarus to the Hindu Epic of the Mahabharata. He also tackled Jules Verne's *From the Earth to the Moon* and found that the novel's premise was infeasible. But in his opinion, the science of the ancient legends *was* feasible.

Rynin himself was walking in the footsteps of Yakov Perelman, who in 1915 published *Interplanetary Journeys*, the world's first book on the science and technology of spaceflight. Years ahead of Western Europe, Perelman was popularizing the idea of rocketry and spaceflight for a Russian audience, resulting in the Soviet Union sending the first man into space in 1961.

Most of the rocket pioneers, including the likes of Hermann Oberth and Werner von Braun, all wanted to use their rocket technology in the hope that it would propel humankind into the depths of the universe, and establish contact with alien life. Instead, their inventions were principally used to fight terrestrial wars.

Constantine Tsiolkovsky (1857–1935) was probably the first person to realize that rocket technology was the means by which to travel into space. Along with Hermann Oberth and Robert Goddard, he is considered to be one of the great theoreticians of spaceflight. In the early 1930s, Dr. Hermann Oberth was not shy in attributing the honor of making people dream of exploring the galaxy to Tsiolkovsky, whom he identified as the father of astronavigation—traveling toward and through the stars.

In 1928, Tsiolkovsky published *Will of the Universe*, in which he wrote, "It is difficult for us to imagine a being superior to earthman. This narrow-minded view prevents us from picturing an intrusion of extraterrestrial entities in terrestrial affairs. Yet a great number of events still remain unexplained because of this attitude. Many curious happenings are recorded in history and literature." Tsiolkovsky was "only" a teacher in a provincial town, but he is considered to be a prophet of science and his papers were often discussed in the highest echelons of academia. He is considered to be the father of the multi-stage rocket, as well as the word *astronaut*.

In an issue of *Messenger of Knowledge* (Moscow, 1930, Nos. 5–6), Rynin and Tsiolkovsky spoke out in defense of aliens visiting Earth, with Rynin writing, "The statement that inhabitants of other worlds have not visited our planet is indeed corroborated by the accepted history of all countries. However, if we turn to the tales and legends of hoary antiquity we shall notice a strange concurrence in the legends of lands separated by oceans and deserts. This concurrence is contained in the fact that many legends speak of the visitation of earth by the inhabitants of other worlds in time immemorial. Why not admit that a grain of truth lies at the bottom of these legends?"

One Small Question for Man...

Fully 35 years later, the status quo of the scientific community on the Ancient Alien Question remained, which is why von Däniken posed it to a Western audience. Though he was, and is, by far the most popular author in the field, he was neither the first nor the only one to pose this question to a Western audience. Italian journalist and writer Peter Kolosimo received the Premio Bancarella, one of Italy's most prestigious literary prizes, for *Non è Terrestre* (*Not of This World*). Published in 1968, it was Kolosimo's fourth book exploring the mysteries of our planet, the first being *Il Pianeta Sconosciuto* (*The Unknown Planet*), published in 1959.

As mentioned, Carl Sagan, with the help of I.S. Shklovski, devoted a chapter of *Intelligent Life in the Universe* (1966) to arguments that scientists and historians should seriously consider the possibility that extraterrestrial contact occurred during recorded history. They concluded that:

- Interstellar travel on par with the rocket technology of the 1960s was within the bailiwick of other extraterrestrial intelligences, and, as a consequence, extraterrestrial visitations to planet Earth should not be ruled out—in fact, they were plausible.
- Legends should be seen as reliable sources, and some legends could indeed describe alien encounters.

In *Broca's Brain* (1979), Sagan nevertheless expressed disapproval of von Däniken, arguing that they had seemingly built on his ideas, not as though they were guarded speculations, but as valid evidence of extraterrestrial contact. It seems Sagan did not see the more than 230 question marks in von Däniken's book.

Sagan posed the Ancient Alien Question after being exposed to reports of hundreds of UFO sightings. One writer, Harold T. Wilkins, combed through ancient literature and legends to find evidence that our ancestors too had seen anomalous objects in the sky. He published on the subject in 1954, with *Flying Saucers on the Moon*. Meanwhile, another British writer, W. Raymond

Drake, went through the same material, scanning it for evidence of ancient aliens. In 1964, Drake published *Gods or Spacemen?*, the title alone clearly showing that the book posed the Ancient Alien Question. Drake said, "I aspired to collect as many facts as possible from ancient literature to chronicle for the past what Charles Fort has so brilliantly done for the present century. I spent many years reading the classics and ancient histories in many languages, and in 1964 published *Gods or Spacemen?*, the first of nine books, wherein I detailed my researches covering most countries of the world, proving, to my own satisfaction at least, that the gods of antiquity were spacemen, who landed and ruled our Earth in a Golden Age, bringing civilization to mankind."[2]

Fully aware of the religious implications of his writings, he felt the need to ascribe to the word *God* at least two meanings: One was for that Supreme Being, the other for the "Space Beings." He also expressed the hope that "this startling conception could prove the fundamental discovery of our century." Almost four decades later, in the teenage years of the 21st century, we know this hope did not materialize.

Before Sagan became a household name, von Däniken featured in a number of popular television programs and series. *In Search of Ancient Astronauts* aired in the United States in 1970, and the German television station SAT-1 ran a 25-part television series with von Däniken in 1993. In 2009, the American production company Prometheus convinced The History Channel to commission *Ancient Aliens*, a two-hour special devoted to the Ancient Alien Question. The show has since become a worldwide phenomenon, proving that posing the Question is part of our Zeitgeist. Clearly, among the general public, the Ancient Alien Question *lives*. So what is the reaction of the scientific community? It can best be summarized by quoting from a blog by Monty Dobson, dated January 21, 2011, titled "History Undoctored":

One Small Question for Man...

The recent trend of presenting pseudoscience as a subject worthy of serious consideration is dangerous to our educational system. As a history professor I am confronted each semester by students who believe the fantasy presented by shows such as The History Channel's *Ancient Aliens*, which perpetuates the notion that extraterrestrials with superior knowledge of science landed on Earth thousands of years ago, sharing their expertise.

This is concerning because the argument is predicated on the insulting premise that people in the past were less intelligent, creative and inventive than we are today. There is an underlying tone of cultural superiority, which implies that 'ancients,' who were likely brown, were incapable of independently developing the sophisticated technology and culture we *know* they had without help [emphasis added].

The show's premise represents a sanitized version of the previous century's colonial and often racist attitudes.

Dobson is typical of the modern scientist, who accuses anyone posing the Ancient Alien Question of being racist. Mudslinging is after all so much easier than a scientific debate. Isn't it ironic that he does not realize that his own belief, namely that he "knows" our ancestors did not receive help, is based on the assumption that science has "superiority" over the "pseudoscience," which is apparently "dangerous to our educational system"? I sincerely hope that the Ancient Alien Question *is* dangerous to the educational system, as well as science. It will be for as long as science ridicules the subject and negates the evidence that suggests that the answer to the Ancient Alien Question is *yes*—We Were Not Alone.

Posing the Ancient Alien Question is not racist, for it was the "people in the past" themselves who specifically said, in their writings, that the path of civilization was not built by them alone, but with the help of gods who contacted them. Civilization, in whichever culture you turn, is seen as a gift of the gods. This is precisely why scientists like Sagan became interested in the Ancient Alien Question. Or, to quote Sagan, "We make our world significant by the courage of our questions and by the depth of our answers."[3] The Ancient Alien Question is a small question for man, but a big question for humankind.

Chapter 2

Ancient Alien Theories

Alien Overlords

Some people believe that the Ancient Alien Question has an easy and straightforward answer: Yes. They were here.

One such person is David Icke. He was a BBC television sports presenter until, in 1990, a psychic told him that he was a healer, placed on Earth with a mission. On April 29, 1991, he appeared on the popular BBC talk show hosted by Terry Wogan, *Wogan*, and proclaimed he was the son of God. He announced to the British nation that evil had been in control of this planet for the past 12,000 years. He would later add that this evil force was reptilian and that underneath the British Queen Elizabeth II was a reptile in hiding (which we could apparently take quite literally, as per the television series *V*, in which alien beings basically had a human mask, which, if torn, would reveal their scaly reptilian hide). Ever since, Icke has traveled across the world, proclaiming that humankind is enslaved by alien overlords. In recent years most of his presentations and theories have focused on conspiracy theories, including those surrounding the events of 9/11.

Icke is typical of those arguing that the answer to the Ancient Alien Question is almost self-evident: From well- or less-known facts, they create a logical whole, in which some of the holes are either obscured or made evident by pointing out that we are, after all, confronted by a vast conspiracy, and that parts of the evidence by default are hidden from us.

For instance, it is a fact that the 400 richest people in America have as much money as the poorest 150 million Americans. Some of this money is "old money," and some of it is new. But for Icke, there is far more to it. He argues that there is a network of families who are today in control of the world, and have always been so. They were the elite installed by our alien overlords, and for more than 6,000 years they have ruled planet Earth. This "bloodline" can be traced from Sumer, via Rome, to the European aristocracy. From there, the bloodline was exported across the world through Colonialism and became the core movers of several secret societies. When these colonies attained independence, according to Icke, this was merely on the surface, as the family bloodlines and secret societies kept control over both Europe and its former colonies—or, in short, the entire world.

Icke therefore believes that events like the attacks of 9/11 have been manipulated, if not staged, to centralize power "to the point where humans are little more than controlled clowns," and throughout his series of books and presentations he compares humans to robots and asks them to rebel and break free from their enslaving, alien-appointed overlords.[1]

As extreme as Icke's conspiracy theory—for he believes everything is intertwined, so there is really only *one* conspiracy—sounds, he is neither the first nor the last to air such theories. Indeed, what Icke believes is what a lot of people believe is the truth about the "ancient alien agenda": In the past, an extraterrestrial race came to this planet and colonized it. At some point, these aliens either left or otherwise removed themselves from the stage, and human manipulators and/or the aliens behind the stage have continued to control humankind, very much like a zoo. That first zoo, it seems, was called the Garden of Eden.

The Gods of Eden

Is there a hidden hand manipulating world events, trying to set humankind against itself, promoting war whenever it can? Author William Bramley felt this was indeed the case, and reported on his findings in his 1989 book *The Gods of Eden*, which is basically about our alleged ancient alien overlords.

The book was advertised as "the chilling truth about extraterrestrial infiltration—and the conspiracy to keep humankind in chains." Bramley reached this conclusion a few years before David Icke. Though their theories are in essence identical—that an unseen hand was making sure we were fighting ourselves all the time, rather than "spiritually set ourselves free"—Icke opted for sensationalist gimmicks, while Bramley adopted a more phlegmatic approach. He wanted to address the greatest paradox of all: Why do religions preach forgiveness, kindness, and peace, but are at the same time one of the principle contributors to war, division, persecution, and oppression? Something was amiss in Eden, and for Bramley, it was the gods who were saying one thing but doing the opposite.

Bramley's thesis thus comes in two parts: First, the conspiracy to keep humankind enslaved. How? By continuously having us fight each other and making sure we are constantly either living in fear and/or slaves to something (in our time, mainly monetary debt). His analysis of the international financial world revealed that no one truly knew who pulled the strings and what the real foundation of worldwide economic policy truly was. It involved a number of "National Banks" that were in essence privately owned, which seemed to charge the various countries interest, which resulted in those countries imposing taxes and regulations on its citizens. For what and for whose benefit was never asked, for if asked, the answer would set the whole of humankind free from what was in essence a game devised by a handful of individuals, behind closed doors, somewhere, at some point in time. "Divide and Conquer" was Caesar's dictum; Bramley saw this as the operating principle across time and across the globe.

The second part of Bramley's theory involved who was behind this. Who were these people behind closed doors? Bramley went all out, and concluded they were alien beings. The idea may seem preposterous, but logically, who else but an alien could manipulate humankind across the globe, throughout time? Only someone who stood above it all...

Bramley noted that "the notion of alien intervention in human affairs is generally tolerated when it is expressed as a work of science fiction, but it is often poorly received when suggested as fact." He added:

> There are few subjects today as full of false information, deceit, and madness as "flying saucers." Many earnest people who attempt to study the subject are driven around in circles by a terrific amount of dishonesty from a small number of people who, for the sake of a fleeting moment of notoriety or with the deliberate intention to obfuscate, have clouded the field with false reports, untenable "explanations," and fraudulent evidence. Suffice it to say that behind this smokescreen there is ample evidence of extraterrestrial visitations to Earth. This is too bad.

Ancient Alien Theories

An in-depth study of the UFO phenomenon reveals that it does not offer a happy little romp through the titillating unknown. The UFO appears more and more to be one of the grimmest realities ever confronted by the human race.[2]

The UFO field is rich with stories of government conspiracies and cover-ups, all claiming that the governments of the world know the truth but actively hide it from their citizens, and that there is an extraterrestrial presence on Earth—and has been for many decades. What is intriguing is that Bramley wrote before the decade when a series of revelations from individuals who claimed to have served in military, intelligence, or government institutions began to "leak" to the public. These people testified to the presence of extraterrestrial races that competed among themselves and with clandestine human organizations for influence over humanity.

The most prominent figure in gathering the whistleblowers' stories is Steven Greer, who published them in *Disclosure: Military and Government Witnesses Reveal the Greatest Secrets in Modern History* in 2001. Greer has gathered the testimonies of more than 100 of these witnesses in written and/or video format, making them available for the general public as well as for a congressional inquiry. One of the most famous whistleblowers is Colonel Philip Corso, who alleged that President Eisenhower signed a treaty with extraterrestrial beings. In *The Day After Roswell*, he writes: "We had negotiated a kind of surrender with them as long as we couldn't fight them. They dictated the terms because they knew what we most feared was disclosure."

Most whistleblowers say that these treaties were established after the 1940s, following UFO crashes or contact being established. They say that it was done quite officially, though secretly. But where Bramley differs from this typical UFO stance is that he states that the aliens have *always* been present, and operate not via secret treaties, but via manipulation of governments, humans, or situations: war.

Bramley began researching the history of human warfare in 1979 and was initially merely going to focus on that phenomenon in his book. It was during this research that he identified a major contradiction: We pretend to be religious human beings, who state that there is a "soul" inside us. But thousands of years of religion still have not been able to create a worldwide paradigm shift to the idea that the soul is far more important than the body. In the materialistic 21st century, the body still reigns supremely. Despite proclaiming to be "spiritual," body characteristics seemed to divide us, specifically something as silly as the color of our skin. Why was it that skin color has been at the foundation of so much hate? For Bramley, the only logical conclusion was that someone very early on in human history had told humankind he was superior to the other skin tones—and told this to *each* group: blacks that they were superior to whites, whites over blacks, and so on. They did this so that whenever we met, we would fight.

"Human history is a seemingly endless succession of bloody conflicts and devastating turmoil," Bramley writes. He found another oddity: "Inexplicably, in the light of astonishing intellectual and technological advancement, Man's progress has been halted in one crucial area: he still indulges the primitive beast within and makes war upon his neighbors." Bramley argued that "it is easy to understand the mental stimuli in two alley cats squabbling over a scrap of food, but it would be a mistake to attribute as simple a state of mind to a terrorist planting a bomb in an airport."[3] Bramley thus felt that we could not simply blame it on the idea that humans will always fight. To underline the idea that we are not animals intent on war, he observed: "The Renaissance was a short period of history revealing that when repression is eased, when intolerance and war-inducing philosophies diminish in importance, and when people are able to think and act more freely, human beings as a whole will naturally and automatically move away from war." He thus concluded that humankind was not naturally prone to war.[4]

It seemed that throughout history, some hidden hand was constantly stirring nations, creating division, a cause for conflict for no apparent reason other than to divide and conquer. As this was a feature of most ages and most locations on Earth, Bramley found it quite logical to assume that it wasn't a group of people, like the Illuminati (the favorite culprits of some conspiracy scenarios), that could be this hidden hand. No, it could logically only be an extraterrestrial civilization. He labeled this hidden hand "The Brotherhood," which consisted of a group of humans with enormous power, but who themselves were controlled by our oppressive extraterrestrial ringmaster.

Bramley felt that very few people realized or even wanted to look at who started wars and for what purpose, simply because they were not looking at the world from the proper perspective: "Most comprehensive history books contain brief references to this type of manipulative third-party activity. It is no secret, for example, that prior to the American Revolution, France had sent intelligence agents to America to stir up colonial discontent against the British Crown. It is also no secret that the German military had aided Lenin and the Bolsheviks in the Russian revolution of 1917. Throughout all of history, people and nations have benefited from, and have contributed to, the existence of other people's conflicts."[5] In short, a conflict between two tribes normally came about when a third party was stirring up trouble behind the scenes. The worst rifts have been caused when an uninvited party decides to act as intermediary, most often whipping both sides into a frenzy, from which an *entente cordial* can never be reached.

Bramley noted that it was The Brotherhood who always, under whatever guise, tried to take control of the world—the stirrer behind the scene. But in the final analysis, *Gods of Eden*, despite its popularity, was never able to prove the existence of an alien brotherhood that had manipulated us from behind the scenes for millennia. But it did show powerful examples of how a few individuals could control many, and how contradictory humanity really is.

The 12th Planet

If aliens are to blame for most of the strife on our blue planet, where are they? Are they indeed, as Icke claims, hidden behind human flesh masks? Or are they instead directing the stage from beyond our planet? That is precisely the best-known and most enveloping of all ancient alien theories, from Zecharia Sitchin. He claimed that the alien rulers of planet Earth originated from an as yet undiscovered planet in our solar system, and that they came to earth hundreds of thousands of years ago.

Sitchin had an interest in ancient history that began as a young boy, when, in a lesson on Hebrew scripture, he asked about the Nephilim. The Nephilim were mentioned twice in the Bible, in Genesis 6:4 and Numbers 13:33, and were described as the offspring of the "sons of God" and the "daughters of men." Who were they? His teacher brushed the question off, and at that point Sitchin began to try to find the answer for himself.

Raised in a Jewish environment, he realized that the Jews were relatively new kids on the blocks and that much of their mythology was borrowed from Babylon and Sumer. He began to study the Sumerian language and weighed the accuracy of their translations, at a time when there were very few scholars in that discipline. In his first book, *The 12th Planet*, published in 1976, he argued that several Sumerian words had been mis-translated and were actually references to spaceships and other alien-related devices. Most importantly, he concluded that these Sumerian texts spoke of the existence of a 12th planet in our solar system, whose inhabitants had colonized Earth more than 400,000 years ago. We, humankind, were a genetic modification, created for specific purposes, which was the availability of a workforce on Earth, which the aliens from the planet Nibiru (the Sumerian name for the 12th planet) had colonized for its mineral deposits, especially gold. The Nephilim were precisely these alien overlords, and Sitchin had finally found the answer he had been looking for since his childhood.

Life on Nibiru faced a slow extinction 450,000 years ago as the planet's atmosphere eroded. When one Nibirian fled to Earth, he discovered our planet rich in gold, which would allow for its homeworld's atmosphere to be replenished. The aliens then began to mine our gold—first extracting it from the Persian Gulf—and sent it back to Nibiru. For this purpose a series of spaceports were created in the Middle East. Sitchin went on to conclude that the Great Pyramid was built by and for the aliens—the gods. He spoke of Pyramid Wars, the division of the Earth between the aliens, and the creation of humankind in a lab around 300,000 years ago as a race that could work in the gold mines for the aliens. Mostly, he sees alien rivalries, before the Anunnaki, a group of Sumerian and Babylonian deities, realize that the demise of Nibiru in 13000 BCE will trigger an immense tidal wave—the biblical flood. The Anunnaki take an oath to keep the impending doom secret from humankind, but one of them breaks rank and informs Noah, beginning an age when humankind is allowed to begin to rule the Earth, whereas the aliens largely maintain a hands-off policy, though they promise that they will return.

Most of the Ancient Alien conspiracy theories can be traced back to Zecharia Sitchin. He either created them, or they were created by others using Sitchin's material. In conspiracy corners, his conclusions are often taken as fact. In *Gods of the New Millennium*, British author Alan Alford writes how he "happened to discover in 1989, Sitchin's contribution to proving the intervention of flesh-and-blood gods in the creation of mankind" and how this "cannot be overstated."

As his research progressed, Alford became one of many who learned that Sitchin's theses did not hold water. When Alford published his dissent from Sitchin's conclusion, he reported that all kinds of allegations were slung his way, including that he had been "turned" by the CIA.

The problem—or advantage—of Sitchin's work is that you are either a total believer or a total skeptic. This is typical of Sitchin's work and his proponents, in the sense that it is an all-or-nothing approach: Sitchin is either totally wrong, or totally right. There is hardly any middle ground.

Sitchin's interpretations were all derived from his understanding of the Sumerian language. Since 1976, no scholar of Ugaritic ever corroborated his claims, and as more experts in the Sumerian language were created, none came even close to endorsing Sitchin. In fact, most noted that Sitchin had greatly mistranslated Sumerian.

One of his most vociferous critics is Michael Heiser, who has an entire website, SitchinIsWrong.com, devoted to refuting Sitchin's theory. From 2001 onward, Heiser invited Sitchin to an open debate, but the latter always refused. Heiser therefore wrote an open letter to Sitchin, inviting him to present evidence in support of his theory. In it, he writes: "The reader must realize that the substance of my disagreement is not due to 'translation philosophy,' as though Mr. Sitchin and I merely disagree over possible translations of certain words. When it comes to the Mesopotamian sources, what is at stake is the integrity of the cuneiform tablets themselves, along with the legacy of Sumer and Mesopotamian scribes. Very simply, the ancient Mesopotamians compiled their own dictionaries—we have them and they have been published since the mid-20th century. The words Mr. Sitchin tells us refer to rocket ships have no such meanings according to the ancient Mesopotamians themselves."[6]

One key term in Sitchin's theories was the word *MU*, which he defined as "an oval-topped, conical object," and "that which rises straight," from which he concluded that it was a space probe, used by the alien astronauts to travel between their orbiting space stations and our planet. However, the Mesopotamian lexical lists define the word as "heaven" and sometimes "rain"—at odds with Sitchin's interpretation.

A century ago, G.M. Redslob pointed out that the translation of the Sumerian *shem* as "name" was incorrect. This was seized upon by Sitchin, who stated that a *shem* was actually a space capsule. But Sitchin was equally wrong. Quite clearly, the word *shem* is related to the word *shamaim*, meaning "heaven." Both *shem* and *shamaim* stem from the word *shamah*, meaning "that which is highward."

Going into more detail on the theory itself, Heiser also queried whether Sitchin could "produce a single text that says the Anunnaki come from the planet Nibiru—or that Nibiru is a planet beyond Pluto? I assert that there are no such texts.... There are 182 occurrences of the divine name Anunnaki. Please show me any evidence from the Sumerian texts themselves that the Anunnaki have any connection to Nibiru or a 12th planet (or any planet)." For almost a decade, Sitchin never answered or addressed the problems raised by Heiser, likely because he was unable to.

How did Sitchin arrive at his interpretations? Though he claimed he was one of the few people in the world able to read Sumerian, it is clear that his understanding was not at all perfect. Sitchin's approach can best be described as multilayered: He would see a depiction, or picture, accompanied by writing, and would then speculate as to how the depiction was evidence of an alien device. He identified pictures that resembled the modules used by the *Apollo* moon missions as Nibirian space modules, and then claimed that the Sumerian word associated with it was simply mistranslated.

Sitchin was therefore highly specific in his exploration of the Sumerian culture, an approach he later went on to apply to other civilizations, each time claiming to find evidence to support his theory. For even though he believed that the gods had initially settled in Sumer, he also argued that the Great Pyramid and the ancient civilizations of America were also created by the occupiers of the 12th planet. Furthermore, he claimed that the Great Pyramid had once been used as a prison for a non-conforming alien!

Though Heiser has clearly shown that Sitchin committed serious linguistic errors, Sitchin's main problem has and will always be astronomy. His 12th planet was said to occupy a highly elliptical orbit in our solar system. It went far into deep space and then swept back to the inner planets of our solar system, in an orbit that lasted 3,600 years. Astronomers have consistently claimed that it would be extremely unlikely for a planet of that size in that orbit to be life-sustaining. More importantly, with today's high-powered telescopes, which did not exist in 1976 when Sitchin first published his theory, we should have been able to see this planet. As a consequence, Sitchin and his dedicated group of followers began to claim there was a worldwide cover-up and conspiracy to keep the existence and approach of this planet a secret.

The plain meaning of *Nibiru* is "ferry, ferryman, or ford," whereby *mikis nibiru* is the toll one has to pay for crossing the river, from *eberu*, "to cross." It was Alfred Jeremias who insisted that Nibiru, "in all star-texts of later times," indicated Canopus, the second-brightest star in the sky, and for the Ancient Egyptians the Southern Pole Star, although de Santillana and von Dechend point out that others have linked Nibiru with other stellar phenomenon, and hence they state that Nibiru has to remain "an unknown factor for the time being."[7]

On occasion, Sitchin and his followers would claim that astronomers were open to the suggestion that our solar system might contain planets in elliptical orbits. But the fact of the matter is that for Sitchin to be correct, such a planet would have to be of a particular size, in an orbit of 3,600 years, and flying in a path that matches his very specific descriptions.

So, because Sitchin had a very specific theory, he needed a very specific answer, and the short answer is that there *is* no such planet. Sitchin is wrong. And because of the manner in which Sitchin himself constructed his theory, in an all-or-nothing approach, Sitchin is *totally* wrong.

The reptilian aliens David Icke wrote about were actually already proposed in 1990 by René A. Boulay in *Flying Serpents and Dragons: The Story of Mankind's Reptilian Past*. Boulay made a special acknowledgment to Sitchin's work, and focused on the physicality of the Anunnaki, as well as analyzing the appearance of gods in other cultures. He observed that "it is no accident that all the early settlements were founded at the mouth of large river systems, where moisture was abundant," which was necessary to the reptile race.[8] However, shall we say, *interesting* his theory is, the problem is that the very foundation of his argument was built on swampy ground. And Boulay is but one of hundreds of theories that have been built on Sitchin's mistranslations.

Erich von Däniken once wrote that "religious people, regardless what faith they belong to, hope for 'salvation from above.'"[9] In the Western world of the 21st century, *god* has become an unpopular word; in fact, one can argue that the Ancient Alien Question was only posed because the weight of the God-word began to wane. But the key issue is that God was once believed to be omnipotent and omnipresent; the problem with many Ancient Alien theories is that most try to make the theories similarly all-encompassing, trying to explain in detail every nanosecond and mystery of our past. Overindulgence is never a good thing.

The Sirius Mystery

The greatest of ancient alien theories does not hold: Sitchin was unable to prove that the Sumerian civilization—as well as all other civilizations—was the creation of aliens who came to planet Earth to exploit its minerals, and who were either still present or at some point in the past had gone back to their homeworld, leaving the Earth and humankind orphaned.

But perhaps there is evidence that contact between humankind and an extraterrestrial being has occurred on a smaller scale? The story that the Dogon, a tribe in Mali, West Africa, had possessed in their antiquity extraordinary knowledge of the star system Sirius achieved worldwide publicity in—once again—1976, through Robert Temple's extraordinary book *The Sirius Mystery*. It was compellingly argued and became one of the most influential books of the 1970s' "ancient astronauts" genre.

Apart from apparently possessing astronomical knowledge about the four moons of Jupiter and rings of Saturn, which the modern world only discovered with the help of the telescope, Temple claimed that the Dogon specifically knew about two smaller stars that are closely related to Sirius: Sirius B and Sirius C. The mystery was how they had obtained this astronomical knowledge, as these companion stars cannot be seen by the unaided eye. He argued that the knowledge the Dogon possessed of Sirius could only have been given to them by extraterrestrial beings that possessed information on that star system.

As the star Sirius was also the brightest star in the sky and hence the most important star for the Ancient Egyptians—who based their calendar on it—the obvious follow-up question was whether the Ancient Egyptians and the Dogon of Mali were somehow related and/or had somehow shared this very specific knowledge about Sirius. Temple concluded that the answer was positive.

Ancient Alien Theories

In 1998, Temple republished the book with the subtitle "New Scientific Evidence of Alien Contact 5,000 Years Ago." The book's reputation was first dented in 1999, when Lynn Picknett and Clive Prince published *The Stargate Conspiracy*, in which they allege that Temple's thinking had been heavily influenced by his mentor, Arthur M. Young, an American inventor, helicopter pioneer, cosmologist, philosopher, and much more. In 1965, Young had given Robert Temple an article written by two French anthropologists, Marcel Griaule and Germaine Dieterlen, on the secret star lore of the Dogon. In 1967, Temple—then age 22—began work on the thesis that became *The Sirius Mystery*. As Picknett and Prince have been able to show, Temple was very keen to please his mentor, who himself believed in extraterrestrial beings from Sirius.

At the core of this theory lies the original anthropological study of the Dogon by Griaule and Dieterlen, who describe the secret knowledge retained by the Dogon of Sirius B and Sirius C in their own book *The Pale Fox*. Griaule claimed to have been initiated into the secret mysteries of the male Dogon, during which they allegedly told him of Sirius (*sigu tolo* in their language) and its two invisible companions. In the 1930s, when their research was carried out, Sirius B was known to exist, even though it was not photographed until 1970.

Griaule and Dieterlen first described their findings in an article published in French in 1950, but at the time they included no comment about how extraordinary the Dogon knowledge of the "invisible companions" was. This step was taken by others, particularly Temple. Peter James and Nick Thorpe, in *Ancient Mysteries*, write: "While Temple, following Griaule, assumes that *to polo* is the invisible star Sirius B, the Dogon themselves, as reported by Griaule, say something quite different." According to the Dogon, when Digitaria (*to polo*) is close to Sirius, the latter becomes brighter. When it is at its most distant from Sirius, Digitaria gives off a twinkling effect, suggesting to the observer that it is actually more than one star. This description of a very visible effect causes James and Thorpe to wonder—as anyone reading this should—whether *to polo* is therefore an ordinary star near Sirius, not an invisible companion, as Griaule and Temple suggest, for, whereas Sirius B is invisible, *to polo* clearly is visible!

The biggest challenge to Griaule, however, came from anthropologist Walter Van Beek. He pointed out that Griaule and Dieterlen stand alone in their claims about the Dogon secret knowledge—no other anthropologist supports their opinions. In 1991, Van Beek himself led a team of anthropologists to Mali and declared that they found absolutely no trace of the detailed Sirius lore reported by the French anthropologists. James and Thorpe understate the problem when they say "this is very worrying."[10] Griaule claimed that about 15 percent of the Dogon tribe possessed this secret knowledge, but Van Beek could find no trace of it in the decade he spent with the Dogon.

Van Beek actually spoke to some of Griaule's original informants; he noted that "though they do speak about *sigu tolo* [interpreted by Griaule as their name for Sirius itself], they disagree completely with each other as to which star is meant; for some, it is an invisible star that should rise to announce the sigu [festival], for another it is Venus that, through a different position, appears as sigu tolo. All agree, however, that they learned about the star from Griaule."[11] Van Beek concluded that this created a major problem for Griaule's claims.

In all claims of conspiracy—in this case, that it is Griaule who gave knowledge about Sirius to the Dogon and then pretended they had given this knowledge to him—there needs to be motive. Although he was an anthropologist, Griaule was keenly interested in astronomy and had studied it in Paris. As James and Thorpe point out, he took star maps along with him on his field trips as a way of prompting his informants to divulge their knowledge of the stars. Griaule himself was aware of the discovery of Sirius B, and in the 1920s—before he visited the Dogon—there were also unconfirmed sightings of Sirius C.

The Dogon were well aware of the brightest star in the sky, but, as Van Beek learned, they do not call it *sigu tolo*, as Griaule claimed, but *dana tolo*. To quote James and Thorpe once again: "As for Sirius B, only Griaule's informants had ever heard of it."[12] Was Griaule told by his informants what he wanted to believe, or did he misinterpret the Dogon responses to his questions? Either way, the purity of the Dogon-Sirius story is clearly spoiled, and it is highly likely that Griaule contaminated the Dogon star knowledge with his own. Carl Sagan also believed that this star lore was not native to the Dogon, but instead had been injected by Griaule and/or Dieterlen. The same conclusion was reached by Peter James and Nick Thorpe.

With this, the Dogon mystery and the possibility of alien contact with a tribe in Central Africa comes crashing down. For more than 20 years, *The Sirius Mystery* influenced speculation about the possibility that our forefathers came from the stars. In his 1998 revised edition, Temple was quick to point out the new discussions in scientific circles about the possible existence of Sirius C, which seemed to make Griaule's claims even more spectacular and accurate. But it is apparent that Temple was either not aware of Van Beek's devastating research, or he decided to ignore it.

The Alien Puzzle

The UFO phenomenon and the Ancient Alien Question have often been mixed and woven into a rich tapestry. The UFO phenomenon is generally agreed to have begun on June 24, 1947, with a sighting by pilot Kenneth Arnold of nine shiny, mostly disc-like objects flying past Mount Rainier (in Washington state) at speeds that Arnold clocked at a minimum of 1,200 miles an hour. Only extraterrestrials, it was concluded, had technology that could fly at such incredible speeds. Since then, most UFO researchers have accumulated evidence, which they see as further confirmation of the extraterrestrial nature of such phenomena. At the same time, leading ufologists like Jacques Vallee, especially in *Passport to Magonia*, and Robert Emmegger, in *UFO's, Past, Present & Future*, have argued that the UFO phenomenon began far earlier than 1947. Apart from pointing at references in the Bible, such as Ezekiel's sighting, Vallee found references from the time of Charlemagne of encounters with tyrants of the air, and their aerial ships. One record, located by Vallee, reads:

> One day, among other instances, it chanced at [the French city of] Lyons that three men and a woman were seen descending from these aerial ships. The entire city gathered about them, crying out they were magicians sent by Charlemagne's enemy to destroy the French harvest. In vain, the four innocents sought to vindicate themselves, saying they were their own country folk and had been carried away a short time since by miraculous men who had shown them unheard marvels. Luckily, the Bishop of Lyons pronounced the incident as false, saying it was true these men had fallen from the sky, and what they [the town folks] said they had seen there was impossible. The people believed what their good Bishop said rather than their own eyes and set at liberty the four ambassadors...from the ship.[13]

It shows that encounters with strange ships at a time when humankind did not fly is not only found in legends, but is a consistent theme throughout our history, and was a worldwide phenomenon long before 1947.

The UFO phenomenon has grown since 1947, when the only available evidence was truly unidentified objects that flew, which were sometimes captured on photographs. These so-called

CE-I—Close Encounters of the First Kind—led to CE-II (in which the object leaves physical traces), CE-III (in which entities are seen), and CE-IV (the so-called alien abductions). The body of evidence presented by UFO researchers suggests that an alien intelligence is here and is interacting with us, and has been for several decades, if not several centuries. The benign or malign purpose of this interaction depends on the coloring of the individual researcher. For the late professor of psychiatry John Mack, "UFO abductees" displayed genuine trauma when he questioned them, suggesting they had an experience that to them was totally real. Mack believed a genuine phenomenon existed, but that whatever was happening was not as straightforward as extraterrestrial beings somehow breeding with the human species, as UFO researcher Budd Hopkins has proposed, and that is largely the standard theory in the UFO field.

Some of the UFO research has taken the phenomenon in the direction of the Ancient Alien Question. In *The Watchers*, UFO researcher Raymond E. Fowler continued his exploration of the intriguing abduction experiences of Betty Andreasson Luca. From this sole woman's account, retrieved under hypnosis, Fowler felt he could argue for the presence of ET on planet Earth. During one abduction experience, Andreasson noted that she saw a hybrid fetus aborted from a woman's womb, "and thrust into a waiting tank of liquid close by. It was at this time I learned these gray beings were called 'Watchers': caretakers of nature and all natural form. They informed me the reason they'd been collecting seed and fetuses was because man would eventually become sterile." She would later have encounters with "beautiful, pale blue–eyed extraterrestrials" which she called the Elders, who were apparently in charge of the Watchers, which were their work force, and which loved the human race.

The abductors' identification of "The Watchers," as Fowler noted, meant that these were the same supernatural or extraterrestrial beings encountered in numerous legends, as well as the Bible. The Chaldeans referred to the Watchers as "Ir." The Egyptian word *neter* means Watcher. And in the Bible, in Genesis 6:1–4, they are listed as the sons of Gods who "fell" for the Earthly women, descended from heaven, chose women, and had children.

Gregory Little was most impressed with Andreasson's revelations and made a study of the Book of Enoch, an ancient Jewish religious work, ascribed to Enoch, the great-grandfather of Noah, currently part of the Bible. The Book of Enoch goes into some depth about the interactions humankind had with these Watchers. Little observed that the Book of Enoch noted that there were Watchers present both at the gates of Heaven and Hell—mimicking the Egyptian neters, who also guarded the gates of Heaven and Hell in the Egyptian Afterlife. Interestingly, the guardians of Sheol—Hell—were described as beings "gray of color, small as children, with a shape that is somewhat similar to the human form." Little observed that this description was not present in the Slavic edition of the book (the most commonly used), but was present in the Hebrew version and was a very good description of "the grays" of UFO abduction lore. Furthermore, Andreasson had described how the Watchers guarded a door. Under hypnosis, she stated how she was shown a "Great Door" and how she was led toward it. The door was an entrance to another world, one of light, of "home," which she also described as the abode of "The One God," whom she met—though at this point she was unwilling to give further details.

Did the Christian Andreasson confabulate stories she might have heard in her childhood and weave them into her claims? Perhaps. But it is clear that she is not the only person who claims to have been abducted. Fowler himself analyzed the Book of Enoch and came upon an intriguing reference on the general UFO abduction phenomenon. In his story, Enoch is home alone, resting in a seat, and falls asleep. Suddenly, he hears talking, though he does not understand what is being said. Two men appear at the end of his feet; they know his name. Enoch wakes up, sees the two men, and is afraid. They tell him not to be afraid, for "you will ascend to Heaven with us." It is in Heaven that Enoch is brought in front of "the Elders" and the rulers of a "stellar hegemony." The events described by Enoch are identical to the events reported in standard UFO abductions stories.

True or not, there are important cultural parallels between the story of Enoch and the modern UFO abduction phenomenon. The Watchers materialized on Earth to have children with female women. The UFO abductors are said to materialize on Earth to abduct people, resulting in pregnancies or a general interest in female genetic material. The consequences of these actions were "giants," to use the Enochian language, or "hybrid babies," to use UFO terminology.

The parallels are there, but what do they mean? Are they ancient legends, adapted to our modern civilization? Or are they genuine events, written down both in ancient and modern times? Is history repeating itself? Or are we merely still intrigued by the same heroic and thrilling stories of our ancestors?

However intriguing and interesting the parallels between the UFO field and the Ancient Alien Questions are, the problem is that you cannot answer one question with another one. Two enigmas do not make for one reality. But they do suggest that two enigmas might be related, or might even be two aspects of a larger enigma—the Alien Question.

Answering that question positively can currently only be done if we look at this question from a certain, skewed perspective. It worked well in the popular television series *The X-Files*, where it was clear that the conspiracy was thousands of years old. But television series like *The X-Files* and so many others use these phenomena to elaborate and entertain, not to prove.

With the all-encompassing theories unable to stand up to scrutiny or lacking in evidence, it is clear that one of the greatest questions humankind is posing—Were We Alone?—cannot be answered easily. To paraphrase my friend Stan Hall, "If it was that easy, someone would already have done so."

Chapter 3

Of Gods and Men

The Protestant bishop James Ussher wanted to provide an accurate history of the Bible, and felt that the best manner in which to do this was to establish an accurate date for Creation. He studied thousands of ancient books and manuscripts, written in diverse languages; by the time of his death, he had a library containing more than 10,000 volumes. After much study, Ussher wrote, "In the beginning, God created heaven and earth, which beginning of time, according to this chronology, occurred at the beginning of the night which preceded the 23rd of October in the year 710 of the Julian period." Transposed to our calendar, that was the year 4004 BCE.

Others have concluded that the Bible contains a code. Or several codes. By selecting letters, certain words and phrases are spelled out. For example, using every 50th letter of the Book of Genesis, the Hebrew word for "bible" is spelled out. This technique was popularized by Michael Drosnin in *The Bible Code*, in which he reported on how computers had successfully been used to find such patterns in the Bible. Drosnin argued that it was exceedingly unlikely that these sequences could have been created by chance. He demonstrated the validity of the code by showing that it wrote of past events that had occurred and made a series of predictions for the future—which proved to be less accurate.

Ussher and Drosnin are but two examples of hundreds of people who have turned to the Bible for answers. They treat the Bible as infallible, quite often literally as the work of God, even though it is known that the Bible has been changed in time, if only through a series of translations. When the Ancient Alien Question first began to be posed, the Bible was mined for evidence to show that some of the encounters with "God" were actually Close Encounters of the Third Kind.

The Spaceship of Ezekiel

Ancient Alien proponents have found places in the Bible where it is clear that something strange is going on. The story of Jonah and the whale is one of the Bible's better-known "fairy tales." In the story, Jonah was swallowed up by a whale but lived to tell the tale. Although the creature is commonly thought to be a whale, it is actually written as a "great fish." And the Bible, in Jonah 2:6, relates how Jonah could walk around in it and breathe and that he even saw "the bottoms of the mountains" while inside this creature—suggesting that it was no creature at all.

Then there is the story of Sodom and Gomorrah. The exact locations of the cities are not known, but it is believed they were at the south end of the Dead Sea, between Israel and Jordan. Genesis 19 records that the cities' inhabitants were so wicked that God rained fire and brimstone on them. Only Lot and his family were spared; they had been forewarned so that they could leave the city. On the evening before the destruction, Lot was visited by two angels who informed him of the upcoming catastrophe. The angels told Lot to flee into the mountains, where he and his family would be safe. They were warned not to look back. Lot's wife did anyway, and she was turned into a pillar of salt. The following day, Lot did look to the land where once two cities rose, and said, "Why, here thick smoke ascended from the land like the thick smoke of a kiln." For Matest M. Agrest, a Russian-born ethnologist and mathematician with a PhD from the University of Leningrad, the destruction of Sodom and Gomorrah was caused by a nuclear blast.

And what to make of this, from 2 Kings 2:11? "And it came to pass, as they still went on, and talked, that, behold, there appeared a chariot of fire, and horses of fire, and parted them both asunder; and Elijah went up by a whirlwind into heaven." This is clearly a traumatic experience for Elisha, who remained behind and never saw Elijah again! Modern ufologists would label it a UFO abduction experience, in which a human being is taken by extraterrestrial beings; medieval folklorists would also call it an abduction, but into the faery realm. So who is the abductor? God? Faeries? Aliens?

The opening chapter of the Book of Ezekiel contains an enigmatic description of a close encounter between the prophet and "the Lord."

> [4] And I looked, and, behold, a whirlwind came out of the north, a great cloud, and a fire infolding itself, and a brightness was about it, and out of the midst thereof as the color of amber, out of the midst of the fire.

> [5] Also out of the midst thereof came the likeness of four living creatures. And this was their appearance; they had the likeness of a man.

⁶ And every one had four faces, and every one had four wings.

⁷ And their feet were straight feet; and the sole of their feet was like the sole of a calf's foot: and they sparkled like the color of burnished brass.

⁸ And they had the hands of a man under their wings on their four sides; and they four had their faces and their wings.

⁹ Their wings were joined one to another; they turned not when they went; they went every one straight forward.

¹⁰ As for the likeness of their faces, they four had the face of a man, and the face of a lion, on the right side: and they four had the face of an ox on the left side; they four also had the face of an eagle.

¹¹ Thus were their faces: and their wings were stretched upward; two wings of every one were joined one to another, and two covered their bodies.

¹² And they went every one straight forward: whither the spirit was to go, they went; and they turned not when they went.

¹³ As for the likeness of the living creatures, their appearance was like burning coals of fire, and like the appearance of lamps: it went up and down among the living creatures; and the fire was bright, and out of the fire went forth lightning.

¹⁴ And the living creatures ran and returned as the appearance of a flash of lightning.

¹⁵ Now as I beheld the living creatures, behold one wheel upon the earth by the living creatures, with his four faces.

Of Gods and Men

¹⁶ The appearance of the wheels and their work was like unto the color of a beryl: and they four had one likeness: and their appearance and their work was as it were a wheel in the middle of a wheel.

The vision is one of seven Ezekiel had throughout a 22-year period, from about 593 to 571 BCE. Ezekiel had been deported by King Nebuchadnezzar in circa 597 BCE to Babylon when he was about 25 years old. He lived in the village of Tel-Abib on the River of Chebar in Chaldea and had been a Temple priest in Jerusalem. All of his visions occurred when Ezekiel was in exile, with his first vision occurring at the age of roughly 35.

What Ezekiel saw in his visions has remained a subject of intense speculation. Astrologers have claimed to understand the vision as a representation of the zodiac, which they see enforced by the mention of a wheel. The faces of a man, a lion, an ox, and an eagle are interpreted as being linked with the fixed signs of the zodiac. But what to make then of the whirlwinds or the creatures that materialized as a flash of lightning, which are clearly not typical of the zodiac? These were precisely the details that inspired Erich von Däniken to include the story of Ezekiel in his book as evidence of possible alien encounters in the Bible.

Josef Blumrich had received a copy of *Chariots of the Gods* while working as a NASA engineer at the Marshfield Space Flight Center in Huntsville, Alabama. He decided to use his 40 years of aerospace engineering knowledge, which included work on Skylab and the space shuttle, to explain how von Däniken had it wrong—for it was clear that the Swiss hotelier had no expertise in the subject area. "It was all rubbish," Blumrich wrote:

> From the wealth of material supplied by von Däniken, I found, when I came to the description of the technical characteristics of Ezekiel's vision, a territory in which I could join in the conversation, so to speak, as I have spent most of my life in the construction

and planning of aircraft and rockets. So I got a Bible to read the complete text, feeling sure that I would refute and annihilate Däniken in a few minutes.[1]

It didn't quite work out that way. From reading the very first chapter, Blumrich began to change his mind.

In his 1973 book, *The Spaceship of Ezekiel*, Blumrich describes how the main body of the spaceship was shaped like an ice cream cone: "It is a rather wide cone with some inward curves—and that main body is carried by four helicopter units." In 1964, Roger Anderson, an engineer of the Langley Research Center in Norfolk, Va., had designed a vehicle with a similar configuration. Anderson had drawn this type of craft because he had been asked to design a vehicle that could make entries into planetary atmospheres.

What he achieved was a series of technical drawings, which suggested that Ezekiel had indeed seen a spaceship. Blumrich concluded that the ship Ezekiel had described was almost possible to construct with present-day technology, and that its shape was largely similar to a *Gemini* or *Apollo* capsule, with the addition of helicopter-like devices to control flight. From his interpretation of the Book of Ezekiel, Blumrich concluded that Ezekiel flew at least three, if not four times, inside this craft.

There is a 20-year gap between Ezekiel's third and fourth encounter, in which he is taken to a temple, which most commentators identify as the Temple of Solomon in Jerusalem. However, it is clear that Ezekiel was intimately familiar with that temple, yet in his vision does not recognize it. Furthermore, some details of the setting of this temple do not match the landscape of Jerusalem. Von Däniken is among those who have proposed that Ezekiel was actually taken to a site known as Chavin de Huantar, in northern Peru, whose measurements and location do correspond with Ezekiel's description. Of course, the most important observation is that it doesn't matter where Ezekiel was taken; that he might have flown with unknown pilots to *any* location is the clincher.

Of Gods and Men

Of equal note for the Ancient Alien Question is that Ezekiel took hundreds of precise measurements of the temple he saw in his vision, which the German engineer Hans-Herbert Beier used to make a detailed model. His conclusion, when incorporating the work of Blumrich, was that the temple was a purely technical construction, to accommodate the housing of the spaceship for maintenance. He believes it was in this "temple" that the nuclear reactor of the spaceship was maintained, and points to Ezekiel's description of the workers wearing protective clothing, as well as the procedures used in replacing the fuel elements of the craft.

Historian Walter Webb has created a modern interpretation of Ezekiel's vision, which, as he describes it, "is a free, imaginative interpretation and as such is purely speculative."[2] This is his reading of the story: Sitting next to the river Chebar in circa 593 BCE, Ezekiel saw a bright, fiery cloud of amber color coming out of the north. As it drew closer, he saw four disk-shaped objects, which he described as "wheels," at least one of which landed near Ezekiel. Four humanoid creatures came out of the craft, each apparently having four "wings," which could have been a device strapped to their back. The devices enabled the creatures to move about rapidly ("and the living creatures ran and returned as the appearance of a flash of lightning"). That the wings were some type of device is suggested by Ezekiel's description that "when they went, I heard the noise of their wings, like the noise of great water." He saw a throne above the ship—a dome-like structure with a pilot's seat?—with the "likeness of a man" seated in it. This frightened Ezekiel so much that he fell on his face. A voice emanated from the ship telling him to get up. He was then taken aboard the ship and heard the "noise of the wheels...and a noise of great rushing" and was carried to Tel Abib, where his fellow exiles lived and where he sat "astonished among them seven days."

Could the "visions" of Ezekiel, which some scientists have argued might be due to temporal lobe epilepsy, be real? That idea is precisely the conclusion reached by Blumrich, a man of science. He is absolutely convinced that what happened to Ezekiel was physically real: He was taken onboard a spaceship, and what he described in his vision were technical details that we are only able to interpret correctly because by the second half of the 20th century, we had the proper framework: the capability to build spaceships.

Giants and Hybrids

One of the most intriguing references in the Bible, at least when it comes to anomalous sightings, is chapter 6 of the Book of Genesis, with its references to "giants," which are clearly non-human, but somehow were able to sexually liaise with human women.

> ¹ And it came to pass, when men began to multiply on the face of the earth, and daughters were born unto them,
>
> ² That the sons of God saw the daughters of men that they were fair; and they took them wives of all which they chose.
>
> ³ And the LORD said, My spirit shall not always strive with man, for that he also is flesh: yet his days shall be an hundred and twenty years.
>
> ⁴ There were giants [Nephilim] in the earth in those days; and also after that, when the sons of God came in unto the daughters of men, and they bare children to them, the same became mighty men which were of old, men of renown.

This is the very passage that set Sitchin on his quest, and it is indeed one of the truly enigmatic passages of the Bible. Taken literally, the Bible states that in those days there were giants on our planet, and it was also at that time that the "sons of God" introduced themselves to "the daughters of men," and had children with them. It clearly reads that this was a meeting of two species, the "sons of God" being clearly not human, but somehow able to create offspring with humans.

The Nephilim are sometimes translated as "giants," sometimes as "fallen," and are therefore sometimes identified as the fallen angels. The story goes that when Lucifer rebelled against God, he was allowed by God to take up residence on Earth and many other angels followed. The Nephilim were present on Earth before the Flood, and one interpretation suggests that God caused the Flood to rid the Earth of the Nephilim, as well as the hybrid creatures the "sons of God" had created with humankind. However, the Bible also suggests that the Nephilim were present on Earth after the Flood.

The translation of *Nephilim* as "giants" comes from the Greek Old Testament, where *Nephilim* was rendered as "gegantes," which looks like *giants*, but would actually be *Titans*. Not coincidentally, the titans were the supernaturally powerful offspring of the union of gods and humans.

The union of "sons of Gods" and women is indeed not unique to the Hebrew Bible. There are hundreds of examples in Greek mythology of a Greek god falling madly in love with a woman. Zeus, the king of the Greek pantheon, married six times and had numerous affairs with mortal women, including Semele, the outcome of which was the famous Dionysus. Another of Zeus's divine affairs was with Alcmene, resulting in the birth of Hercules. According to Ovid's *Metamorphoses*, her labor lasted seven days and she had great difficulty giving birth to such a large child.

The Greek myths are usually taken as allegorical, whereas the Bible is often used for more literal interpretations. The Nephilim, as "fallen," have been identified with the Greek Grigori, or the Watchers of Book of Enoch fame, and have led scholars to argue that the Nephilim/Watchers/Grigori/sons of God are fallen angels—otherworldly creatures that ended up living on planet Earth after a dispute with God (or someone who went down on paper as God, but might not have been the Almighty).

There are other interpretations of this passage, such as the one held by St. Augustine in the fourth century, which argued that "sons of God" referred to the line of Seth, while "daughters of men" referred to the line of Cain—two biblical patriarchs. Still others interpret "sons of God" as meaning a line of priests—men in the service of God.

Other parts of the Bible also suggest there were indeed giants living on the Earth. Genesis 14 and Deuteronomy 2 speak of two tribes, the Rephaim and the Anakim. The Anakim were directly connected with the Nephilim, and were said to be descended from a giant named Anak. In Numbers 13:33, it is said that this tribe was so tall that spies who were sent in felt like "grasshoppers, and so we were in their sight." Moses is said to have killed Og, king of the Rephaim and "the last of the remnant of the giants," according to Deuteronomy 3. Og had a bed nine cubits long, which, depending on which cubit was used, measured between 13.5 and 15.5 feet. And we are all familiar with the story of David fighting Goliath, who was about 9 feet tall. In 2 Samuel 21:20 and 1 Chronicles 20:6 we read of "still another battle, which took place at Gath," where "there was a huge man with six fingers on each hand and six toes on each foot—twenty-four in all," showing that these giants were clearly described as being largely human, but having a much larger size, plus extra fingers and toes. But the giants were clearly of flesh and blood, as many episodes of the Old Testament detail how the Israelites came upon many of these giants in Canaan and killed most of them, thus claiming the land of Israel as their own.

In isolation, the passage from Genesis 6 could indeed mean anything, and could be interpreted literally or symbolically. But placed in a larger context, it is clear that references to nonhuman or superhuman creatures breeding with human women is a common theme throughout many myths and legends. One can argue that all of these should be seen in a symbolic manner, but it is equally valid to argue that they should be interpreted literally.

Biblical Longevity

One of the more intriguing aspects of the Bible is the list of prediluvian patriarchs and their ages. Methuselah, for example, was said to have lived to the impressive age of 969 years, though "the First Man," Adam, lived for a solid 930 years—respectable for any prototype.

Detailed recordkeeping of people's dates of birth and death is a relatively recent—and still largely Western—practice. But from the available records, it is clear that humankind's age limit seems to lie somewhere between 115 and 120 years—however few attain it. The oldest attested person on record is the French Jeanne Calment, who lived to be 122 years and 164 days, born as she was on February 21, 1875, and dying on August 4, 1997. Interestingly, this outside limit is on par with what is said in Genesis 6:3, "his days shall be a hundred and twenty years."

The list of biblical patriarchs as given in Genesis 5 goes as follows:

- Adam: 930 years; begetting a son at the age of 130.
- Seth: 912 years; begetting a son at the age of 105.
- Enos: 905 years; begetting a son at the age of 90.
- Cainan: 910 years; begetting a son at the age of 75.
- Mahalaleel: 895 years; begetting a son at the age of 65.
- Jared: 962 years; begetting a son at the age of 162.
- Enoch: 365 years before walking with god; begetting a son at the age of 65.
- Methuselah: 969 years; begetting a son at the age of 187.

📖 Lamech: 777 years; begetting a son at the age of 182.

📖 Noach: 950 years; begetting a son at the age of 500.

Faced with these superhuman ages, the faithful are often encouraged to accept the veracity of these life spans that far exceed modern man's life expectancy as well as anything that the archaeological record have uncovered. For Martin Luther, these patriarchs had a better diet and sounder bodies, and experienced a less developed impact of sin on the physical creation, hence allowing them to live longer. Others have proposed that there was a different climate prevalent on Earth that would have allowed for these extended life spans. For those who turn to the Bible for every answer, on this point, it does not provide an explanation as to why these patriarchs lived so long. As to a "less developed impact of sin," the Fall happened during Adam's lifetime, so the fact that his descendents still lived long does not seem to have a logical explanation. The Bible furthermore does not attribute anything special to these people—except a long life, and living before the Deluge.

Others, in the quest to understand and make the biblical account acceptable, have tried to reduce these hard-to-imagine life-spans to more mundane possibilities. One of these interpretations is a lunar solution. This would mean that to obtain the "real age," as we calculate someone's life-span today—by solar years—their ages need to be divided by 12. This would make Methuselah just shy of 81 years old when he died. Suddenly, the impossible seems not only possible, but likely.

This therefore offers an appealing solution to the problem. However, as soon as one mystery seems solved, a new problem arises: the age at which these people fathered children. The eldest, Methuselah, waited until he was 187 years old to have a child, which in solar years would be 16 years. No real problem there. But the youngest dad, Mahalaleel, would have been just shy of 5 years old when he became a father—rather young, and apparently not an exception, for his father and grandfather had started at roughly the same time! And that makes the "most logical solution" hard to accept.

When we take the Bible out of its isolation, various parallels once again become apparent. In ancient Egypt and Sumeria, there are known lists of kings. Several of these begin with a series of kings who ruled before a flood or, in the case of Egypt, before the unification of Upper and Lower Egypt. Some of these deities lived even longer than Methuselah, to several thousands of years. In Sumerian accounts we read that the kingship descended from heaven to Eridu. In Eridu, Alulim became king and he ruled for a staggering 28,800 years. It seems that if Alulim had heard that Adam had died at the age of 930, he would have said he died in his infancy.

Here is the Sumerian list:

- Alulim of Eridu(g): 8 sars (28,800 years).
- Alalgar of Eridug: 10 sars (36,000 years).
- En-Men-Lu-Ana of Bad-Tibira: 12 sars (43,200 years).
- En-Men-Ana: This name is not present on all lists.
- En-Men-Gal-Ana of Bad-Tibira: 8 sars (28,800 years).
- Dumuzi of Bad-Tibira, the shepherd: 10 sars (36,000 years).
- En-Sipad-Zid-Ana of Larag: 8 sars (28,800 years).
- En-Men-Dur-Ana of Zimbir: 5 sars and 5 ners (21,000 years).
- Ubara-Tutu of Shuruppag: 5 sars and 1 ner (18,600 years).
- Zin-Suddu: This name is not present on all lists.

It's no wonder that these kings were seen as gods. That is precisely what authors such as Zecharia Sitchin have argued: We should take both the Bible and these lists of kings at face value; they show a reality—namely that we are face-to-face with alien beings.

A lot of ink has gone into puzzling out the purpose of Genesis 5, with some researchers noting that the list of patriarchs functions merely as a bridge between one narrative and the rest, largely there to fast-forward the story a few millennia. They argue that the Sumerian King List may have served as inspiration for this exercise, for during their Babylonian captivity, the Jews would definitely have stumbled upon it, and they may have decided to incorporate this information into their own creation myths.

The Sumerians had a different system of counting, based on the number 60. Some have tried to align Genesis 5 with the information of the Sumerian King List, while the Jewish exegete Cassuto suggested that the figures in Genesis 5 (and 11) were "multiples of five with the addition of seven."[3] An earlier attempt noted that the figures for the antediluvian patriarchs could be computed by 39 times 42 years, and the period of time from creation to Abraham's entry into Canaan by $6 \times 7 \times 7 \times 7$, or 42 times 49 years. It is clear that we are coming perilously close to a Bible Code, in order to "explain" something that we cannot take, or don't want to take, at face value.

In this interpretation, we are midway between a literal interpretation and the atheist viewpoint, which is that the Bible as a whole is a literary invention, and hence pure fiction. But if fiction, why not make it more believable, or at least give a moral or logical explanation why characters who had hard-to-believe life-spans were inserted into the story?

Elsewhere, in China, we find that the first dynasties are referred to as those of the Five Monarchs, which confusingly involved nine rulers, whose combined reigns lasted from 2852 to 2206 BCE—or an incredible 70 years each! In Vedic accounts, it is related that until circa 3000 BCE, the human life-span was roughly 1,000 years.

In the late 1800s, theologians sought ways to make the Bible conform to the claims of Darwinian evolution and uniformitarian geology. One novel way was to offer the idea that the names of the patriarchs were used to refer to entire dynasties, clans, or tribes, and not to actual individuals. This would mean that when the Adam clan had exercised dominion for 130 years, a person was born in the Adam clan who eventually either ruled or was the progenitor of the Seth clan. The Adam clan continued to be powerful for an additional 800 years, and then the Seth clan took over. This idea doesn't sound too logical, and would be a nightmare from a legal point of view within tribal matters: having to go back 800 years within a clan to find out who could succeed whom?

Others have suggested an astronomical interpretation. For example, Michel Barnouin proposed that the life-spans were actually the synodic periods of the planets—the time required for a body within the solar system to return to the same position relative to the sun as seen by an observer on the Earth. The life-span of Lamech, 777 years, would be related to the cumulative synodic periods of Jupiter and Saturn; 962, the life-span of Jared, would be the cumulative synodic periods of Venus and Saturn.

Another astronomical inroad is the possibility that each patriarch was assigned a star "kingdom"—a distance from one star to another. Their age would then be the number of days to be calculated between the rising and setting of certain stars. For example, Seth is born to Adam and Eve after the birth of Cain and Abel, which have been linked with Castor and Pollux in Gemini, when Adam is 130 years. If the left lower corner star of the Great Square is the heliacal rising star at dawn, it takes 130 days until Sirius—named Sothis in Egypt, and which could be the Seth of the Jews—is the dawn's rising star. Continuing in this scheme, from the star Sirius (Seth), it is 912 days—its life span—to the star Altair in Aquila. The star Altair sets as the star Sirius rises—coinciding with the notion of "dying." From this foundation, the entire series of kings in Genesis 5 and 11 has been linked to certain prominent stars and constellations.

As calculated by William Walker III, this system of identifying patriarchs with star regions only applies at around 42.5 degrees latitude—the Black Sea—thus identifying that area as the likely origin of this system.

This "third alternative" thus sits in the middle of the two standard theories: one asking for total faith in the Bible, the other skeptical, arguing that the Bible is fiction. It argues that the Bible is true, but that the patriarchs are not mortal men, but gods—stars. Their "ages" are correct, and they are even lifespans, but of stars and their visibility in the night's sky. Hence, the Bible is correct—but so are the skeptics.

Of course, there is a fourth possibility, which is that the patriarchs did indeed live hundreds of years, but that their ages were then adjusted to incorporate astronomical knowledge, which would mean that the Bible is not truly factually correct, but an amalgamation of various, diverse knowledge, woven together.

But taken as a whole, it is clear that the Bible does suggest that something strange was going on: There are numerous, quite straightforward references to giant beings living in Canaan, which the incoming Israelites had to fight and defeat before they could reclaim the land. The Israelites named these creatures "Nephilim," and it is clear that wherever they came from, they were clearly not "human," as in Homo sapiens. As a whole, Jewish and other legends spoke of how these beings were linked with the gods. The central question is: Were they Gods, or gods?

Cargo Cults

Could it be that nonhuman, but nevertheless not divine, entities were mistaken for or labeled as gods? The answer to this question is a simple yes, because there are numerous examples of that "mistake" having been made.

Of Gods and Men

The natives of Tanna, an island of Vanuatu, in the South Pacific Ocean, developed a cult around John Frum. Local legend has it that the king of a far-off nation called America visited Tanna and lived among the natives. His name was John Frum. He gave the natives coin and paper money, a helmet, and other objects, including a photograph. He explained lightning to them, as well as sound, wind, and the constellations, and he spoke in a strange language. The people have tattoos on their skin that read "USA."

The religion practiced by the people of Tanna is what is known as a "cargo cult," a religious cult that has appeared in many traditional, pre-industrial tribal societies in the wake of interaction with more technologically advanced cultures. The cults normally focus on obtaining the material wealth—the "cargo"—of the advanced culture. Many of these cargo cults emerged around World War II, when many of the islands in the South Pacific suddenly saw 300,000 American troops pouring in from the skies and seas. These "gods" indeed brought the locals what seemed to them to be endless supplies of food and goods—including Jeeps, washing machines, radios, canned meat, and candy—so much so that they believed it was all summoned by magic. After all, none of it was made locally, so where did it come from?

After the war, America lost interest in these islands and the locals saw an end of their "Golden Age." They therefore began to construct piers and created airstrips in their fields, in the hope that these "temples" would entice the gods—the Americans—to return. Indeed, the locals prayed for the return of the ships and planes, for with the return of the gods, a new Golden Age would come.

Whether or not there ever was a real John Frum is unknown. There are variant spellings: Jon Frum and John From. He is normally described as an American World War II serviceman, sometimes black, sometimes white.

He is not the only man whom the people of Tanna have mistaken for a god. The Yaohnanen tribe of Tanna believe that Prince Philip, the Duke of Edinburgh, is a divine being. He is in fact taken to be the pale-skinned son of a mountain spirit and the brother of John Frum. Whereas common knowledge in Britain holds that Prince Philip was born in Corfu, Greece, on June 10, 1921, the Yaohnanen believe that he was born in Tanna, then traveled over the seas to a distant land where he married a powerful lady and would in time return. And return he did....

It is not clear when the cult was formed, but it is believed to have been sometime in the 1950s or 1960s. It probably occurred when Queen Elizabeth II was somehow depicted as paying particular attention to Prince Philip during a public function, which the natives of Tanna either saw on television or as a photograph, and took Prince Philip as one of their own.

When the royal couple visited Vanuatu in 1974, the Yaohnanens' beliefs were reinforced, though the Prince himself was at the time not yet aware of the fact that he was considered to be a local deity. A few years later, when he was told of the tribe, the Resident Commissioner got Prince Philip to sign a photograph, which was then given to his worshippers, who responded by sending him a traditional nal-nal club, with which the prince duly posed, sending the photograph back to the Yaohnanen.

The Papas of New Guinea called the first seaplane they saw "the devil who came down from the sky" and the first steamboat "God Tibut Amut smoking a long cigar." During his expedition to New Guinea in the 1920s, Frank Hurley noticed that the natives from the village of Kaimari began to fashion small wooden replicas of his seaplane as toys, which were distributed to all the households. Natives from the Eastern highlands were seen making radio masts from bamboo—copying the Persian Oil Company's transmitter. Following World War II, the natives of a small New Guinean island built a ghost airport near the village of Wewak, complete with bamboo airplanes, to entice the gods to return.

Of Gods and Men

The Leahy brothers went to the highlands of Papua New Guinea in the 1920s to make a documentary about the cargo cults. In it, Mike Leahy recounts the story that a small group of adventurers had landed on the island and begun to clear a section of the jungle so that the aircraft could land. When they made contact with the locals, they told them they did not come to steal, but needed to make room so that the "barlas" could land—a big bird that came from the sky and made lots of noise. Grabowski, the pilot, was a tall fellow. Leahy observed:

> Wearing a pilot's flight suit, white helmet and black protective goggles, he opened the hatch and got out of the plane, while about 2,500 natives were standing in dumbfounded silence along the airstrip. No one uttered a word. They had no idea what was going on. To them, Grabowski was a god. A god who arrived in a celestial bird, also a type of divine creature.[4]

What we see on these South Pacific islands is something that shows that men have been mistaken for gods; specifically, that an advanced technological civilization posed such a radical break from their traditional framework that the cargo and the men involved were deified. This is definitive proof that humankind could, and in fact has, numerous times, mistaken other humans—and maybe, by extension, nonhuman intelligences—for God.

John Frum was prophesied to one day return to the islands, when the Golden Age of the Gods would return. The existence of a Golden Age, when the Gods lived among humankind and taught them sciences, including the constellations, is precisely what we read in the legends and myths of our ancient civilizations. Later on, we will see the story of the Babylonian civilizing god Oannes, who appeared out of the waters of the Persian

Gulf, spoke to the local people, and offered them knowledge, including knowledge of the constellations. It precisely echoes the story of John Frum and the cargo cults. Like the Americans after World War II, some of these gods too promised to one day return.

It is therefore possible that men of flesh and blood, whether human or extraterrestrial, could be mistaken for gods. It is possible that the meeting Ezekiel had with God was truly with the pilot and operator of a spaceship. However, all legends can be interpreted in a number of ways. In the Bible, it is clear that there is a body of evidence that together clearly argues for the presence, in biblical times, of a race of giants. But the presence of these giants in itself is not proof that ancient aliens once bred with human women.

Legends, by default, cannot be proof, but we *can* accept them as evidence. And when we take the whole, rather than individual details, it is clear that there is substantial evidence to suggest that "gods" once came to our ancestors, interacted with them, on occasion guided them, and also seem to have helped them in the endeavor known as civilization. In the case of the gods of Vanuatu, we know that the Western world and America, the land of their gods, was technologically advanced and possessed the "cargo" to impress the natives. But when we turn to ancient Egypt or Sumer and their claims that gods once ruled their nation, or that Oannes taught them civilization, we cannot look elsewhere on planet Earth and find evidence of a civilization far enough advanced to have sent missionaries to these cultures. Nor have we ever found evidence of creatures that lived a thousand or maybe tens of thousands of years. But, again, whereas a case can be made that the God(s) of the Bible and other legends are truly extraterrestrial beings, there is currently no hard proof. If we need hard proof, then we need to investigate the archaeological record of planet Earth.

Chapter 4

Old Buildings, New Techniques

The search for evidence to answer the Ancient Alien Question has always been focused on buildings or artifacts that our ancestors left behind. The question is whether they created it themselves, or were helped or inspired by alien visitors. Erich von Däniken's series of questions in *Chariots of the Gods* is specifically directed to these structures, which at the time were clearly not adequately explained by scientists and archaeologists. The official descriptions seldom explained the intricacies and wonders of a given site.

Now 40 years later, the situation has somewhat improved, but many of the original questions remain, and none more famous than those surrounding the greatest building on planet Earth constructed by our ancestors: the Great Pyramid.

The Greatest Pyramid

The Great Pyramid is the only remaining wonder of the ancient world. It is officially said to have been built as the tomb for Pharaoh Khufu, a king of the Fourth Dynasty who ruled from around 2589 to 2566 BCE, but there are skeptics who argue that there is no evidence that Khufu was ever involved with the construction of this pyramid. They point out that the sarcophagus inside the King's Chamber was found empty, and there are no inscriptions anywhere in or on the pyramid to link it with him. Hence, they argue, the stories that the Great Pyramid is far older could definitely be true. The Arab writer Abu Zeyd el Balkhy actually stated that the Great Pyramid was built when Lyre was in the constellation of Cancer, which would take it to about 73,000 years ago.

The Great Pyramid of Khufu is the only surviving wonder of the ancient world. Many believe that the scale and precision involved in building this gigantic monument was simply outside the scope of the ancient Egyptians. Recent discoveries have shown that the method and science involved in its construction are so advanced that the how was only recently discovered.

Old Buildings, New Techniques

There is, however, evidence that Khufu definitely *was* involved with the construction of the pyramid. In the relieving chambers above the King's Chamber, there is a cartouche containing Khufu's name, which clearly shows that Khufu's men were there. These relieving chambers were never meant to be entered and had in fact been sealed at the time of the pyramid's construction. Hence, they date back to the time the pyramids were built. The discovery of Khufu's name inside thus provided definitive evidence that this pharaoh was responsible for the Great Pyramid.

In Zecharia Sitchin's *The Stairway to Heaven*, published in 1980, the chapter "Forging the Pharaoh's Name" argues that Colonel Richard Howard Vyse did not discover but instead *forged* a cartouche containing the name of Pharaoh Khufu. Vyse was credited with this groundbreaking discovery that placed his name in the annals of Egyptology in his book *Operations Carried on at the Pyramids of Gizeh in 1837*. Sitchin said that the cartouche had not been seen by previous visitors to the relieving chamber in question. How could they have missed what Vyse so easily found? Furthermore, Sitchin writes, "Wasn't it odd, I thought, that for centuries no markings of any kind were found by anyone, anywhere, in the pyramid, not even in Davison's Chamber above the King's Chamber—and only Vyse found such markings where only he first entered?"

Next point of debate: The cartouche was executed in red paint. The experts had difficulty distinguishing it from other—recent—inscriptions, and its possible status as a recent addition wasn't helped with claims that people had been seen entering the structure with red paint. Perring's memoirs, *The Pyramids of Gizeh*, do state that the red paint "was a composition of red ochre called by the Arabs *moghrab* which is still in use.... Such is the state of preservation of the marks in the quarries that it is difficult to distinguish the work of yesterday from one of three thousand years."

But the best evidence, Sitchin argued, was that the name of Khufu was misspelled—conforming to a notorious misspelling in a book to which Vyse had access. He claims that the inscription reads Ra-ufu, not Khufu. This mistake would have been unthinkable for ancient Egyptian writers to make, but it is explainable if the inscription was done in 1837. That year, an academic book about hieroglyphics called *Materia Hieroglyphica* had been published, in which the name of Khufu was erroneously entered. The lines of the sieve were so close together that they appeared in the print like a massive disc, which is in fact another way of writing "Ra." It is known that Vyse had this book with him.

Definitely, Vyse had the opportunity to commit this fraud. But in any crime, motive is an important consideration—and Sitchin is able to provide one: Vyse's expedition was running short of funding, and had not uncovered any major revelation that would grab headlines, which is what he needed to receive more funding. The discovery of the cartouche was therefore a gift from heaven. Too good to be true?

Perhaps. However, it seems that accusations of forgery work both ways. Sitchin's opponents have pointed out that the visual evidence for the misspelling that Sitchin provides is erroneous at best, and some claim Sitchin has actually forged evidence in support of his conclusions of forgery! His opponents point out that various other photographs, including those circulated by Rainer Stadelmann when he was working on the ventilation system in the Great Pyramid in the 1990s, reveal that the correct sign was used in the writing in the relieving chamber—hence, Ra-ufu is in fact Khufu. In their opinion, Sitchin, not Vyse, is guilty of forgery.

In Sitchin's possible defense, when he first published his accusation in 1980, several photographs now in existence, including Stadelmann's, had not yet been made; only drawings existed, and perhaps these showed the inaccuracy as well? Unfortunately for Sitchin, that is not the case: A sketch of the cartouche appears

Old Buildings, New Techniques

in Perring's book, published in 1839. Sitchin gives no precise source from which he got the cartouche, but as Perring is listed in the bibliography, most assume it was his book that provided Sitchin with a drawing of the cartouche. And, as such, the conclusion drawn by those antagonistic towards Sitchin is that he purposefully faked the story of a forgery in an attempt to predate the pyramid to several millennia before Khufu.

The Great Pyramid is also the subject of isolationism: It tends to be seen in isolation. But it is not. The Pyramid of Khafre next to it is almost as big, as is the Red Pyramid at Dashur. If aliens built the Great Pyramid, then it needs to be argued that they were also responsible for at least some of the other pyramids in ancient Egypt.

Just slightly smaller than the Great Pyramid, the Pyramid of Khafre has retained some of its cover stones at the very top of the pyramid. It therefore allows one to imagine how brilliant—literally—these pyramids would have looked in their heydays.

So is there no mystery to the Great Pyramid? Actually, there is. The evidence suggests that though Khufu was responsible for its construction, he had at his disposal technology and information that official archaeology does not credit the Ancient Egyptians with. It is technology that was millennia ahead of its time, helping to build the pyramid with an accuracy that defies modern standards.

The Great Pyramid has been measured in extraordinary detail, which has revealed how purposefully everything to do with this pyramid was executed. Early on, explorer W.M. Flinders Petrie found that the internal volume of the sarcophagus in the King's Chamber was 1,166.4 liters (about 308 gallons), and the external volume was precisely twice that: 2,332.8 liters (616 gallons). This clearly underlines that whoever built this had access to advanced technology and mathematics. Accurate measurements of the Great Pyramid give its dimensions as 230.2506 meters (755.43 feet) on the North Base, 230.35869 meters (755.77 feet) on the West Base, 230.45318 meters (756.08 feet) on the South Base, and 230.39222 meters (755.88 feet) on the East Base. The maximum deviation from perfect square is therefore 0.09812 meters, or 0.80 feet, which is an accuracy of 0.0004 centimeters per meter, or 0.0015 inch per foot. The deviation from the 90-degree angles of the four corners of the pyramid is 0 degrees 00'02" (northwest), 0 degrees 03'02" (northeast), 0 degrees 3'33" (southeast) and 0 degrees 0'33" (southwest)—an extraordinary accuracy. The slopes of the pyramid are at an angle of 51 degrees, which is known as the "perfect" angle, as it embodies the mathematical ratios of pi and phi—two ratios the ancient Egyptians allegedly did not possess as they were "only" discovered by the Greeks. Yet their usage is on display throughout the pyramid complex. Such accuracy is stunning, far exceeding modern building achievements. No wonder, therefore, that as early as John Taylor in 1859, its construction was ascribed to a divinely inspired race of non-Egyptian invaders, though Mark Lehner in *The Complete Pyramids* (1997) only ventured as far as to question "Why such phenomenal precision?", arguing that the answer eluded us.

Old Buildings, New Techniques

Choosing to remove the responsibility for construction of the Great Pyramid—or any other monument—from the native culture is a dangerous exercise that today will greatly upset the scientific establishment. Indeed, it is clear that, for science, keeping all buildings "native" to the culture in which they are found is far more important than actually going with the available evidence. And in the case of the Great Pyramid, it was its accuracy, which far exceeded the accuracy of other buildings of its time in ancient Egypt, that has prodded so many to conclude it was built by non-Egyptians. But the available evidence actually suggests that Khufu, an Egyptian, did build it, but that somehow he had at his disposal information and building techniques that did not seem to have been used before. That is the true great mystery of the Great Pyramid.

Detail of the section of the Pyramid of Khafre where the Arabs abandoned their work in removing the cover stones. It reveals the extraordinary precision involved in the building work of this and other pyramids.

It is a fact that not a single pyramid has ever been found in which a mummy was present. Egyptologists are quick to point out that grave-robbers are responsible for this, but in truth intact pyramids *have* been found, and when their sarcophagus was opened, no mummy lay inside. So, if not a tomb, the question is what the pyramid could be. The most vociferous answer in recent years has come from engineer Christopher Dunn, who, in *The Giza Powerplant*, argues that the pyramids are power plants.

Flinders Petrie inspected the King's Chamber and argued that it had been subject to a violent disturbance, which had shaken it so badly that the entire chamber had expanded by 1 inch. The culprit was identified as an earthquake, the only natural force capable of creating sufficient force. But as Dunn highlights, the King's Chamber is the *only* room affected by this event; the Queen's Chamber remained unaffected. Dunn says he has seen no evidence of laser cutting in ancient Egypt, but the rocks display evidence that *some* machinery was used. Flinders Petrie estimated that a pressure of 1 to 2 tons on jewel-tipped bronze saws would have been necessary to cut through the extremely hard granite; Dunn found evidence of lathe turning on a sarcophagus lid in the Cairo Museum. Petrie himself found evidence of spiral drilling in granite, measuring the feed rate as 1 in 60, which is incredible for drilling into a material like granite. Petrie was impressed with this feed rate, as he was confronted with an engineering anomaly. The ancient Egyptians could not have achieved this by using the tools ascribed to them. Dunn's analysis revealed that the ancient Egyptian drill performed 500 times greater per revolution than modern drills! He observed that ultrasonic drilling would be capable of the feats seen by Petrie in the Valley Temple, but the ancient Egyptians of course did not possess ultrasonic drills.

What if the stones of the Great Pyramid were not quarried, but "made" on site? Joseph Davidovits first aired this theory in 1974. Professor Davidovits is an internationally renowned French scientist, who was honored by French President Jacques Chirac with one of France's two highest honors, the Chevalier de l'Ordre National du Mérite, in November 1998. Davidovits has a French degree in chemical engineering and a German doctorate degree (PhD) in chemistry, and was also a professor and founder of the Institute for Applied Archaeological Sciences, IAPAS, Barry University, Miami, Florida, from 1983 to 1989. He was a visiting professor at Penn State University, Pennsylvania, from 1989 to 1991, and has been professor and director of the Geopolymer Institute, Saint-Quentin, France, since 1979. He is a world expert in modern and ancient cements, as well as geosynthesis and man-made rocks, and is the inventor of geopolymers and the chemistry of geopolymerization. He is, in short, a scientific genius and the expert in his field, sometimes referred to as the "father of geopolymers."

These are just the highlights; his CV is longer than most books. But the reason I list his career's distinctions is that all of his scientific credibility has made virtually no dent in Egyptological circles, where archaeologists have largely disregarded his findings about how the pyramids—or at least the Great Pyramid—were *really* constructed. In his expert opinion, backed up by experiments and analysis, the stones of the Great Pyramid were not hewn from quarries and then transported; instead, rough stone was quarried, but then placed in a (wooden?) container with other materials, causing a chemical process that made what in simple terms some might call cement, but which in fact is a type of stone that even experts in the field have a hard time telling apart from natural rock.

From an engineering perspective, this technique would make the construction of the Great Pyramid much easier: There were no immense limestone blocks to be moved; there was no real need for a ramp, and the transportation of the stone material could be done faster, as less care was required in moving the limestone; it was merely an ingredient, and if it broke, no one cared. Furthermore, the technique could also explain how the tremendous accuracy in the construction of the pyramid was achieved—the famous "no cigarette paper is able to be fitted between two stones." Rather than figuring out how two hewn stones were perfectly fitted to each other on site, instead, we would have wooden molds that were placed next to a completed "block," upon which "cement" was poured into the mold, then left to dry, before the next stone was made. This guaranteed that each one fitted perfectly to the next.

This theory also fits in with the evidence on the ground. Some of the blocks that were allegedly hewn have large lumps trapped within the mass; others have wavy strata; others have differences in density between the stones of the pyramids and the natural stones as located in the quarries; and there is a general absence of any horizontal orientation of the shells in the pyramid blocks, when normal sedimentation would be expected to result in shells lying flat. All of these are telltale signs for an expert like Davidovits that the stones were cast, not hewn.

For us to accept that the blocks were cast, the only missing ingredient is whether or not the ancient Egyptians were familiar with such "rock making," of geopolymerization. Davidovits is the world expert in this technology, and it is fair to say that not a single Egyptologist was aware of it until Davidovits first proposed his hypothesis. Specifically throughout the past three decades, Davidovits has been trying to educate this group of scientists, but they remain largely unwilling students, even though he sold more than 45,000 copies of his book when it appeared in 1988. The general public wanted to understand, but Egyptologists lacked the credentials to criticize his work, and they chose to ignore it. Today, there seems to be something of an Anglo-Saxon conspiracy against his theories, as Davidovits's books are easily published by respected houses in France and other countries, yet *They Built the Great Pyramid* was self-published in its English edition.

First aired as a hypothesis in 1974, his theory has come a long way. Davidovits was given samples of the Great Pyramid by Egyptologist Jean-Philippe Lauer in 1982, which he identified as fragments of geopolymers. In more recent years, his work has received the backing of several other experts in the field, and when his team gave samples of modern reagglomerated stone produced at the beginning of the year 2002 to two leading geology laboratories for blind analysis, the scientists stated that the sample was natural limestone! When even geologists get it wrong, it underlines how difficult it is for Egyptologists who—as mentioned—remain unwilling to venture where they truly should go, to understand.

Davidovits has used chemical analysis to show that the stones of the pyramids are different from the native stone in the quarries, demonstrating that the traditional stance of the Egyptologists can, from a scientific standpoint, no longer be maintained. The analysis shows that the stones did not just come from nearby quarries, but are indeed cast. To quote Davidovits:

> The results [of the quarry samples] were compared with pyramid casing stones of Cheops, Teti and Sneferu. The quarry samples are pure limestone consisting of 96–99% Calcite, 0.5–2.5% Quartz, and very small amount of dolomite, gypsum and iron-alumino-silicate. On the other hand the Cheops and Teti casing stones are limestone consisting of: calcite 85–90% and a high amount of special minerals such as Opal CT, hydroxy-apatite, a silico-aluminate, which are not found in the quarries. The pyramid casing stones are light in density and contain numerous trapped air bubbles, unlike the quarry samples which are uniformly dense. If the casing stones were natural limestone, quarries different from those traditionally associated with the pyramid sites must be found, but where? X-Ray diffraction of a red casing stone coating is the first proof to demonstrate the fact that a complicated man-made geopolymeric system was produced in Egypt 4,700 years ago.[1]

That is an extraordinary claim to make: that a science that we thought was invented in the last few decades was actually already in use in Egypt 4,700 years ago. And furthermore that the ancient Egyptians used the best building technique ever designed: creating stone blocks that are so identical to natural rock that, from a chemical position, geologists often cannot tell them apart! Davidovits is therefore convinced that this method of stonemaking was the origin of alchemy. He points out that the deity specifically linked with Khufu was Khnum, which means "to bind," "to join," "to cement," "to unite," and which typifies the process of geopolymerization.

Egypt was seen as the birthplace of alchemy, but for Davidovits, it is also the cradle of chemistry. He argues that certain names, such as *mafkat*, which Egyptologists have been unable to translate or explain, were "invented words"—that is, technical terms—as they described compounds that ancient chemists had constructed. He believes that when Imhotep is credited as "the inventor of the art of constructing with cut stones," it is actually a mistranslation of the Greek *xeston lithon*, which does not translate as "cut stone," but rather means "the action to polish stone." For Davidovits, Imhotep is actually the inventor of working with geopolymers, and it was specifically for that reason that he was considered to be a god. In short, Imhotep was an Ancient Egyptian who somehow created a science 4,700 years ahead of his time. Without this invention, the Egyptian Pyramid Age would not have been. The key question is, therefore, how Imhotep accomplished this seemingly impossible feat.

Davidovits believes that Imhotep created two different chemical formulas: a very simple one for the casting of the limestone core blocks, and another one to produce the high-quality stones of the exterior layer. The first and major ingredient in these techniques is soft limestone. Soft limestone can be easily disaggregated either under pressure or by diluting it in water. To that end, he writes, "shallow canals were dug in the soft limestone

Old Buildings, New Techniques

along the Nile, forming ideal basins for producing large quantities of muddy limestone. Imhotep's men began disaggregating the clayish soft rock with its water, until the lime and the clay separated, forming a mud with the fossil shells at the bottom."[2] Next, a substance called natron salt (sodium carbonate) was poured in. Salt is a very reactive substance that has a petrifying effect, which is why it is used to avoid the putrefaction of organic tissue by mummification. Natron is found in great quantities in the desert and in the Wadi-El-Natron (60 miles northwest of Cairo and named after the substance) and Davidovits has shown that the ancient Egyptians of the Pyramid Age used it in massive quantities.

Next, more lime, the mineral that binds, was added. Lime is a powdery residue obtained by burning and reducing to ashes sedimentary rocks such as limestone and dolomite. The fire oxidizes and converts the rocks into a powdery residue, which is lime. Lime mixed with natron and water produces a third substance, a much more corrosive one, which sparks off a strong chemical reaction and transforms other materials. The water dissolves the natron salt and puts the lime in suspension, forming caustic soda. Caustic soda is the catalyst Imhotep needed to trigger off a powerful chemical reaction, one that would produce the fast integration of silica and alumina.

According to Davidovits, the ancient Egyptians then mixed the ingredients in the canals until a homogenous binder paste was obtained. Imhotep now had a water-based cement, which he then had to convert into concrete. For this, he added more fossil shells, limestone rubble, and silt from the river Nile, producing a concrete paste, which was carried to where hundreds of small wooden molds had been prepared. These molds had been smeared with rancid oil to facilitate the release of the concrete once hardened. The mixture was rammed into the molds, becoming a dense re-agglomerated limestone, which was left to dry in the shade, to avoid its cracking under the hot sun.

The preceding description is a proven chemical procedure, but was it known to Imhotep? For an untrained eye, the process seems terribly complex. How could it have been known millennia ago?

Davidovits thinks that ancient records have left us clues that this was indeed the manner in which the pyramids were built, as well as showing the total cost of the mineral mixing ingredients required in the process. He believes that this information was actually left behind on the pyramid covering stones and pointed out to Herodotus when the Greek writer visited Giza. Herodotus reported that a sum of 1,600 talents, or roughly the equivalent of 150 million dollars, was spent on garlic, onions, and radishes, which he and everyone else considered a phenomenal amount of money for what seem to be secondary dietary requirements for the workforce. As such, the story is taken with...a pinch of salt, and the argument that Herodotus was lied to by his locally hired tourist guide. But Davidovits believes that those names ("garlic, onions, and radishes") were misinterpretations of what was actually written on the pyramid. We have to remember that our ancestors mostly referred to substances based on their colors: "rubber" comes from the Latin word for "red," as rubber was red. And so Davidovits argues that these words are not "garlic," "onion," or "radish," but technical terms whose true meaning had become lost. Davidovits has used other inscriptions, including several stelae from the Fourth Dynasty, to show that specific mining venues were exploited during the Pyramid Age, but that the materials quarried there have no clear purpose within the traditional methodology of constructing the pyramids—but they do make sense within his theory.

Is there hard evidence to credit Imhotep and his colleagues of the Third and Fourth Dynasty with the invention of geopolymers? Perhaps. The Famine Stele, found on the island of Elephantine in southern Egypt, does describe the invention of building with stone through processing different minerals and ores, which could be chemicals involved in the fabrication of man-made stone. On the Giza plateau, Davidovits has shown that several stones have weathered unnaturally: One single block was sometimes left unfinished for the day, and thus it hardened overnight before being brought to the desired height the following morning. This meant that one block was made in two phases, with slightly different materials, and created under different circumstances. Six millennia later, it means that sometimes the lower section of a stone has weathered badly, but the higher section has not, even though the stones next to it do not reveal such lower weathering. Such weathering does not conform to the traditionalist view of quarried blocks.

There is also circumstantial evidence. For example, we know that the ancient Egyptians were familiar with cement as such: At several places in the Great Pyramid, remains of 4,500-year-old cements are found, and are still in excellent condition. This ancient mortar is far superior to the cement used in modern buildings, as well as the cement used to restore the ancient Egyptian monuments—much of which has already degraded and cracked after only 50 years.

Davidovits has gained some acceptance from Egyptologists for his idea that some Egyptian artifacts, specifically some vases, were geopolymers. Thus, it is accepted that the ancient Egyptians had the necessary chemical and technical knowledge (of copper, alkalis, and ceramics) to mold vases in this way. Davidovits argues, "So if the Egyptians knew how to make such a high-quality cement for vases and statues, what was there to stop them adding aggregates such as fossil shells to produce a high-performance reagglomerated limestone? Clearly, nothing."[3]

The most recent support (and headlines) for Davidovits's findings has come from Linn W. Hobbs, professor of materials science at the Massachusetts Institute of Technology (MIT). Hobbs has stated that he believes that mainstream archaeologists have been too contemptuous of work by "other scientists"—read:

Davidovits—suggesting the possibility of concrete. "The degree of hostility aimed at experimentation is disturbing," Hobbs said. "Too many big egos and too many published works may be riding on the idea that every pyramid block was carved, not cast."[4]

In 2006, research by Michel W. Barsoum at Philadelphia's Drexel University confirmed Davidovits's conclusion that samples of stone from parts of the Khufu Pyramid were microstructurally different from limestone blocks. Barsoum, a professor of materials engineering, said microscope, X-ray, and chemical analysis of scraps of stone from the pyramids "suggest a small but significant percentage of blocks on the higher portions of the pyramids were cast" from concrete—thus confirming Davidovits's conclusions.[5]

When Barsoum, a native of Egypt, went public with these findings, he said he was unprepared for the onslaught of angry criticism that greeted the peer-reviewed research by himself and scientists Adrish Ganguly of Drexel and Gilles Hug of France's National Center for Scientific Research. "You would have thought I claimed the pyramids were carved by lasers," Barsoum said.[6] Egyptologist Zahi Hawass's reaction was typical of the onslaught: "It's highly stupid," he said. "The pyramids are made from solid blocks of quarried limestone. To suggest otherwise is idiotic and insulting."[7]

These are just a few examples in a long list of evidence that argues that the most likely method of construction was the use of geopolymers, and not hewn limestone slabs that were perfectly moved into position. As recently as 1951, the German Egyptologist Otto Neugebauer argued that "ancient science was the product of very few men; and those few happened not to be Egyptian."[8] Neugebauer's statement was in sharp contrast with men like Aristotle, who saw Egypt as "the cradle of mathematics," crediting Egyptians with inventing geometry, astronomy, and arithmetic. Eudoxus, like Pythagoras, studied in ancient Egypt before being admitted to Plato's Academy in Athens,

Old Buildings, New Techniques

showing that the ancient Greeks throughout their history knew that Egypt held certain knowledge that was of vital importance for an educated Greek—and that was apparently a type of knowledge that they were unable to attain in Greece itself.

Though it has been studied by so many, it is clear that the Great Pyramid has not yet given up all of its secrets. These are just a few more of its peculiarities:

- Flautist Paul Horn has noted that the granite sarcophagus in the King's Chamber resonates at a frequency of 438 cycles per second (Hz).

- Acoustics engineer Robert Vawter claims that the King's Chamber was designed specifically as a resonant chamber in which the sound of specific frequencies would resonate.

- The granite of the King's Chamber contains silicon-quartz crystals; aswan granite contains 55 or more percent quartz crystals. Dee Jay Nelson and David H. Coville write that this "would allow a 'piezotension' upon these parallel surfaces and cause an electromotive flow. The great mass of stone above the pyramid chambers presses downward by gravitational force upon the granite walls thereby converting them into perpetual electric generators.... A man within the King's Chamber would thus come within a weak but definite induction field."[9]

Traditionalists might argue that these phenomena are unintentional, but what if they *were* intentional? What if someone was meant to put himself in this sarcophagus and lay there? Might something truly special happen? It is a question that takes us beyond the analysis of the building of the Great Pyramid, which has shown us that aliens are unlikely to have built it, but that it was clearly built with technology far ahead of its time, in the possession of Imhotep. So did he discover it, or was he given this knowledge?

Baalbek

The temple of Baalbek lies only 50 miles northeast of the Lebanese capital of Beirut. It was once the greatest Roman temple in the world, and people came from all over the Roman Empire to visit it. Today, because of three decades of warfare and terrorism in the region, hardly anyone makes it to Baalbek.

In Roman times, the city was known as Heliopolis, The City of the Sun. The temple complex is situated in the fertile Bekaa valley, but historians have long wondered why the largest Roman temple was built here. There was clearly some attraction to Baalbek, and the answer seems to be that the area had long been deemed to be sacred and the Romans were only the latest in a long line of powers that incorporated it into their heritage.

The complex is dedicated to the worship of a triad: Jupiter, Mercury, and Venus, the first of which the Romans associated

The temple complex of Baalbek in Lebanon became the home of the largest Roman temple. But it is the platform below the Roman complex that is one of the great enigmas of the ancient world, as it holds stones that weigh hundreds of tons. No one knows how they were transported.

with Ba'al, after whom the site was named. *Ba'al* is a Semitic word, meaning "lord," and it therefore has covered a number of deities; in this case, the Lord of the Bekaa valley—Ba'al-bek, who is generally identified with Hadad, a storm and rain god.

The Arabs believe that Baalbek was the place where Nimrod rebelled against God and constructed the Tower of Babel, but there are other traditions that link the construction of the complex with Cain, who built it after Jahweh had cursed him. All of these legends share one common component, which is that the temple of Baalbek is considered to be the oldest building in the world. Apart from being old, it is also huge. The Acropolis of Baalbek is much bigger than the Acropolis in Athens. In fact, even the second-largest temple in Baalbek is bigger than the Parthenon in Athens.

It is the megalithic ruins between the temple that have attracted speculation as to how our ancestors could have created Baalbek. Most interesting is the stone platform on which the Romans built the Temple of Jupiter. Its walls consist of about 24 monoliths at their lowest level, each weighing 300 tons. There is a trilithon (a grouping of three blocks, two vertical with a horizontal block atop them) in the southwest wall of the platform, known as the "Marvel of the Three Stones," each more than 62 feet high and weighing an estimated 800 tons! A fourth stone nearby is 80 feet in length and weighs 1,100 tons! They are thought to be the world's biggest blocks of cut stone. As in so many other places, the stones are precisely cut and were somehow transported from a quarry several miles away from the temple complex. Michel Alouf, the former curator of the site, observed that, "In spite of their immense size, they are so accurately placed in position and so carefully joined, that it is almost impossible to insert a needle between them. No description will give an exact idea of the bewildering and stupefying effect of these tremendous blocks on the spectator."[10]

The so-called Stone of the South, which lies in the quarry, is 69 feet long, and is estimated to weigh 1,200 tons; another stone in the quarry, The Stone of the Pregnant Woman, weighs 1,000 tons. With the technology that science has accredited to the builders, it would take 40,000 men to move this single block! This is logistically impossible, as a 69-foot-long block does not offer sufficient holds and spaces for 40,000 men to put their hands on it. So clearly *some* form of technology was used in moving this stone; it is the only possible conclusion. Not only were the stones moved from the quarry to the platform, but they were also lifted up 30 feet in the air.

Roger Hopkins, a stone mason, has suggested that the trilithon stones and 300-ton blocks were all moved with wooden rollers, and he has been invited to demonstrate his suggestion in a number of television programs. However, Hopkins was using

The Stone of the South, still in the quarry of the Baalbek complex. It is 69 feet long, and is estimated to weigh 1,200 tons. It is among the most gigantic stones ever to have been carved. How these and similar stones were ever meant to be transported is unknown, and poses challenges even to our modern equipment.

Old Buildings, New Techniques

10 people for a 2-ton stone in his demonstration, which was done on a concrete platform—a very smooth surface compared to the landscape around Baalbek. For a stone weighing more than 10 tons, Hopkins agrees he requires more than 100 people to move it.

Archaeologists already have difficulty explaining how the Romans built the temple itself. The Temple of Jupiter consisted of 54 columns, though only six now remain after millennia of earthquakes. It is believed that the platform was actually constructed to make the entire temple complex more resistant to earthquakes, but this is faulty logic, as the temple complex was clearly *not* resistant to earthquakes, whereas the platform itself has withstood the test of time. A more logical scenario is that the platform was chosen by the Romans to build their temple, as they knew that it would offer a better chance for their temple to remain intact.

The architrave and frieze blocks of the Temple of Jupiter weigh up to 60 tons each, with one corner block weighing more than 100 tons, and all of them raised to a height of more than 60 feet above the ground. Though archaeologists argue this was done using Roman cranes, these cranes were not capable of lifting such weights. They therefore suggest that combining multiple cranes may have allowed the builders to lift these stones, but in the truth, this is speculation. Archaeologists do not even speculate as to how the 800-ton stones were moved, for there is no evidence from any known civilization that such technology was available to our ancestors—but someone clearly accomplished it, somehow!

British author Alan Alford, in *Gods of the New Millennium*, contacted Bob MacGrain, the technical director of Baldwins construction company, who confirmed that modern technology was just about able to lift and place 1,000-ton stones on a support structure that was 20 feet high, but this technology had just come about in the 1990s, when Alford wrote the book.

Because of its location, Baalbek is largely off-limits, so the ability to understand our ancient past has become one of the victims of the warfare that has typified this region. Is it a coincidence that the Romans all of a sudden excelled in their building techniques in a location where humankind had excelled before? Or is it possible that when the Romans erected their temple, there was still a body of knowledge locally available that they made full use of? That could more easily explain the enigma of the largest temple of the Roman Empire, though it does not explain the mystery of the platform itself.

For that mystery, we need to go back to the beginnings of civilization. With stories of the Tower of Babel and folklore that this was the oldest building in the world (which, in biblical terms, the Tower of Babel obviously is), Baalbek presents some of the best evidence from the ancient world to demonstrate that at a point in time before the Roman Empire, someone in the Bekaa valley was far more advanced than anyone else, and constructed a stone platform that truly defies belief. Whoever built it possessed technology and/or knowledge that cannot be accredited in a normal manner to our ancestors, as Baalbek's platform is truly extraordinary—out of the ordinary. No wonder, therefore, that the Russian scientist Matest Agrest in 1959 proposed that Baalbek was used as a launch platform for extraterrestrial spaceships. Indeed, until NASA moved the gigantic Saturn V rocket to its launch pad on a huge tracked vehicle, no one had transported such a weight as the stones of Baalbek.

Carnac

In Brittany, France, Carnac and its neighboring villages still contain about 4,000 megalithic stones. Archaeologists believe that the original amount was probably closer to 10,000 stones. Carnac is especially famous for the thousands of stones that have been grouped into so-called alignments—stone rows. Though

The French town of Carnac is primarily famous for its stone rows. More than 4,000 remain. But the area once also had the tallest standing stone in the world, weighing 340 tons and measuring 60 feet high. This incredibly large stone has since fallen and broken into various parts.

the stone rows of Carnac are not unique—they are found elsewhere in France and abroad—Carnac does have the most impressive and most gigantic stone alignments in the world.

Archaeologists date the stone rows as being 5,000 to 6,000 years old, making them approximately 1,000 years older than the Great Pyramid of Giza, in Egypt. It should therefore come as no surprise that, locally, the stone rows are compared to a "Neolithic cathedral."

It is known that the largest stones on display here weigh more than 20 tons. Modern reconstructions, using tools and techniques that were known to our Neolithic ancestors, have shown that a group of approximately 20 people were able to create a stone of such size. But this is not the real enigma of Carnac. The enigma is that the stones are still standing. The surface of the Neolithic Age is barely 10 inches below the present ground level, and a further 10 inches below is granite—one of the hardest rocks on the planet. This means that the stones were placed on soil with a maximum depth of 10 inches, before they hit solid rock. In this tiny hole, the builders had to create all the required balance to keep the stone upright. Despite the long odds, they managed to succeed in this, as is evidenced by the thousands of *standing* stones that make up the stone rows.

Whereas many megalithic remains have been seriously damaged and been the subject of vandalism, the key to the survival of the Carnac megaliths might be the fact that they were largely invisible until the 17th century. Documents written before that time do not refer to them; most likely they were hidden by foliage that masked them from passers-by. But in the 17th century there was a need for more agricultural ground, which led to the discovery of the megaliths. Whereas in other parts of the world the megalithic blocks were often moved (if possible) or toppled and then buried, in Carnac, there were so many of them that it was an impossible task for any farmer, which meant that they remained intact.

Major archaeological interest in the stone rows only began in the latter half of the 20th century. These archaeologists originally believed that, rather than a series of stone rows, there was in origin just one major stone row, covering a distance of more than 5 miles. Soon, research revealed that this "single stone row" theory did not float; it seemed instead that there were five stone rows, four of which contained approximately 1,000 stones. However, more recent research, which I will come back to shortly, suggests there is indeed a "great plan" to Carnac, and that it could be considered as one single stone row.

One concentration of stones can be found near Erdeven; the other concentration of stones stands back-to-back to the north of Carnac. The most western is that of Le Menec, where there are 1,099 standing stones in 11 rows. One stone towers above all others, measuring 12 feet, and is thus labeled "the giant." Most of the stones are, however, relatively small—at least in comparison to the stone row of Kermario, to the east of the row of Le Menec.

The stone rows of Kermario number 1,029 stones, distributed in 10 rows. The field where they stand measures 3,675 feet, showing that the stones are roughly one yard apart. This field has the most gigantic stones, and is continued in the field of Kerlescan, where there are 594 stones, in 13 rows, spread out over 2,900 feet.

There are further stone rows: those of Sainte Barbe, which is a stone row of 50 stones, in four rows, oriented south to north; and the most northern stone row of Kerzerho, which numbers 1,130 stones in 10 rows, measuring an impressive 7,000 feet in length. Near the camping of Kerzerho, some of these stones measure no less than 19 feet in height. They are the highest standing stones in the entire region.

Apart from stone rows, there are also other megalithic constructions here, like the dolmen at Crucuno, which makes for an impressive sight as it leans against a wall of a farm; its covering stone weighs 40 tons. Archaeologists have dated it as contemporary with the stone rows, at around 4000 BCE.

There is one standing stone that was 60 feet high, weighed in at 340 tons, and was moved over a distance of 4 miles to its present location. It should come as no surprise that this stone is no longer standing. But this stone does underline the knowledge and technology of this culture, which erected stones on a scale not seen anywhere else.

What are they? Archaeologists have excluded the possibility that these are graves. Neither did they serve a military purpose, though the American soldiers, during the Second World War, did mistake the stone rows for a German defense line. According to the legend, a French soldier who was aware of the situation had to intervene, as otherwise the stone rows would have become the target of intensive bombing raids.

Excluding funerary and military purposes, archaeologists conclude that the only purpose could have been religious. Modern archaeologists think that it is likely that the stones were used as the framework for a procession, and whereas this is possible, in the final analysis, all archaeologists have to agree that they simply do not know why Carnac was built.

One man, Howard Crowhurst, has been able to demonstrate how Carnac was constructed and has revealed that the builders were great mathematicians, who were also very familiar with astronomy. Crowhurst has demonstrated that a number of stone rows were aligned to solar and lunar phenomena. Kermario, for example, is aligned to the sunrise at the summer solstice—something Kermario has in common with that other great marvel of the megalithic world, Stonehenge.

Crowhurst moved to the Carnac region in 1986, and his three decades of mapping the stones—more recently aided by the arrival of Google Earth and its satellite photographs—has revealed to him a master plan. When he analyzed the stone rows, he realized that there was great intricacy in their design. He noticed that the construction method of the stone rows at Carnac involved squares: Sometimes two squares were used to create a rectangle, and sometimes three. What Crowhurst realized, for example in Le Menec, was that the short side of this rectangle was aligned perfectly north–south, and the stone rows were aligned along the diagonal of this rectangle. This insight revealed Carnac's master plan, which is marked by an extreme accuracy in design and planning, whereby its builders used advanced mathematics, and were also able to plot and measure pieces of land over distances of several miles, before they began to place thousands of megaliths. In short, the region of Carnac was carefully mapped, measured, and plotted, so that these stone rows would be accurately directed to certain lunar, solar, and maybe other astronomical phenomena—likely some that are not yet discovered.

This means that our ancestors could plan almost to the inch plots of lands that stretch for several miles. In his analysis of Carnac, Crowhurst confirmed that this civilization used the so-called megalithic yard. This megalithic yard was first proposed by Professor Alexander Thom, who made detailed surveys of

Old Buildings, New Techniques

600 megalithic sites in Britain, Ireland, and France. The megalithic yard is equal to 2.72 feet. Thom also proposed another unit, which he labeled the megalithic rod, and which was 2.5 megalithic yards. Whereas archaeology is largely preoccupied with trying to find ammunition with which to attack Thom's conclusions, Crowhurst is one of several who have found further evidence of this unit of measurement. At Kermario, he found that the three most important stones present were 500 megalithic rods apart. He has measured the Scottish Ring of Brodnar (on the Orkney Islands, off the northern coast of Scotland) and found its diameter is 50 megalithic rods, a distance he also found in the diameter of the stone circles surrounding the Irish megalithic complex of Newgrange and the two stone circles in Avebury, near Stonehenge. All these sites are identified as the most important megalithic monuments of Western Europe, making Crowhurst's observations extremely important.

Alexander Thom suggested that "there must have been a headquarters from which standard rods were sent out but whether this was in these islands or on the Continent the present investigation cannot determine."[11] What can be determined is that there definitely was a central HQ, which covered both France and Britain, and this from as early as 4500 BCE.

Whereas some conservative archaeologists such as Aubrey Burl have poured scorn over Thom's megalithic yard, more progressive archaeologists have actually boldly gone where even Thom did not go. Archaeologist Euan Mackie noticed similarities between the megalithic yard and a unit of measurement that was in use in Mohenjo Daro, in modern Pakistan, as well as ancient measuring rods used in mining in the Austrian Tyrol. He has also suggested similarities with other measurements such as the ancient Indian gaz and the Sumerian šu-du3-a, and is one of many who have noted that the megalithic yard is the diagonal of a rectangle measuring 2 by 1 Egyptian remens. The "diagonal of a rectangle" is of course precisely the "secret of Carnac" that Crowhurst has uncovered.

The emerging scenario is therefore that the ancient world used several units of measurement, but several cultures actually shared common units of measurement, or units that were related—most specifically, that Egypt and the megalithic civilization were somehow using a related unit of measurement. Throughout Western Europe, all megalithic monuments share not only a similar appearance, but also made use of the same system of measurement and mathematics.

We know that human hands could have built Carnac, but that is not the real mystery of the site. The revelation of Carnac is that our ancestors were—once again—far more advanced in mapping the landscape, measuring it, and building to an incredible accuracy, for reasons unknown. Crowhurst has identified that our ancestors seemed to realize the landscape came with certain energies, and he feels adamant that is why certain megaliths were placed in the locations they can now be found. Megalithic Europe incorporated certain natural features (such as mountains) into an artificially enhanced landscape, which had been constructed according to a mathematically complex and precise master plan. It involved careful alignments to astronomical phenomena, but also played with the energies of the earth—which is likely one of the reasons why the stones of Carnac were placed on top of a granite surface. Certain energies were harnessed here, but how and why remains a question that can only be answered in the future. What we *can* say is that the site shows that the builders of Carnac—in 4500 BCE—possessed knowledge with which official archaeology refuses to credit them.

Flying Machines in Ancient India

Ancient India has made one of the greatest contributions to the concept of ancient flight: the vimana. At the World Space Conference on October 11, 1988, in Bangalore, India, Dr. Roberto Pinotti addressed the delegates and spoke on ancient

Old Buildings, New Techniques

Indian vimanas, telling them what the vimanas were and that they should take the subject seriously: that the vimanas should be studied as real flying machines. He was largely addressing the foreign delegates, for many Indian traditions hold the belief that their ancestors possessed technology that gave them the ability to fly.

References to vimanas can be found in the Yuktikalpataru of Bhoja (12th century CE), the Mayamatam, in 150 verses of the Rig Veda, the Yajurveda, and the Atharvaveda, as well as literary passages belonging to the Ramayana (fifth century BCE), the Mahabharata (sixth century BCE), the Puranas, the Bhagavata (ninth century CE), the Rahuvamsam, and references in the drama Abhijanaakuntalam of Kalidasa (second century BCE), the Jatakas (third century BCE), and several more. Some of these documents even give details on the mechanism of the vehicles. Chapter XXXI of the Samarangana Sutradhara contains details of the construction of this machine, and it has been found that one manuscript of this treatise is as old as 1610 CE. There are 230 stanzas dealing with not only their construction, but also with take-off, their ability to cruise for distances of thousands of miles, and the danger of bird strike!

Since the 1960s, a number of organizations and experts have done complete books on the vimanas, including technical drawings, several of which are in English. In fact, B.G. Talpule wrote a book in Marathi entitled *Vimana Kalecha Sodha* in 1907, in which he described the vimana, which he said he had constructed in 1895. It is the first printed text on flying machines in India, but Swami Dayananda Saraswati had previously argued that there were aerial flying machines in ancient Indian texts, and he interpreted verses of the Veda from that perspective.

The Vedas say that the Rbhus built an aerial chariot for the use of the twin Asvinas, the physicians among the gods. The craft was comfortable and could move everywhere, including the heaven and sky. The vehicle could fly faster than the mind, was triangular, large, three-tiered, uneven, and piloted by at least three people. It had three wheels, and was made of gold, silver, or iron, though it was most often described as gold. It would come down with a great sound, and when it did, it was said that many people gathered to see its landing. It was said to also be able to land on the sea and then come to shore. When it moved on land, it left marks of its wheels. Apart from the three pilots, it could accommodate seven or eight people. It had scheduled flights: three at night and three during the day. Its departure was accompanied by loud sounds, which were said to make buildings tremble as well as uproot trees and small plants. The parallels between this story and the "vision" of Ezekiel are quite clear; maybe, indeed, Ezekiel was visited by a vimana?

Apart from vimanas, the Mahabharata also contains references to missiles, armaments, war machines, and like. These weapons were said to have caused colossal destruction, comparable only to modern nuclear warfare.

Passages of the Mahabharata read:

...[It was] a single projectile

Charged with all the power of the Universe.

An incandescent column of smoke and flame

As bright as the thousand suns

Rose in all its splendor...

...It was an unknown weapon,

An iron thunderbolt,

A gigantic messenger of death,

Which reduced to ashes

The entire race of the Vrishnis and the Andhakas.

...The corpses were so burned

As to be unrecognizable.

The hair and nails fell out;

Pottery broke without apparent cause,

And the birds turned white.

After a few hours

All foodstuffs were infected...

....to escape from this fire

The soldiers threw themselves in streams

To wash themselves and their equipment.

A detailed study into the question of whether vimanas and the related passages from the ancient Indian accounts are evidence of crafts with flight (if not spaceflight) capability was done by Richard L. Thompson, a scientist with a PhD in mathematics from Cornell University. He found that the numerous Indian texts gave accurate dimensions for the diameter of the Earth and even the plane of the ecliptic. The Puranas spoke of 400,000 humanlike races living on various planets and of 8 million other life-forms. Many of these races were said to possess *siddhi*, which humans could master, but were not born with. These siddhi were what in the West are labeled paranormal abilities, such as mental communication, but they also involved a number of techniques, such as changing the size or weight of objects, levitation, or moving objects through the ether without being impeded by physical obstacles, as well as entering another human being's body and taking control of it.

On the subject of vimanas, Thompson found references to a vimana in the possession of the ancient Indian King Salva, which he had acquired from Maya Danava, an inhabitant of a planetary system called Talatala:

Salva chose a vehicle that could...travel anywhere he wished to go, and that would terrify the Vrsnis. Lord Silva said, 'So be it.' On his order, Maya Danava, who conquers his enemies' cities, constructed a flying iron city named Saubha and presented it to Salva. This unassailable vehicle was filled with darkness and could go anywhere. Upon obtaining it, Salva went to Dvarakak, remembering the Vrsnis' enmity towards him. Salva besieged the city with a large army.... From his excellent airship he threw down a torrent of weapons, including stones, tree trunks, thunderbolts, snakes and hailstones. A fierce whirlwind arose and blanketed all directions with dust.[12]

Dr. Dileep Kumar Kanjilal finds that if you delve into the literature of India, you come away with descriptions of modern tanks, armored cars, places for missiles on multi-wheeled carriers, sound-interceptor missiles, ground-to-air and air-to-ground missiles, laser beams, and mass-destruction weapons similar to nuclear bombs. The Vanaparvan speaks of Arjuna's weapon, the Pasupata, which had the potential to destroy the entire world. Arjuna was strictly forbidden to use this weapon against human beings. He also possessed the Narayana weapon, mentioned in the Dronaparvan. This, too, could create total destruction, and it killed instantly all life at the epicenter. The heat generated was equivalent to 100 times the power of the sun; the sky became filled with dust and strong winds, while trees were incinerated and the sound caused people far away to tremble with fear. In fact, there is a tradition that the war mentioned in the Mahabharata occurred in either 3127 BCE (according to the Aihole inscription from the seventh century CE) or circa 1500 BCE (according to modern scholars). Indeed, from around 1500 BCE to 500 BCE (the birth of Lord Buddha), no literary or historical records are found, and it is clear that a real dark age reigned over India.

Mohenjo Daro literally means "Mound of the Dead." Sometimes referred to as a metropolis of the ancient Indus Valley Civilization, it was built around 2600 BCE and was one of the early urban settlements in the world. Whereas most Ancient Alien Questions focus on the origin of civilization, at Mohenjo Daro, the question has to do with how and why the city was abandoned around 1500 BCE.

Old Buildings, New Techniques

The site was rediscovered in 1922 when an officer of the Archaeological Survey of India, Rakhaldas Bandyopadhyay, was led to the site by a Buddhist monk. A decade later, excavations began. And as the excavations progressed, they found hundreds of scattered bodies—in the middle of the street, some still holding hands. People were just lying, unburied, in the streets of the city; there seemed no one available to bury them.

What could cause such devastation? Why did the bodies not decay or get eaten by wild animals? Furthermore, Alexander Gorbovsky, in *Riddles of Ancient History* (1966), reported on the discovery of at least one human skeleton in this area with a level of radioactivity approximately 50 times greater than it should have been due to natural radiation. Also, thousands of fused lumps, christened "black stones," have been found at Mohenjo Daro. These appear to be fragments of clay vessels that melted together in extreme heat, around 2,550–2,910 degrees F. The centers of both cities bear the traces of an explosion or something resembling it. The buildings are literally leveled. Whatever ended Mohenjo Daro, it was sudden, and extreme.

Albion W. Hart was one of the first engineers to graduate from the Massachusetts Institute of Technology (MIT). During an engineering project in Africa, he and his colleagues were traveling through the desert. Margarethe Casson, in an article on Hart's life in the magazine *Rocks and Minerals* (no. 396, 1972), writes, "At the time he was puzzled and quite unable to explain a large expanse of greenish glass which covered the sands as far as he could see. Later on, during his life, he passed by the White Sands area after the first atomic explosion there, and he recognized the same type of silica fusion which he had seen 50 years earlier in the African desert."

Robert Oppenheimer was an American theoretical physicist and is often called the "father of the atomic bomb" for his role in the Manhattan Project, the World War II project that developed the first nuclear weapons. Oppenheimer had studied Sanskrit.

He obviously witnessed the first atomic bomb detonation on July 16, 1945, in the Trinity test site in New Mexico. Afterward, he quoted from the Bhagavad Gita: "I have unleashed the power of the Universe, now, I am become Death, the destroyer of worlds." In 1952, at a press conference at the University of Rochester, he was asked whether the Trinity test was the first ever nuclear detonation carried out. He replied, "Yes...in our times."

It is clear that Oppenheimer was convinced of the reality of the ancient Indian accounts and felt that what he had accomplished at the Manhattan Project was merely the rediscovery of a science. And so, whereas our ancestors were clearly capable of building the most beautiful and largest of structures, they clearly were also able to wipe them out.

Chapter 5

A Brave New World

Terra Preta

Since the latter half of the 20th century, two leading thoughts have come to the forefront of the world's consciousness: One is the possibility that we could destroy our planet (including whether or not our industrialized economy is *already* killing the planet); the second is the idea of "terraforming" other planets—making them suitable for human habitation. Both "techniques" transform an existing ecosystem but reside in opposite camps—destruction, and creation.

Though topical (and for many perhaps theoretical), terraforming is not a purely modern issue, nor an outcome of our conquest of space, nor merely the science fiction of the generations that have grown up in the 20th century. Indeed, during that same century, it has become clear to science that two millennia before humankind went into space, people in the Amazon created and used similar techniques.

"Terra Preta de Indio" (Amazonian Dark Earths) is the local name for certain dark earths—literally: dark-colored soil—in the Brazilian Amazon region. These dark earths occur in several countries in South America (Brazil, Ecuador, and Peru) and possibly beyond. As ecologically rich as the rainforest may appear, the soil it stands in is unsuitable for farming—largely a result of the incessant rain washing away all nutrients. But those pockets of soil that are Terra Preta are suitable for farming and thus form an out-of-place patch of fertility in an otherwise-harsh environment.

In fact, this soil has the ability to maintain nutrient levels throughout hundreds of years. According to Bruno Glaser, a chemist at the University of Bayreuth, "If you read the textbooks, it shouldn't be there." And according to a study led by Dirse Kern of the Museu Goeldi in Belem, Terra Preta is "not associated with a particular parent soil type or environmental condition", suggesting it was not produced by natural processes.[1]

Typical Terra Preta pockets in the Amazon are seldom larger than 2 acres, reaching down to a depth of approximately 25 inches, with traces going down to 6 to 9 feet deep. Terra Preta, in short, is like a small pocket of different soil, stretching over a small area of land, and not going to any depth. Still, when the various pockets are added up, about 10 percent of the Amazon landmass contains Terra Preta (though some argue that only 0.3 percent of the basin is covered)—a space roughly the size of France, or twice the United Kingdom.

As a rule, Terra Preta has more plant-available phosphorus, calcium, sulfur, and nitrogen than is common in the rain forest. The soil is specifically well-suited for tropical fruits. Corn, papaya, mango, and many other foods grow at three times the normal rate of tropical soil. Fallows on the Amazonian Dark Earths can be as short as six months, whereas fallow periods on Oxisols (tropical rain forest soils) are usually eight to 10 years long. Only short fallows are presumed to be necessary for restoring fertility on the dark earths. However, precise information is not available, because farmers frequently fallow the land due to an overwhelming weed infestation and not due to declining soil fertility. In 2001, James B. Petersen reported that Amazonian Dark Earths in Açutuba had been under continuous cultivation without fertilization for more than 40 years.

What's more, the soil behaves like a living organism: It is self-renewing and thus acts more like a super-organism than an inert material. But the most remarkable aspect of Terra Preta is that it is *man-made*, created by pre-Columbian Indians between 500 BCE and 1500 CE, and abandoned after the invasion of Europeans. (Other dating suggests 800 BCE to 500 CE.)

Francisco de Orellana, of the Spanish Conquistadors, reported that as he ventured along the Rio Negro, hunting a hidden city of gold, his expedition found a network of farms, villages, and even huge walled cities. When later Spanish settlers arrived, none could find the people of whom the first Conquistadors had spoken. Had they been lured here with a lie? And if the farms did not exist, a "city of gold" seemed to have been an even bigger lie. Later, scientists were skeptical of Orellana's account, as in their opinion, the Amazonian soil could not support such large farming communities. These scientists were speaking at a time when Terra Preta was not yet identified, and it is now accepted that these vast cities were indeed there—Orellana wasn't lying.

Wim Sombroek of the International Soil Reference and Information Centre in Wageningen, Netherlands, has identified one of the biggest patches of Terra Preta near Santarem, where the zone is 3 miles long and half a mile wide. The plateau has never been carefully excavated, but observations by geographers Woods and Joseph McCann of the New School in New York

City indicate that this area would have been able to support about 200,000 to 400,000 people.

Terra Preta was first discovered in 1871, but was misidentified as "terra cotta." In 1928, Barbosa de Farias proposed that Terra Preta sites were naturally fertile sites. Camargo (in 1941) speculated that these soils might have formed on fallout from volcanoes in the Andes, because they were only found on the highest spots in the landscape. Another theory went that they were a result of sedimentation in tertiary lakes or in recent ponds. A natural explanation remained the best-liked flavor until the 1950s, when the camp became divided and more and more began to favor an anthropogenic (in other words, caused by humans) origin. During the 1960s and 1970s, Terra Preta sites all over the Amazon basin were mapped and investigated with respect to the physical and chemical parameters of the soil, which supported the anthropogenic origins of the material. The fact that most of the sites are not too far from navigable waterways, where people would be expected to settle, added to this conviction.

So was it a byproduct of habitation, or was it a clear example of terraforming, intentionally created for soil improvement? That question remained unanswered, though most now argue that people altered the soil via a transforming bacteria. In the 1980s, it was thought that Terra Preta was made as a kind of kitchen-midden, which acquired its specific fertility from dung, household garbage, and the refuse of hunting and fishing. The soil was also full of ceramic remains, another clear sign of human intervention. The preferred conclusion was therefore that biological waste products had been gathered and then used as fertilizer, resulting in Terra Preta. However, how the compost gained its stability and special properties remained subject to speculation. Could it really be true that this almost magical ability was an advantageous but totally accidental byproduct?

A Brave New World

At the end of the 1990s, investigations on the molecular level showed that Terra Preta contained tremendous amounts of charring residues, which are known to contain high amounts of nutrients and to persist in the environment for centuries. This is a 21st-century problem that has been brought to worldwide attention due to its importance for the global climate. Soil organic carbon is an important pool of carbon in the global biogeochemical cycle. Because Amazonian Dark Earths have high carbon contents that are five to eight times higher than the surrounding soil, Terra Preta could, in some theories, be considered as "bad" soil. And if we were tempted to see this as contaminated earth, we should note that the areas that are enriched in organic matter are not 5 to 10 inches deep, as in surrounding soils, but may be as deep as 3 to 6 feet. Therefore, the total carbon stored in these soils can be one order of magnitude higher than in adjacent soils.

The Amazonian basin is not the only site where Terra Preta has been found. The terrain of the Bolivian Llanos de Mojos is savannah grassland with extreme seasons: floods in the wet, fires in the dry. Crops are hard to grow and few people live there. But back in the 1960s, archaeologist Bill Denevan noted that the landscape was crossed with unnaturally straight lines. Large areas were also covered with striped patterns. Clark Erickson, a landscape archaeologist, was drawn to the numerous forest islands dotted across the savannah, which he found littered with prehistoric potsherds, similar to the ceramics found in Terra Preta soil. Some mounds were as much as 54 feet high, and much of the pottery was on a grand scale as well. Together with his colleague, William Balée, Erickson realized that the entire region must have been linked with agriculture, but they needed evidence for their conviction. They soon found that some of the mounds were still inhabited by indigenous people and that their language had words for staple crops like maize, as well as cotton and dye plants. The straight lines they had observed turned out to be canals for irrigation, next to which were found causeways. These canals themselves are a masterwork of engineering: The ancient engineers had wedged diamond-shaped rocks in the bottom of the canals, so that they would remain free from sediment. The water flow itself would clean the canals, and so a human agent was not required.

As to the mounds, Erickson's interpretation is that they were built to offer protection from floodwaters, with the most sacred buildings always at the center of the mound on the highest level. There is historical evidence for this: A Spanish expedition of 1617 remarked on the extent and high quality of a network of raised causeways connecting villages together. The area is so vast that it could have sustained hundreds of thousands of people. Erickson believes that the Mojos Plains were home to a society that had totally mastered its environment.

But how did they do it? Orellana reported that the indigenous people used fire to clear their fields. We know that the Bolivian savannah has also been the "victim" of fire—though perhaps we should argue that it was "blessed" with fire. Bruno Glaser has found that Terra Preta is rich in charcoal, which is incompletely burnt wood. Terra Preta contains up to 64 times more of it than the surrounding red earth. He believes that the charcoal holds the nutrients in the soil and sustains its fertility from year to year. In experimental plots, adding a combination of charcoal and fertilizer into the rainforest soil boosted yields by 880 percent compared with fertilizer alone. With this information, we have made an important step toward understanding one of the great secrets of the early Amazonians: Set the soil on fire, and it will regenerate. Of course, though science may have long forgotten about this technique, in the highlands of Mexico, these techniques can still be seen at night, when local farmers set parts of their fields alight. But the science of Terra Preta is not nearly as simple as that. A simple slash-and-burn technique does not produce enough charcoal to make Terra Preta. Instead, a "slash-and-char" technique must have been used. Named by Christopher Steiner of the University of Bayreuth, this technique does not burn organic matter to ash, but incompletely, whereby the charcoal is then stirred into the soil. Carbon is, as mentioned, a key ingredient in this process. When a tree dies or is cut down, the carbon stored in its trunks, branches, and leaves is released, but when plants and trees are reduced to charcoal, the carbon remains in the charcoal, apparently for periods up to 50,000 years, according to research by Makoto Ogawa. This explains the high levels of carbon in Terra Preta.

Today, we know that the distribution of Terra Preta in the Amazon correlates with the places that Orellana reported were zones where farming occurred. Today, as in the past, Terra Preta holds great promise for the Amazonian population—as well as other areas of the world—where modern chemicals and techniques have failed to generate significant food from Amazonian soil in a sustainable way. Though some of the secrets of this soil have been discovered and will provide great help to many impoverished regions, some ingredients of Terra Preta remain unidentified—or at least difficult to reproduce. In fact, one missing ingredient is how the soil appears to reproduce. Science may not know the answer, but the Amazonian people themselves argue that as long as 10 inches of the soil is left undisturbed, the bed will regenerate in about 20 years. A combination of bacteria and fungi are believed to be the transformative agents, but the exact agents remain elusive from science's microscopes.

So in the Amazon and on the Bolivian plains, we have a terraforming substance that someone in the distant past knew and developed, but whose secrets have been lost (though modern farmers in those regions know how to work with the manmade soil). The people who created it just disappeared. The communities Orellana saw were gone some decades later. What became of them? Tragically, Orellana's and other groups were responsible for their demise. Such visitors brought diseases to which the natives had little resistance: smallpox, influenza, measles, and so on. So even though perhaps hundreds of thousands of people could survive in the New World for millennia by transforming the land they lived on, they had no protection against the new viruses that were brought in by the Europeans. Contact with our own kind, after thousands of years of separation, is dangerous; what to think of making contact with an extraterrestrial species?

Crystal Skulls

It took 15 years before Harrison Ford, George Lucas, and Steven Spielberg agreed on what *Indiana Jones and the Kingdom of the Crystal Skull*, the fourth installment of the Indiana Jones saga, had to be. The problem was not which object to have Indy chase; that decision had been made: crystal skulls. The problem was the realization by Lucas that this installment would have to involve extraterrestrials. Ford and Spielberg disagreed on this point, and it was a debate that carried on for several years. In the end, Lucas proposed that he would call the beings "intra-dimensional," rather than extraterrestrial. But when Spielberg asked, "What are they going to look like?" Lucas replied, "They'll look like aliens!"

Crystal skulls are not "just" objects like Indy's prior treasures, the Holy Grail and the Ark of the Covenant. Crystal skulls are said to contain knowledge, and psychics who have come in contact with them have heard these skulls speak. Indeed, some believe them to be alien communication devices. But the interest in crystal skulls is more recent than the interest in the Ancient Alien Question. It was only in the 1980s, when U.S. citizens like Nick Nocerino traveled through what was once the Mayan heartland and found that local shamans were offering crystal skulls, that their story began to emerge in the Western world. Since the late 1980s, crystal skulls have become a popular subject of intrigue, some allegedly having been carved by a lost—if not alien—civilization.

The British Museum Skull in London is one of the most popular items on display in one of the greatest collection of artifacts in the world. The label on its case reads, "Originally thought to have been Aztec, but recent research proves it to be European," of late 19th-century fabrication. The museum obtained the skull for 120 pounds in 1897 from Tiffany & Co. As to how Tiffany had acquired it, speculation was that it originated from a soldier of fortune in Mexico.

In 2004, Professor Ian Freestone, of the University of Wales at Cardiff, examined the skull and concluded that it was cut and polished with a wheeled instrument, which he said was not used by the Aztecs. Freestone argued that the sculpture was therefore of modern, post-Columbian origin, further noting that the crystal used was common in Brazil, but not Mexico—the Aztec homeland—and that "the surface of the skull, which contains tiny bubbles that glint in the light, is more sharply defined than softer-looking Aztec crystal relics with which it has been compared."[2] However, Freestone said that even though there was strong circumstantial evidence suggesting the artifact was 19th-century European in origin, this did not amount to cast-iron proof.

In recent years, the story of how the British Museum acquired the crystal was investigated by Dr. Jane MacLaren Walsh of the U.S. Smithsonian Institution. She concluded that the British Museum Skull and the one at Musée de l'Homme (Museum of Man) in Paris were both sold by Eugène Boban, a controversial collector of pre-Columbian artifacts and an antiques dealer who ran his business in Mexico City between about 1860 and 1880. Though it is indeed likely that Boban placed the British Museum Skull at Tiffany for auction, there is no hard evidence. However, such evidence does exist for the Musée de l'Homme Crystal Skull, which in 1878 was donated by collector Alphonse

Pinart, who had bought it from Boban. Boban's 1881 catalogue does list another crystal skull, "in rock crystal of natural human size," selling for 3,500 French francs—the most expensive item in the catalogue. It is possible it was never sold, and hence was offered to Tiffany to sell at auction.

Having established these facts, however, Walsh then argues that the skulls are not genuine artifacts but were instead manufactured between 1867 and 1886 in Germany, as German craftsmen were deemed to be the only people with the skills to be able to carve these skulls.

Though Boban was indeed a controversial figure, he was no different from all the other operators on the antiquities markets in those days—some of whom made deals for treasures such as the Rosetta Stone or the Elgin Marbles that continue to upset entire nations from which they were "exported." No one disputes that the Elgin Marbles are genuine, but the same cannot be said for crystal skulls. There is *no* evidence—not even circumstantial—that Boban sourced these skulls from Germany. That is only a tenuous connection made by Walsh. Is it not more logical to conclude that, as Boban operated in Mexico, he may have acquired the skulls in Mexico? It would be completely logical to assume that, if they are Aztec in origin, they were offered on the Mexico City antiques market, where Boban then picked them up. This is the most logical scenario, yet academics seem to prefer the modern German fabrication theory for which there is no evidence. Why? Because science and crystal skulls is not a happy marriage.

As to the fact that the skulls were polished with a wheeled instrument, Professor Freestone himself argued that this in itself does not mean they are modern fabrications. Though Freestone, Walsh, and others have suggested that this overturns the likelihood that the skulls are pre-Columbian, other experts like Professor Michael D. Coe of Yale University stated that evidence of wheel markings in no way proves that the skulls are modern.

A Brave New World

He actually said that although it has long been accepted that no pre-Columbian civilization used the rotary wheel, new evidence contradicts this scientific dogma, which Walsh and Freestone continue to adhere to as it seems to suit their agenda. Wafer-thin obsidian ear-spools are now known to have been made using some rotary carving equipment and to be dated to the Aztec/Mixtec period. When Coe was asked about the opinions of Walsh on the subject, according to Chris Morton and Ceri Louise Thomas in *The Mystery of the Crystal Skulls*, Coe concluded: "People who sit in scientific laboratories don't know the full range of the culture they're dealing with. We really don't know half as much about these early cultures as we think we do. People need to reexamine their beliefs."

Walsh and some of her colleagues have largely presented Boban as a charlatan, but they've failed to report that he was known to have owned genuinely ancient artifacts as well as a collection of rare books and early Mexican manuscripts. He had even written a scientific study, *Documents pour server à l'histoire du Mexique (Documents to serve the history of Mexico)*, in 1891. Furthermore, he personally crusaded against frauds and fakes, such as in 1881 when he spoke out against forgeries that were being made in the suburbs of Mexico City. Would he shoot himself in the foot that same year by listing a fraudulent crystal skull in his catalogue?

Mentions of the German connection and claims of Boban's dishonesty come from a single letter from one of Boban's competitors, Wilson Wilberforce Blake. He wrote how they should buy from him, not Boban, who was, as he said, not honest, and he made accusations that the skull Boban had sold was a forgery, insinuating that the skull had been made in Germany instead. However, no evidence was ever produced for any of these claims, and Blake had an obvious motive for smearing Boban's character: He was after Boban's share of the market.

In short, Walsh has uncovered good indications that Boban had skulls and sold them, but regarding the German connection, she has relied on the words of a man who was out to smudge Boban's character, and this is not evidence. The story of the way the crystal skulls have been treated by academics has—alas—all the usual hallmarks of the way the scientific establishment treats all anomalous finds: It pushes them aside, labeling them fakes.

But could these skulls be genuine archaeological finds? As Morton and Thomas pointed out, Boban's artifacts went on sale at a time when Teotihuacán, just north of Mexico City, was being excavated. Teotihuacán is one of the most important archaeological sites in the Americas, containing pyramids—and a pyramid layout—on par with the pyramids of the Giza Plateau.

Boban is known to have visited the excavations; in fact, he did so in the company of Leopoldo Batres, the Inspector of Monuments. Interestingly, if we look at Blake's incriminating letter a bit more closely, he claimed that Batres, too, was "not only a fraud but a swindler."[3] Is it even possible that Boban got the skull from Teotihuacán? If so, the finger of guilt should point to Batres, and because Batres sold other finds he made at this site, why not a crystal skull as well? In those days, half of the finds the excavators made ended up on the black market, and the other half became part of the "archaeological record." It is known that even the great Howard Carter, in his exploration of the Tutankhamen tomb—heralded as the greatest archaeological discovery of the 20th century—fell victim to this scheme. Nonetheless, concluding that the skulls are genuine archaeological treasures is more logical—and better documented—than speculating about a theoretical German connection.

It was not only archaeologists who were selling crystal skulls. The Mayans themselves were selling them, too. Entire Mayan villages are known to have been financially supported by the sale of archaeological goods that at one point they had placed on the black market. Nick Nocerino claims that he met a shaman in

1949 while traveling in Mexico, who led him to a Mayan priest who said he was authorized to sell crystal skulls because the village needed money for food. Nocerino didn't buy any of the skulls, but he did study them. With such things on offer, why would Boban need to source a German crystal skull, only to have great difficulty selling it? Walsh will have you believe that the reason is that there *are* no genuine crystal skulls and that the entire subject area is a modern myth. That is simply not true.

The Mitchell-Hedges Crystal Skull

Scientists argue that none of the crystal skulls were found during an archaeological excavation—that is, apart from the so-called Mitchell-Hedges Crystal Skull, which was mentioned in *Indiana Jones and the Kingdom of the Crystal Skull*. Of all the crystal skulls, this is—rightfully or not—seen as the most intricate and is definitely the most controversial. "Believers" see it as the one crystal skull that is impossible to have been made by human hands—leaving only one possibility: that the skull was made by a non-terrestrial intelligence.

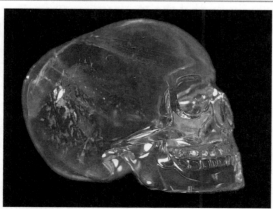

The Mitchell-Hedges Crystal Skull is the most enigmatic of all crystal skulls. Its detachable jaw, made from the same piece of crystal as the rest of the skull, has posed an impossible challenge for those looking for a simple explanation.

The skull was named after its discoverer, the adventurer F.A. "Mike" Mitchell-Hedges, if we believe the "official" version of its find. The official version goes that the skull was found in the ruins of Lubantuun in Belize (then British Honduras) in 1924 during an archaeological survey of the site. This "Skull of Doom," as Mitchell-Hedges labeled it, was not referenced until 1931, and the seven-year gap has been used by skeptics to argue that the story of its discovery is a lie.

In his autobiography, *Danger My Ally* (1954), Mitchell-Hedges stated that "The Skull of Doom is made of pure rock crystal and according to scientists it must have taken 150 years, generation after generation working all the days of their lives, patiently rubbing down with sand an immense block of rock crystal until the perfect skull emerged." He continued, "It is at least 3,600 years old and according to legend was used by the High Priest of the Maya when performing esoteric rites. It is said that when he willed death with the help of the skull, death invariably followed. It has been described as the embodiment of all evil."

So, Mitchell-Hedges associated this crystal skull with the Maya in 1600 BCE—when the Maya were not yet around. Noting Mitchell-Hedges' interest in finding evidence for a lost civilization of Atlantis, many people have argued that the skull is therefore a relic of *this* earlier civilization. You can imagine what the skeptics have made of this theory.

In 1936, eminent anthropologist G.M. Morant and Adrian Digby, a future Keeper of the Department of Ethnology at the British Museum, analyzed the Mitchell-Hedges Skull and argued that it is not of modern workmanship. Digby wrote, "...in neither case [including the British Museum Skull] is there any trace of identifiable tool marks, and it is certain that neither specimen was made with steel tools. On the teeth there is no trace of a lapidary's wheel which would betray one or both specimens as being of comparatively recent origin."[4] This is at odds with the conclusions drawn by Walsh, who saw clear evidence of tool marks. She argues that Morant and Digby's tools were far inferior to hers, which is true, but what Walsh fails to note is that in the intervening decades the Mitchell-Hedges skull is known to have been polished by art restorer Frank Dorland, who is known to have used modern tools. Writing in the journal *Man* in July 1936 (Vol. 36), Morant and Digby both commented that the skull's detachable lower jaw would have taken the creator—whoever it was—many hundreds if not thousands of hours of extra work, and that thus there would have to have been an important reason why the jaw had to be detached—more than purely artistic reasons.

In 1964, Anna "Sammy" Mitchell-Hedges—the adventurer's adopted daughter and custodian of the Skull of Doom—lent the skull to Frank and Mabel Dorland, famous art experts and restorers. Dorland commenced his study by taking many photographs from various angles. He also used a binocular microscope to create a three-dimensional image of the skull. It was during this scientific analysis that the skull began to reveal a magical dimension.

One evening, Dorland finished his work too late for the skull to be returned to its vault in the Mill Valley Bank. So he took the skull home, placing it next to the fire he had lit for the evening. He then noticed how the light of the fire was reflected through the eyes of the skull. This made him realize that the skull allowed certain optical effects to be produced—though other stories state that throughout the evening the house was also a hive of poltergeist activity.

Dorland discovered that the optical effects were the result of the way the skull had been carved, which gave him further insights into the precision of the workmanship. He observed that there was a type of "layering" on top of the skull, which made it behave like an amplifying glass. The back of the skull channeled the light through the eye sockets at the front of the head.

Although no one would be able to see what was happening from behind the skull, anyone looking at the face would perceive a spectacular series of images that would appear to come from within the skull itself.

Dorland also discovered two holes at the bottom of the skull that are invisible when the skull is positioned upright. The holes allow the skull to be swung without falling over. This was a further indication, along with the detachable jaw, that this skull was not a mere display object but had been created to perform certain functions: to move, if not pretend to speak (via the detachable jaw), and to project certain images to the observer standing in front of it.

In December 1970, Dorland took the skull to the laboratories of Hewlett-Packard in Santa Clara, California, which was at the time one of the world's most advanced centers for computers and electronics. The lab technicians there were specialists in the production of precision quartz crystals, which were used in various high-tech instruments. They were perfectly suited to figuring out how the skull could have been made. One of their tests revealed that the skull was made out of one piece of quartz—including the detached jawbone. The lab technicians stated that they were unable to create a skull like that with the technology available to them in 1970.

Their analysis further showed that the skull exhibited three different types of workmanship, and hence they suggested that work on it was carried out over three generations, or a period of 60 to 70 years—about half the time Mitchell-Hedges argued it would have taken to make. The idea that three generations would have worked day in and day out on creating one skull was an unlikely scenario, and thus the skull was proposed to have been created with "unknown technology"—which soon became interpreted as "of alien origin," or from a previous civilization that was technologically superior to ours, which quickly got linked with Atlantis. This was what Mitchell-Hedges had always claimed: that this skull was physical evidence of a lost advanced civilization.

Larry LaBarre, one of the testers at Hewlett-Packard, added to his observations a decade after the 1970 tests. He said that the quartz of which the skull was made was very hard, measuring nine out of a possible 10 on Moh's scale, meaning that only a diamond would be able to cut it. The quartz, though of one piece, was furthermore composed of three or four growth phases, each with a different axis. Cutting it would have been extremely difficult, as hitting upon a new axis might shatter the crystal if the cutter was not careful. In short, whereas it was easy to say it would have taken 60 to 70 years to make, it could only have been made with diamond tools, and the slightest error would have shattered the entire object! That some form of unknown technology was therefore involved in the creation of the Mitchell-Hedges skull was evident.

But one vital question remained: How did Mitchell-Hedges get it? The skull's owner, English adventurer Frederick A. "Mike" Mitchell-Hedges, writes in his autobiography, "How it came into my possession I have reason for not revealing"—and he never did. But Mike's secrecy was not shared by his adopted daughter, Anna, who inherited the skull from her father upon his death in 1959. She would state that it was she who found it, in the Mayan city of Lubaantun (in British Honduras/Belize), on the occasion of her 17th birthday, January 1, 1924. If true, it begs the question as to why her father was so reluctant to reveal this rather mundane and innocent discovery.

An analysis of Mitchell-Hedges' autobiography reveals—very much like a polygraph test—one area of his life about which he lied. He states that in 1913, when working for Mike Meyerowitz, a diamond merchant in New York, he announced that he was leaving for Mexico, and by November 1913, he had made it to a tiny village a few miles inside the Mexican border, where he was taken captive by General Pancho Villa's troops on suspicion of espionage and taken to the general himself. This account suggests that Mitchell-Hedges must have been one of the most unfortunate men ever. But his fortune soon changed, for the general believed Mitchell-Hedges when he said he was not a spy. Indeed, soon he became a member of Villa's army, for a period of 10 months.

Already the story is somewhat unbelievable, but some people do have a run of bad luck, and Mitchell-Hedges may have suffered from a form of Stockholm syndrome. Then again—imagining the impossible—could he have gone to Mexico expressly to be captured and to spend as much time, as closely as possible, with the great Mexican revolutionary? All this theory would require is the acceptance that Mitchell-Hedges was not a man out for adventure—an Indiana Jones—but, instead, a James Bond, sent by his government to provide an insider's perspective on the Mexican Revolution. Analysts have argued that Mitchell-Hedges lied about this period of his life, and lying is a prime attribute for any intelligence operative. Villa fought 15 battles while Mitchell-Hedges was allegedly with him, yet in *Danger My Ally* not one of these campaigns is mentioned. Why leave out details of events with which his readership would have been more than impressed, especially as it showed how danger truly was his ally?

One author, Sibley S. Morrill, in *Ambrose Bierce, F.A. Mitchell-Hedges, and the Crystal Skull* (1972), has underlined the period of late 1913 to 1914, when Mitchell-Hedges was with Villa, as the likeliest time for him to have acquired the crystal skull. He added, without providing further details, that "some high officials of the Mexican Government are of the unofficial opinion that the skull was acquired by Mitchell-Hedges in Mexico," and that it was illegally removed from the country. This scenario could explain why Mitchell-Hedges never said how he'd obtained the skull, as well as why his daughter might have felt it prudent to relocate the place of the skull's discovery to a different country—British Honduras (Belize).

A Brave New World

A fact that is rarely discussed is that Mitchell-Hedges wrote a novel, *The White Tiger*, published in 1931, which tackles the subject of crystal skulls. The novel is about "White Tiger," the leader of the Mexican Indians, who turns out to be an Englishman who was unhappy with his existence in England and immigrated to Mexico. Early on in the novel, the main character argues that he met White Tiger when he had discussions with the Mexican president, at which time the chief left him his diary, which he then published as this novel, while changing certain locations mentioned in the diary.

The most interesting part of the book is when White Tiger recounts how he was elected leader of the Indians—a position that required an initiation involving being shown the lost treasure of the Aztecs in a lost city of pyramids. So White Tiger, now their king, is shown the treasure, which includes "crystal heads"—plural—hidden in an underground cave complex:

> As they passed into the temple, the priest impressively led him to one of the massive walls, placing his hand in a certain manner upon what appeared to be a solid block of stone. At his touch it rolled slowly back, disclosing a flight of steps down which they passed.... On and on down countless steps—into the very bowels of the earth until again the priest pressed the apparently solid rock barring their progress. With scarcely a sound the stone block turned as easily as if on oiled hinges and before them yawned a long tunnel. Passing through this they descended another flight of steps. For a third time the priest touched the wall and a huge stone rolled aside. Then in the dim light of the lantern the White Tiger saw that he was in an immense vault cut out of the living rock.
>
> Before him, piled in endless confusion, lay the treasure of the Aztecs. Gold chalices, bowls, jars and other vessels of every size and shape; immense

plaques and strange ornaments all glittered dully. Of precious stones there were none, but many rare chalchihuitl (jadeite pendants) [sic]. Masks of obsidian and shells beautifully inlaid were all heaped together with heads carved from solid blocks of crystal. Legend had not exaggerated the treasure of the Aztecs. Almost boundless wealth lay at the disposal of the White Tiger.

The suggestion is that this is not fiction but what really happened to Mitchell-Hedges: He was White Tiger and was given the crystal skull by Mayan priests, just as Nick Nocerino would be offered crystal skulls a few decades later.

Finally, one of the rumors that circulate around the skull is that the then Mexican president, Porfirio Díaz, owned a secret cache of treasures, among which were two crystal skulls that found their way to Pancho Villa. It is even said that he had two of these skulls on his desk. Though the rumor has never been validated, it is a remarkable story because *The White Tiger* opens inside the Mexican president's office, where the main character meets White Tiger. Noting that later on in *The White Tiger* he is the one who sees crystal skulls inside a cave complex, we can only wonder whether the rumor, the novel, and the truth are all one and the same.

Interestingly, shortly before his death in August 1975, Sibley Morrill wrote to *Ancient Skies*, the newsletter of the Ancient Astronaut Society, stating, "My new book, *Ambrose Bierce, Mitchell-Hedges and the Crystal Skull*, may interest you because of the very real possibility (not mentioned in the book) that the famous crystal skull either had an extraterrestrial origin or was produced by people who either were extraterrestrials here on Earth or received their extraordinary knowledge from them. It is definitely established that the Maya were remarkable astronomers. It is also completely certain that neither the Maya nor any other ancient race could have made the crystal skull unless they possessed technology and instruments they are no longer known to have had."

Today, there are a large number of crystal skulls in circulation, most of which are of modern fabrication, either from China or Brazil. But a century ago, there were hardly any. The likeliest scenario for these skulls is that they were genuine, found during archaeological excavations or given to the likes of Mitchell-Hedges by the native people. In the case of the Mitchell-Hedges skull and some others, it is clear they were not made by a technology we know and their origins have to be found in a lost or unknown—if not alien—civilization. The evidence suggests that these skulls date back to the Mayan world, and that one or two may actually have come from Teotihuacán, the City of the Gods. Is it a coincidence that in Mayan creation mythology, there was a mystical skull said to be that of a god, and that this god—this mysterious skull—spoke to the Mayan people?

Teotihuacán, the City of the Gods

According to Mayan mythology, in 3112 BCE, the gods convened in Teotihuacán, just outside of Mexico City. However, according to accepted archaeology, the city only existed three millennia later, from 300 to 600 CE, and covered 7.7 square miles, holding a massive population of 200,000 people. The name *Teotihuacán* means "place of the gods" or "where men were transformed into gods," and was given to the site by the Aztecs.

The central focus of the complex is a series of pyramids: the Pyramid of the Moon and the Pyramid of the Sun, which, together with the Temple of Quetzalcoatl, are the axis along which the city developed. The actual central axis is the Avenue of the Dead, running from the plaza in front of Pyramid of the Moon past the two other features, and beyond, originally more than two miles long. It was named "Avenue of the Dead" because of archaeological discoveries alongside it. Still, the name may betray a mythical aspect, as ethnographer Stansbury Hagar suggested that the Avenue may be a representation of the Milky Way—normally seen as a Way of the Soul.

Hagar went further and stated that the entire complex was a map of heaven: "It reproduced on earth a supposed celestial plan of the sky world where dwelt the deities and spirits of the dead."[5] His conclusions were in line with those of Hugh Harleston Jr., who mapped the complex in the 1960s and 1970s and believed that the entire complex was a precise scale model of the solar system.

If the center line of the Temple of Quetzalcoatl was taken as the position of the sun, markers laid out northward from it along the axis of the Avenue of the Dead indicate the correct orbital distances of the inner planets, the asteroid belt, Jupiter, Saturn (the Sun Pyramid), Uranus (the Moon Pyramid), and Neptune and Pluto, represented by two mounds further north. Harleston's suggestion fueled speculation of extraterrestrial intervention in the Mayan civilization, as the planet Uranus had only been discovered in 1787, and Pluto as late as 1930, with the help of telescopes, a technology officially unknown to the Maya. How did the Mayans therefore acquire this knowledge?

Harleston also concluded that the entire site was constructed according to a system of measurement that he named the STU, for Standard Teotihuacán Unit, which equals 3.47 feet. This unit features in the length of a side of the Pyramid of the Sun and the Pyramid of the Moon, as well as in the distance between the two pyramids, showing that the entire complex was carefully laid out in a very scientific and mathematical manner. Where have we observed that before?

Others went beyond even these observations. Alfred E. Schlemmer stated that the Avenue of the Dead might never have been a street, but instead was a series of linked reflecting pools, filled with water that descended through a series of locks from the

A Brave New World

Pyramid of the Moon, at the northern extreme, to the Citadel in the south. British author Graham Hancock added, "The street was blocked at regular intervals by high partition walls, at the foot of which the remains of well-made sluices could clearly be seen. Moreover, the lie of the land would have facilitated a north-south hydraulic flow since the base of the Moon Pyramid stood on ground that was approximately 100 feet higher than the area in front of the Citadel."[6]

The Teotihuacán mapping project demonstrated that there were a series of canals and waterways that formed a network between the city and ran to Lake Texcoco, currently 10 miles away, but possibly closer in antiquity. Was it purely for economic reasons, or was it part of "religious engineering" involving the Avenue of the Dead?

These theories have added to the body of evidence, which suggests that the master plan for the site was a visual representation of astronomical knowledge. The Pyramid of the Sun is aligned with a point on the horizon where the sun sets on May 17th and July 25th, the two days of the year in which the sun sits exactly over the peak of the pyramid at noon (zenith), uniting the heavens with the center of the world. This orientation explains the zenith's 17-degree deviation from the north-south alignment of the Avenue of the Dead.

At the time of the equinoxes, March 21st and September 21st, the passage of the sun from south to north resulted at noon in a perfectly straight shadow that ran along one of the lower stages of the western façade of the pyramid. The whole process lasts just longer than a minute. It is possible that the spectacle occurred on all sides, but as only the western side now remains somewhat intact, it is impossible to draw any further conclusions. The other sides were excavated up to a depth of 20 feet, by Leopoldo Batres.

Several authors, including Zecharia Sitchin and Graham Hancock, have repeated each other's argument that there are major correspondences between the pyramids of Giza and those of Teotihuacán. For example, the Pyramid of the Sun is 225 meters (738 feet) wide and 65 meters (213 feet) high, constructed out of five successive layers of mud. Its ascent is via 242 stairs. This floor plan is rather close to that of the Pyramid of Khufu at Giza. The Pyramid of the Moon is much smaller: 42 meters (138 feet) high and 150 meters (492 feet) wide, yet its summit is as high as that of the Pyramid of the Sun, because it sits on the site's highest point. This feature can also be seen in Giza, where Khufu's and Khafre's pyramids reach an equal height, even though one is taller than the other.

The most obvious comparison, however, is that the layouts of the three pyramids at Giza and the three main structures of Teotihuacán represent the Belt of Orion. The Pyramid of the Moon compares with the smallest pyramid on the plateau; the Pyramid of the Sun compares with Khafre's pyramid; and the Temple of Quetzalcoatl, which has the largest ground plan but was never built into a full pyramid, compares with that of the Great Pyramid. Though there are individual differences, I would suggest that the same ingredients were used at both sites, answering to the same general ground plan: to represent the Belt of Orion, which in ancient Egypt was linked with their mythology and in the Mayan culture was part of the creation mythology.

On May 17, circa 150 CE, the Pleiades star cluster rose just before the sun in the predawn skies. This synchronization, known as the heliacal rising of the Pleiades, only lasted for a century or so. It is now suggested that this event was the reason why the pyramid complex of Teotihuacán was constructed. The sun and the Pleiades are important in the religious rituals of the Mayans; the Sun-Pleiades zenith conjunction marked what is known as the New Fire ceremony. Bernardino de Sahugun's Aztec informants stated that the ceremony occurred at the end of every 52-year Calendar Round. The Aztecs and their predecessors had carefully observed the Pleiades, and the ceremony was performed precisely at midnight on the night when the constellation was supposed to pass through the zenith.

The story is in line with the creation myth, which states that the gods gathered together at Teotihuacán and wondered anxiously who was to be the next Sun. This conclave occurred at the end of the previous World Age, which had just been destroyed by a flood. Now, only the sacred fire could be seen in the darkness, still quaking following the recent chaos. "Someone will have to sacrifice himself, throw himself into the fire," they cried; "only then will there be a Sun." Two deities, Nanahuatzin and Tecciztecatl, both tried the divine sacrifice. One burned quickly, the other roasted slowly. Then Quetzalcoatl manifested himself and was able to survive the fire, ensuring a new World Age. It is this age that began in 3112 BCE and that was predicted to end on December 21, 2012 CE. It is this creation myth in which the "Hero Twins," Nanahuatzin and Tecciztecatl, were confronted with a magical skull of the gods that spoke to them. It is known that Mayan ceremonial sites, like Teotihuacán, were three-dimensional renderings of the creation myth. It is therefore logical to conclude that there was a real divine skull present there. A crystal skull? A related question is therefore whether Batres was the man who might have sold such artifacts to Boban.

Batres was also involved with another sale, namely that of sheets of mica that were found between two of the upper levels of the Pyramid of the Sun. The discovery occurred in 1906, when the complex was restored. But the mica was removed and sold as soon as it had been excavated, by Leopoldo Batres, the man in charge of the project. Its economic value was clearly seen to be much higher than its archaeological value.

More recently, a "Mica Temple" has been discovered at Teotihuacán, but this time, the mica has remained in situ. The temple sits around a patio about 300 yards south of the west face of the Pyramid of the Sun. Directly under a floor paved with heavy rock slabs, archaeologists found two massive sheets of mica. The sheets are 90 feet square and form two layers, one laid directly on top of the other. As it sits underneath a stone floor, its use was obviously not decorative, but functional. The question is what possible use the builders of Teotihuacán could have had for mica.

Mica is a substance containing different metals, depending on the kind of rock formation in which it is found. The type of mica found at Teotihuacán indicates a type that is only found in Brazil, more than 2,000 miles away. The same South American mica was found in Olmec sites. The Olmecs are often seen as a civilization separate from the Mayans, preceding them, but new thinking suggests that *Olmec* is a misnomer and they should really be seen as an early stage of the Mayan civilization of Central America. It is clear that the mica's presence in Teotihuacán involved a lot of effort—and it thus must have played an important role—but what was that role? Archaeology has been unable to provide a consistent answer. Alternative historians have outlined Teotihuacán's clear parallels to other pyramid complexes, such as Giza, but both sides of the debate fail to identify the purpose of the site. As we shall see, the answer fits in with the Ancient Alien Question, and reveals the true framework in which the question needs to be asked.

The Nazca Lines

However interesting and important Teotihuacán is, nothing in the New World is as famous as the Nazca lines when it comes to the Ancient Alien Question. Nazca is approximately 250 miles south of the Peruvian capital of Lima. It is home to enigmatic lines, some measuring 5 miles in length, with one line even continuing for 40 miles. Situated in an area where it almost never rains—a few drops per year on average—the lines have been impressively preserved since they were created almost

The Nazca lines in Peru are one of the billboards for Ancient Alien theories. Their patterns are reminiscent of modern airport layouts, and many tourists are doing aborted approaches via airplane so they can experience the full excitement.

2,000 years ago by removing the top soil, thus revealing the white soil underneath.

These lines appear in an area that covers more than 300 square miles and come in various forms and shapes; apart from long lines, there are also depictions of animals, including an ape, a whale, a snake, and a llama, a human being, a flower, and many more. But the most prominent features are the lines, etched here throughout a period of one millennium, from 500 BCE to 500 CE.

The designs are so vast that little can be seen from ground level. Small portions are visible, but the entire scope of the Nazca lines is only visible from the air. The logical question is therefore why this complex was constructed when it was to all intents and purposes invisible from the ground—and the people who created it had not yet discovered flight. It was this quagmire that Erich von Däniken stirred up, suggesting that those who had constructed the complex *did* know the secret of flight. He also pointed to the straightness of the lines: Throughout a distance of 1,500 meters (4,921 feet), the lines never deviate more than 4 meters (about 13 feet). He also observed that the complex looked similar to the design of modern airports. Could the Nazca lines have been an airport for extraterrestrial deities who came to visit the civilizations of Southern America?

Rather than answer the question with a stern *no*, scientists preferred to laugh at von Däniken's suggestion. As a point in their favor, they were aware that the ground itself was very uneven and rough, which would mean that any plane would immediately have a severe accident during landing. So, though it looked like an airport, it was not. The question remains whether it could be part of an indigenous cargo cult, the Nazca culture having created the lines because they had seen their gods build genuine airports.

Today, owners of local airplanes offer tourists the experience of making an "aborted landing" on the lines: The pilots prepare for a landing as if the lines are an airport, and just before the landing, the plane pulls up again. The attraction exists because of the fame that von Däniken's best-selling books bestowed on the lines.

Though von Däniken popularized the lines, they were not unknown before his arrival. Maria Reiche was a German mathematician with an interest in the lines since shortly after World War II; since the 1950s, she had lived near the lines in an effort to understand what they meant. For many years, she tried to bring the lines to the attention of the scientific community. Though she largely failed where von Däniken succeeded, in retrospect, both Reiche and von Däniken are now considered to have been pivotal in bringing the lines to public awareness.

Reiche believed that the lines had an astronomical function: They were there to determine the position of the stars. Unfortunately, a subsequent scientific analysis of her theory proved it incorrect; though some lines were indeed marking astronomical features, the correspondence was nothing outside of the normal odds: There are a large number of stars and a large number of lines, so some should be aligned to some stars—by accident. Until her death in 1998, Reiche nevertheless continued to defend her theory.

Reiche's biggest preoccupation was the conservation of the lines. She knew that every touch to the ground, even a normal stroll through the area, left marks in the surface that remained visible for many years afterwards. Reiche was therefore appalled to find that the lines had become a tourist destination—in sharp contrast with the local people, who looked to the tourists as a new source of desperately needed income. The "aborted landings" of the pilots made her shiver, fearing one day a plane would crash and destroy some of the lines. For most of her life, she also found that the local authorities were not interested in the lines, and she fought to make the lines a listed national monument. In the end, her struggle proved successful. But her theory as to what the lines were was incorrect. Von Däniken's theory of an airstrip was equally impossible. So where does this leave the Nazca lines?

The problem is simple: If a plane ever did manage to land on the lines, on the rough terrain, the sheer displacement of air would result in the lines being blown off. The top soil would once again cover the scraped-off areas, and the white lines of the soil underneath would disappear. As extraordinary as they are, and as much work has gone into them, in the end, the Nazca lines are "just" a bit of sand that was dusted off to reveal the ground below. It is the extraordinary meteorological conditions that reign in this part of Peru that have preserved the lines for millennia.

Von Däniken's idea that the lines should be viewed from the air inspired travel writer Jim Woodman and balloonist Julian Nott, who theorized that though an aircraft was unlikely, perhaps a hot air balloon would do. Remarkably, rock paintings near the lines do show a balloon. Also, at the ends of several straight lines are blackened rocks, suggesting they had been fired—perhaps repeatedly. Perhaps they were sites of sacred fires, or perhaps they were sites where hot air was created to fill a balloon in order to get liftoff? To test their theory, Woodman and Nott built a primitive balloon, based on the depictions on an ancient vase. They also used material that would have been available to the local people. In 1975, their "Condor I" became airborne. The balloon flew for approximately 20 minutes and covered a distance of three miles. It was practical proof that the Nazca people could have used a balloon from which they would be able to see the lines. But "could" does not mean they did...

British explorer Tony Morrison, who has made extensive expeditions in the region and knew the theories of von Däniken, Reiche, and many others, realized that most Nazca enthusiasts were too focused on their own research and paid too much attention to the lines themselves, and not the features that were on, along, and near them. Morrison spoke to the local people, who had retained stories of how their distant ancestors had constructed the lines. He learned that certain sections of the network continued to be used by the local people for religious purposes. Perhaps this was the key to unlocking the mystery of the Nazca lines?

Morrison's research revealed that the network was a type of cemetery. The desert area, where nothing could live, where no rain fell, was an area delineated by the local people for use in contacting their ancestors. This should not have come as a surprise, if we also know that the local cultures were in origin shamanic, because contacting one's ancestors is of primary importance in shamanic tradition. For the Nazca people the land of the dead was similar to Earth, but was found in another dimension, contactable by those equipped with the right techniques, yet invisible to our eyes. The lines were an ingenious system that aided the shaman in his voyages to the Otherworld, where he established contact with the gods. And so, it seems, von Däniken was at least partially right.

Morrison argued that the lines often converged in certain nodes, from which they continued. On these nodes and at regular intervals along the lines, small altars could be found, sometimes little more than a small heap of stones and earth. Morrison, and later British researcher Paul Devereux, remarked that the most important aspect of the lines had not been sufficiently focused upon: The lines were *straight*. Straight lines were specifically and uniformly linked with the voyage of the shaman in the Otherworld. Souls were said to only be able to travel in straight lines. (Similarly, in the Christian tradition, roads termed "dead straight roads" often linked the church with the cemetery, in those cases where the cemetery was not immediately next to the church.) That this road was "dead straight" was no accident; it was because of the popular belief, found in so many cultures across the world, that the dead could only travel in straight lines.

When Tomasz Gorka of Munich University in Germany analyzed five geoglyphs near the city of Palpa, a lesser-known neighbor of the Nazca lines, he found other lines, in the interior of the trapezoid structures, that were not visible from the air. He argued that the geoglyphs visible today are only the most recent stage of a prolonged construction process, during which the whole complex of drawings was constantly added to, remodeled, obliterated, or changed by use. As some of the lines produced stronger magnetic anomalies than others, Gorka and Karsten Lambers of the University of Konstanz in Germany argued that the soil beneath was compacted by people walking back and forth during prayer rituals, which would tie in with the known practice of placing ceramic vessels at key shrines along the lines. The prayer rituals, of course, were linked with the worship of the dead: The living walked this sacred landscape to contact their ancestors.

Though this theory seems to explain the straight lines, what to make of the accompanying figures of animals and other forms and shapes? It is currently believed that the animals predate the lines. Their size is often massive; one figure measures 100 feet. Remains of animal sacrifices have occasionally been found next to these animal images.

Research into this area had been carried out by anthropologist Marlene Dobkin de Rios, who published a scientific thesis in 1977 on three areas in the New World where she had found drug-using cultures that had created designs on the landscape: the Hopewell Indians of North America, the Olmecs of Mexico, and the Nazca culture of Peru. She argued that the animal depictions were magical protectors—charms—for the shamans. They also acted as tribal boundaries, so that shamans of other tribes would not enter a certain territory. Archaeologist Evan Haddingham built upon this research and learned that similar practices continue to be observed by the local people in and around Nazca to this very day.

Dobkin de Rios notes that the design of the Nazca lines is also found on pottery and other objects of the Nazca civilization; they often depicted the return of a god. But rather than an extraterrestrial being, she argues that it is the return of the shaman from his sacred duty, the soul voyage. She also identified the cactus "San Pedro" (*Trichocereus pachanoi*) as the plant that induced the shaman's vision. This plant was also depicted on various pots and even on ancient temples.

So von Däniken was right when he suggested that the animals and lines had to be seen from the sky: They were seen during the shaman's flight, on his voyage to the Otherworld. Shamanic theory states that the shaman leaves his body and "floats" or "soars" through the sky, where often the eagle or another animal is his totem animal—the animal mimics or symbolizes the flight of the soul. He was right that these lines were an airstrip; they were an airstrip for the soul to take off to and return from the Otherworld.

The Sacred Valley: The Footsteps of Viracocha

Peru is known as the cradle of the Inca civilization, a culture that the Spanish called "diabolical," and, until recently, was deemed to have been primitive. (The Inca civilization was not often included in school curricula in Western Europe.) Von Däniken posed this central question in the 1960s: If the Inca were primitive or stupid, how had they been able to create their often complex buildings, such as Sacsayhuaman or Ollantaytambo, the former of which has stones weighing as much as 361 tons? These two complexes stand at altitudes where today the modern tourist has difficulty breathing when walking, let alone hauling large stone blocks that weigh tons.

The site of Sacsayhuaman, located just above Cuzco, displays some of the largest and most extraordinary stones. The stones have several differently shaped sides, which somehow all fit perfectly together. This technique was necessary because of the severe earthquakes prevalent in the region. The Inca's construction technique has proven to withstand these quakes when no other buildings did.

Four decades later, it is now clear that the Inca were not stupid. It has also become clear that the Inca built upon centuries of knowledge available to their predecessors all across the continent. They were the last indigenous group of rulers who had toiled on the land for hundreds of generations, if not thousands of years. Nevertheless, the question of *what* their civilization represented is still largely unanswered. The main work of answering this question has been carried out by a small number of Peruvian archaeologists, as well as a certain amount of visiting scientists, but their conclusions have not yet become common knowledge.

Two key people in this quest to understand the Inca civilization are Fernando and Edgar Elorrieta Salazar. They have straightforwardly identified that the Inca civilization considered an area known as the "Sacred Valley" to be the heart of their civilization. It was sacred because it was linked with the gods.

The Sacred Valley of Peru descends from Lake Titicaca, via Cuzco and Ollantaytambo, to Machu Picchu and beyond. It was the path walked by the civilizing deity Viracocha, which is why the valley is sacred. Based on the extraordinary engineering features found in the various monuments, the idea of an otherworldly interference is not incredible.

A Brave New World

The Sacred Valley begins at the Bolivian altiplano around Lake Titicaca, continues to Cuzco (literally the "navel" of the Inca world), to Machu Picchu, the best-known Inca structure, rediscovered by Hiram Bingham in 1911. Situated at an altitude of 12,000 feet, Lake Titicaca is the highest navigable lake in the world. It was on an island in this lake, the Island of the Sun, that the Inca legends state that the creator god, Viracocha, appeared on Earth, and it was here that Viracocha's voyage to spread civilization to the people of this region began.

Lake Titicaca is the highest navigable lake in the world. It is seen as the site where the Inca deity Viracocha emanated on this planet. The borders of the lake hold some of the most extraordinary archaeological sites, specifically Tiahuanaco and Puma Punku.

In April 2004, I was fortunate enough to follow in the footsteps of Viracocha, using a lovely single-track train that runs through some of the most spectacular scenery in the world. From Lake Titicaca, which is so high that it is physically hard to breathe, the valley descends to 11,155 feet in Cuzco and 9,186 feet in Machu Picchu. From here, Viracocha continued on his path, walking southeast to northwest, until he reached the Pacific Ocean and disappeared, his mission accomplished.

The legend of Viracocha and how he "walked" the Sacred Valley brings us face to face with the enigmas of the Inca civilization. The structures that we see today at Ollantaytambo or Cuzco are reminders in stone of the "Holy Road" traveled by the Creator God.

Ollantaytambo is built at an altitude that makes it almost impossible to believe that such gigantic stones went into the construction of the temple complex. But its location here was predicated on the presence of a sacred feature on the hill that overlooked the site: Its slope revealed a face, which was that of the god Viracocha himself.

At Ollantaytambo, the profile of a human being, identified with Viracocha, can clearly be distinguished in the mountain that overlooks the complex. The Salazar brothers have furthermore identified that the temple at Ollantaytambo is aligned to certain notches in that hill, the alignment of which coincides with important sunrise events in the calendar. This complex contains massive stones, specifically the so-called Wall of the Six Monoliths, which is precisely what the name suggests: a wall made up of six gigantic monoliths, apparently left unfinished, even though this area was the main structure of the Temple Hill, commonly known as the Fortress because of the gigantic blocks used in its construction. Parts of this temple were constructed with huge red porphyry (pink granite) boulders. The stone quarry for this extremely hard type of stone was 2.5 miles away, on the other side of the valley in which runs the Urubamba River. Stated that way, it might not sound

A detail of the hill that overlooks the temple complex of Ollantaytambo. A section of the hill clearly reveals a face, which has been linked with the god Viracocha, the civilizing deity of the Inca.

like much, but when you are standing on the Fortress and looking in the direction where these stones came from, it feels like an impossible task. The valley is deep, the mountain altitude high—just under 9,000 feet. A. Hyatt & Ruth Verrill, in *America's Ancient Civilizations*, sum up the enigma: "How were such titanic blocks of stone brought to the top of the mountain from the quarries many miles away? How were they cut and fitted? How were they raised and put in place? No one knows, no one can even guess. There are archaeologists, scientists, who would have us believe that the dense, hard andesite rock was cut, surfaced and faced by means of stone or bronze tools. Such an explanation is so utterly preposterous that it is not even worthy of serious consideration. No one ever has found anywhere any stone tool or implement that would cut or chip the andesite, and no bronze ever made will make any impression upon it."

The stone face of Viracocha towering over Ollantaytambo is the key to why massive blocks were positioned here; his face shows that the Creator God is still present, watching over his people. But whereas most attention goes to the massive stone blocks of the Temple Hill, the Salazar brothers have identified that in the valley below, the first beam of the sunrise falls on the so-called Pacaritanpu, the House of Dawn, where the gods became "God." This structure is hardly identifiable, unless it is looked upon with the "right eyes." At first, there appears to be nothing but a cultivated field near the river. Though dating from the Inca time period, it is hardly recognizable as important. But a second glance will reveal that the entire field portrays a gigantic pyramid; this two-dimensional structure is viewed as a three-dimensional pyramid. And this is not a mere trick of the eye, as the position where the sunbeam hits the ground has been clearly and uniquely marked by a stone structure.

Such subliminal images in the Inca structures are not unique. Elsewhere, the Inca used the same technique, often in city planning. The Salazar brothers have identified various animal forms in the hills and designs of Machu Picchu. The design of the capital Cuzco is equally ingeniously created to form the image of a puma, the royal animal. Many of these constructions were achieved by using a mixture of natural shapes, which were then augmented—"stressed"—by human intervention, often by creating fields in very specific shapes.

The notion that sacred geography underlines Inca city planning is not a new observation. The Jesuit Father Bernabe Cobo, in his book *The History of the New World* (1653), wrote about "ceques" in Cuzco. These were lines on which "wak'as"—shrines—were placed and which were venerated by local people. Ceques

A Brave New World

When Machu Picchu was discovered in 1911, its beauty and majesty made it a must-visit place. Though the stones used in its construction are not as massive as elsewhere in Peru, its location makes it part of a sacred pattern that involved the wanderings of the civilizing deity Viracocha.

had been described as sacred pathways, similar to the straight lines that can be found in Nazca. Cobo described how ceques radiated outward from the Temple of the Sun at the center of the old Inca capital. These were invisible lines, only apparent in the alignments of the wak'as. The ceques radiated out between two lines at right angles, which divided the city into four zones and extended farther out into the Inca Empire, which is how the empire got its name: Tawantinsuyu, meaning "Four Quarters of the Earth."

Cuzco was the Inca capital; its original Quechua name was Qosqo, meaning "navel." It is here that some of the most impressive stone masonry of South America is on display. The Dominican Priory and Church of Santo Domingo were built on top of the impressive Coricancha (Temple of the Sun), in an effort to prevent the local population from continuing to worship Viracocha. When the Spaniards arrived in Cuzco, they saw 4,000 priests serving at the Coricancha. Ceremonies were conducted around the clock. Little remains of the Coricancha today, but what is left shows how impressive it was. The granite walls were once covered with more than 700 sheets of pure gold, each weighing around 4.5 pounds. The courtyard was filled with life-size sculptures of animals and a field of corn, all fashioned from pure gold. Even the floors of the temple were covered in solid gold. Facing the rising sun stood a massive golden image of the sun, encrusted with emeralds and other precious stones. At the center of the temple was the true navel—the Cuzco Cara Urumi, the "Uncovered Navel Stone." This was an octagonal stone coffer covered with 120 pounds of pure gold.

Remarkable stonework built by pre-Inca people who lived in Peru can be seen in various locations, but one of the more interesting and accessible sites is the streets around the Coricancha in the "navel" of the Inca capital of Cuzco.

As at Ollantaytambo, the true miracle of the Coricancha is its massive granite blocks. A major earthquake on May 21, 1950, caused severe localized damage in Cuzco. The buildings from the colonial era were affected, but the city's Inca architecture withstood the earthquake. Many of the old Inca walls were at first thought to have been lost after the earthquake, but what truly happened was that the earthquake merely exposed the original granite retaining walls of the Coricancha. The superiority of these stones is on display in the streets around the Coricancha. Here, the lower levels of the stones are monolithic and with complex angles, engineered so as to withstand earthquakes. On top are smaller stones. Archaeologists here imitate the work of their colleagues in Baalbek: They obscure the extraordinary difference between the layers, pretending somehow that both layers were the work of the Inca civilization. It is clear that the walls around the Coricancha are evidence of two distinct building techniques, the foundations showing that whoever built them possessed advanced engineering knowledge of working with stone, which was clearly lost by the time the upper layer was built.

When the Spanish Conquistadors discovered the Coricancha, the Temple of the Sun, in the heart of the Inca capital of Cuzco, they stripped all of its walls of their gold. Little remains of the temple, but what does reveals the extraordinary workmanship that went into it, including this doorway.

All of these massive building projects were carried out for one reason: This was the path walked by Viracocha. Modern research has looked at the legend of Viracocha and the Sacred Valley of the Vilcamayu and Urubamba rivers and has concluded that the Sacred Valley symbolized the Milky Way. The Milky Way was the Path of Souls. Cuzco is situated between the two rivers, and on a stellar map of the Milky Way this corresponds with the "dark gate" north of Sagittarius, which was seen as an entry to the Otherworld: a navel indeed!

These radical interpretations that are being put forward will no doubt require time before being accepted by each and all. Still, they sit within a worldwide phenomenon of creator beings walking the land and sculpting it as they go.

It will take even longer before their influence and novel approach is adapted and adopted by archaeologists. Meanwhile, several tourists continue to walk the Sacred Path of Viracocha: Many travel from Tiahuanaco to Cuzco, onward to Ollantaytambo, and finally make the arduous trek to Machu Picchu. The path is a natural way of moving about the country and has been walked for hundreds of generations, from the earliest farmers to the Inca kings—but it is said that it was first walked by Viracocha.

Fewer tourists, however, visit Tiahuanaco, which author Igor Witkowski has described as "the city that breaks all the rules." It does. Its most famous feature is a tremendous stone construction known as the Gate of the Sun, with a central image of Viracocha carved into it, showing how this city sits firmly within the bailiwick of the Sacred Valley. It is here that Viracocha is said to have landed on planet Earth.

Officially, the origins of Tiahuanaco date back to 1500 BCE, but its heyday is normally placed in the first centuries CE. It was built in an area that was virtually infertile, and therefore the Tiahuanacos created farming platforms. They first placed large rocks on the land to form a base, and then a layer of clay to waterproof it. Then they added a layer of gravel, sand, and soil to create farmable land. Then a series of irrigation ditches were created and filled with water so that agriculture could provide for the local people. The extent of the work involved to make this area inhabitable suggests that there was a very good reason for people to go to so much trouble. Otherwise why didn't these people simply live somewhere else, where life was easier? The answer to that question was Viracocha.

In the 19th century, when Frenchman Augustus LePlongeon found seashells at Tiahuanaco he concluded that the city had been a seaport in antediluvian times and had likely been located at a far lower altitude. Then somehow, a cataclysm—the Deluge—had lifted up the entire mountain range. Arthur Posnansky was the next to claim that Tiahuanaco was antediluvian. He labeled it the oldest city on Earth. Posnansky calculated it to date back to 15000 BCE. Various university professors, such as Dr. Hans Ludendorff, director of the Astronomical Observatory of Potsdam, were intrigued by Posnansky's interpretation and held a three-year study, between 1927 and 1930, and concluded that Posnansky was right. Today, scientists state that Posnansky has been proven incorrect.

LePlongean and Posnansky weren't the first to give Tiahuanaco such an eminent distinction. When chronicler Pedro de Cieza de Leon asked the natives there whether the Inca had built Tiahuanaco, they "laughed at the question, affirming that they were made long before the Inca reign and...that they had heard from their forebears that everything to be seen there appeared suddenly in the course of a single night." Another Spanish visitor added that his information said that the stones had been miraculously lifted off the ground, and "carried through the air to the sound of a trumpet."[7]

But the most enigmatic feature of the Tiahuanaco complex is Puma Punku, a structure that proponents of the Ancient Alien Theory almost uniformly hold as among the best available evidence for it. One of the construction blocks here weighs an

Puma Punku is one of the world's most enigmatic sites. The stones are not only gigantic in size, but they also show chiseling that is so precise and intricate that it is beyond the means of ordinary tools, but required machinery on par with our most modern equiptment.

Even though we could reproduce some of the chiseling in the rocks, there are so many diverse shapes, channels, tubes, and holes that it is not simple to ascertain their purpose.

estimated 440 tons, and others weigh between 100 and 150 tons. Many of these monoliths were fixed with I-shaped metal clamps. However, it is not the size of the blocks that is of primary interest but the precision of the stonecutting—to one 10th of a millimeter, roughly the thickness of a piece of paper. Each stone has three-dimensional edges; modern cutting machines do not allow us to make the sharp edges we see here. There are a series of complex blocks, the so-called H-letter-type blocks, which have almost 80 surfaces each—rather than the usual six surfaces on a normal brick. The precision of these blocks rules out manual processing: The sides are smooth, have exactly the same diameter, and are precisely parallel. One block contains a precise groove that has a semi-elliptical cross section, 4.5 millimeters wide and around 1 meter long. In it, distanced at 28 millimeters, is a row of holes, with a diameter slightly less than that of the groove. All the holes have the same diameter of 4 millimeters, and the deviations in depth between the holes do not exceed 0.1 millimeters—stunningly precise. Only extremely sophisticated machining can accomplish such a block today. What made these stones in Puma Punku? Science has no answer, and wishes Puma Punku to remain largely unknown—in stark contrast with the fame Tiahuanaco had among the Inca.

Pedro de Cienza de Leon, the Chronicler of the Incas, wrote in 1553 about Tiahuanaco, stating that the sun emerged from the Island of Titicaca. The Inca said that there appeared from the south a large white man who performed miracles, and whom they called Maker. He taught the people to be good and to love one another. As he traveled north, he became known as Tici-Viracocha. Later, another white man appeared, performing miracles, and he was given the name Viracocha. In the province of Cocha, however, the locals wanted to stone him, so he knelt and raised his head to the sky, and at that very moment a large fire approached in the sky and the natives feared for their lives. Viracocha then ordered the fire to cease, but the fire and heat had already scorched the surrounding stones, making them light as cork, so that even the biggest of stones could be easily picked up.

And so with Viracocha, we are once again confronted with a civilizing deity, whose cult involves some of the greatest stone blocks ever carved, and some of them most intricately carved. We are once again confronted with a legend that is on par with other cultures elsewhere in the world. Wherever we turn, the common denominator of these anomalies is that they were built by or as a result of a foreigner, in the possession of extraordinary techniques and technology. That is the conclusion that all the available evidence suggests. Instead, what science *believes* is that there is nothing to see; that we should quickly move on, for all of this is merely the hard work of the indigenous people.

The Quest for the Metal Library

Sometimes it is not a case of what you know, but who you know. In 1973, Erich von Däniken, at the height of his fame following the success of *Chariots of the Gods*, claimed that he had entered into a gigantic subterranean tunnel system in Ecuador, which he was told spanned the length of the continent. Surely this was evidence that our ancestors were highly advanced, or that the builders of this network were extraterrestrial? The structure was believed to house a library in which books were made out of metal. This in an area where today there is nothing but "primitive" Indian tribes with no written language. Is the library evidence of a lost civilization? Or an extraterrestrial presence on planet Earth?

The story centers around Janos "Juan" Moricz, an aristocratic Argentinian-Hungarian entrepreneur who claimed that he had discovered a series of tunnels in Ecuador that contained a "Metal Library." In a signed affidavit dated July 8, 1969, he spoke about his meeting with the Ecuadorian president, where he received a

A Brave New World

concession that allowed him total control over this discovery—provided he could produce photographic evidence and an independent witness that corroborated the discovery of the underground network. Moricz, it seemed, felt that von Däniken was the best witness he could have.

In 1972, Moricz met with von Däniken and took him to what Moricz claimed was a secret side-entrance, through which they could enter into a large hall within the underground complex. Apparently von Däniken never got to see the library itself, just the tunnel system. Von Däniken included the visit in his book *The Gold of the Gods*: "The passages all form perfect right angles. Sometimes they are narrow, sometimes wide. The walls are smooth and often seem to be polished. The ceilings are flat and at times look as if they were covered with a kind of glaze.... My doubts about the existence of the underground tunnels vanished as if by magic and I felt tremendously happy. Moricz said that passages like those through which we were going extended for hundreds of miles under the soil of Ecuador and Peru."

Then, one of the world's biggest potential discoveries soon turned sour. Journalists from the German publications *Der Spiegel* and *Stern* interviewed Moricz, who now denied ever having been in the cave with von Däniken. This undermined von Däniken's credibility (though skeptics will argue he had none to begin with), and, for many, the incident was proof that von Däniken was a fabricator of lies. But no one pointed out that if von Däniken had been lying, he would not have left such an easy trail to Moricz. He could have claimed that he could not reveal the name of his source, and *Der Spiegel* and *Stern* would have been none the wiser. Instead, it seemed that something was amiss with Moricz, who had landed von Däniken in an international controversy from which his career never really recovered.

There are in fact several oddities with this story. First, Moricz merely denied having taken von Däniken there; the existence of the network itself he did not deny. In *Der Spiegel*, March 19, 1973, we can read:

Der Spiegel: "How did you discover the [metal] library?"

Moricz: "Somebody took me there."

Der Spiegel: "Who was this guide?"

Moricz: "I can't tell you."

Moricz further stated that the library was guarded by a tribe. So, in short, Moricz claimed to von Däniken that he had discovered caves, and he showed these to him. Now Moricz claimed to have seen the caves, having been led there by a guide whom he could not identify, but denied having taken von Däniken there. The logical conclusion seems to be that Moricz had shown something to von Däniken, was now caught by the fact that everyone seemed to know he had done so, and had to make sure that whoever had shown him did not bear any grudges against him, no doubt because Moricz himself would most likely have been asked not to show anyone else the site.

By 1975, the story of the Metal Library had killed the career of a notorious author, so who would dare to tread in his footsteps? The answer: Neil Armstrong, the first man on the moon. And before him, Stan Hall, a Scotsman who wanted to change the status quo of the controversy.

Stanley "Stan" Hall read von Däniken's book and subsequently befriended Moricz, who confirmed that he *had* met von Däniken in 1972 and had taken the Swiss author from Guayaquil to Cuenca, where they met Padre Carlos Crespi and saw his collection of enigmatic artifacts. The Crespi Collection, now largely discarded after the padre's death, was an enigmatic collection of metal plates and other objects suggesting that South America's past was vastly different from what the official history tells us. The Crespi Collection is often labeled a hoax, because there is no archaeological evidence to suggest that the civilizations of South America could have created the items in it.

After this visit, Moricz claimed, there was insufficient time to take von Däniken to the "true location," so instead he decided to show him a small cave some 30 minutes from Cuenca, claiming it connected to the network. This seemed to clear up the von Däniken–Moricz controversy, but not the enigma of the Metal Library itself. Where was it? Moricz's 1969 expedition had ventured into the Cueva de los Tayos, which Moricz identified as the cave that led into the Metal Library. But in 1969, no Metal Library had been uncovered during an expedition led by Moricz. So Hall decided to organize an Ecuadorian-British expedition that would explore the Cueva de los Tayos; it would be a purely scientific expedition.

The Tayos Cave was wrongly identified as the site of the famous Metal Library, one of the greatest treasure troves waiting to be discovered. But when the Tayos Cave was explored in 1976, there was nevertheless a series of important discoveries, with some hints that sections of the complex were manmade.

I met Stan Hall a few times throughout the course of a decade, without knowing that the person I was speaking to was Stan Hall. He was a member of the audience at the Scottish

Saunière Society conferences. He blended into the background and was unlikely, if not unwilling, to stand out. It was by pure accident that I found out I knew Stan Hall—*the* Stan Hall, who furthermore lived near where I lived at the time. This gave me the opportunity to get a personal perspective on the story, and resulted in a friendship that lasted until his untimely death in 2008.

From Hall I learned that, though originally set up to take place in 1977, the 1976 expedition occurred at a time when von Däniken's public profile had been damaged by Moricz—and Hall was apparently about to endorse Moricz's claim. This left von Däniken feeling wary about Hall for more than 20 years, until both men realized they were kindred spirits rather than mortal enemies.

Why did Hall do it? He wanted to create a framework: If there was indeed a Metal Library, the first step would be to map the site. That was the main and only goal of the expedition; there was no treasure-seeking. Hall used his professional expertise as a project manager to create a three-week exploration of this famous cave: a joint venture of the British and Ecuadorian armies, supported by a team of geologists, botanists, and other specialists.

So how did Neil Armstrong get involved? "The expedition needed an honorary figurehead," Hall said. "The name of Prince Charles, who had recently received a degree in archaeology, was proposed, but I knew Neil Armstrong had Scottish connections. My mother was an Armstrong and via another Armstrong in Langholm, where Neil had been made an honorary citizen, I made contact. Months later, I got a reply that Neil Armstrong was more than willing to join us on this mission. It's when the expedition suddenly became a life's challenge."

On August 3, 1976, when the expedition was winding down, Armstrong entered the tunnel system of the Tayos Cave. The team was *officially* not looking for a metal library, and in fact did not stumble upon one. Had they done so, the discovery would have altered humankind's perspective on our history and origins. For Armstrong, it could have been his second great contribution to humankind's exploration, but it was not to be. However, the team did catalogue 400 new plant species as well as a burial chamber inside the cave, in which a seated body was found. The chamber was later dated to 1500 BCE, and it was believed that at the time of the summer solstice the sun illuminated this tomb. Both the date and the alignment show that the history of Ecuador is far older and more intricate than what is officially believed.

Stan Hall (left) and Neil Armstrong at the Tayos Cave basecamp, after Armstrong had entered the cave. If the Tayos Cave had been the location of the Metal Library, Armstrong would not only have been the first man on the moon, but also among the first to find evidence of one of the greatest enigmas on this planet.

When the expedition was finished, Stan Hall returned to his day job. Until 1991, the year Moricz died, the Metal Library continued to elude him. Had it not been for Hall, the story of the Metal Library would probably have died there. He knew that Moricz was not the originator of the story, as von Däniken noted on page 53 of his book. In the 1973 interview with *Der Spiegel*, Moricz confirmed that an unnamed person had shown him the cave. But who was this person? Hall decided to track down this third man, who had seemingly disappeared into the shadows. Hall had a name—Petronio Jaramillo—but nothing more.

"Moricz died in February 1991," said Hall. "I had a name and a telephone directory. But there were an awful lot of Jaramillos in Quito. Finally, I found him—or, rather, his mother. It was September 1991 when she gave me the phone number of her son. I phoned him. He told me that it had taken 16 years before our paths crossed. He was willing to meet me, and stated that he needed three days to fill me in."

When they met, Jaramillo confirmed that when Moricz arrived in Guayaquil in 1964, he teamed up with lawyer Dr. Gerardo Peña Matheus. Through acquaintances, Andres Fernandez-Salvador Zaldumbide and Alfredo Moebius, Moricz met Jaramillo in Moebius's house, and from there Moricz ran with Jaramillo's story. Hall was annoyed with himself when he realized that various people had tried to direct him toward Jaramillo as early as 1975, but it took until 1991 for the two to finally meet.

Jaramillo and Hall realized that had it not been for Moricz, who focused attention on the Cueva de los Tayos, the 1976 expedition could have resulted in the discovery of the century—and what a track record for Armstrong it would have been! And yet also, had it not been for Moricz, the story would never have come out the way it did. Hall also remembered how he had shown Moricz a manuscript about the 1976 expedition, which Moricz then point-blank refused to return. The incident actually ended their friendship, but Hall never understood why Moricz did it—until 1991, when he realized that the manuscript mentioned Jaramillo. It was a name Moricz did not want to see published, as he had confirmed in the 1973 German newspaper interview.

A Brave New World

Jaramillo and Hall became friends, though both agreed Jaramillo would not reveal the location of the site. Still, he was willing to talk in detail about its contents and any other aspect of it Hall wanted to discuss. From Jaramillo, Hall was able to learn the true story of the Tayos library—which was not in the Cueva de los Tayos at all! Jaramillo stated that he had entered the library in 1946, when he was 17 years old. He was shown it by an uncle, whose name has gone unrecorded but who was known as "Blanquito Pelado" (a loving description of the man's appearance). He was apparently on friendly terms with the local Shuar population, who invited him to see a secret in gratitude for the kindness and goodness he had shown toward the tribe. The story, of course, brings back memories of what likely happened with Mitchell-Hedges and the Mayan descendents who showed him the cave that contained crystal skulls.

Jaramillo entered the system at least once after that. On that occasion, he saw a library consisting of thousands of large, metal books stacked on shelves, each with an average weight of about 45 pounds, each page impressed from one side with ideographs, geometric designs, and written inscriptions. There was a second library, consisting of small, hard, smooth, translucent—what seemed to be crystal—tablets, grooved with parallel channels, stacked on sloping shelves of trestled units covered in gold leaf. There were zoomorphic and human statues (some on heavy column plinths), metal bars of different shapes, and sealed "doors"—possibly tombs—covered in mixtures of colored, semiprecious stones. There was a large sarcophagus, sculpted from a hard, translucent material, containing the gold-leafed skeleton of a large human being. In short, an incredible treasure.

On one occasion, Jaramillo took down seven books from the shelves to study them, but their weight prevented him from replacing them. This also meant that they were too heavy to remove from the library and reveal to the world. Jaramillo never produced any physical evidence for his claims, which may explain why he wanted to live in the shadows of this story. He had seen it with his own eyes, but would anyone else *believe* it?

Hall did ask him why he never took photographs: "He said that it would not prove anything," Hall told me. Still, Jaramillo stated that he had left his initials in these seven books so that, if the library were ever discovered, it could be proved that it was he who had entered it.

Jaramillo and Hall wanted to combine forces to see whether the Metal Library could be opened: One knew the location, and the other had a proven track record of organizing proper expeditions. First, contact with various ambassadors and politicians was established; then the scientific community was brought in. The plan was for Jaramillo to lead the team to the site, where they would remain for a period of three to four months (during the dry season), cataloguing the contents of the site and guaranteeing that nothing went missing. Everything would remain in situ. A report with recommendations would be the only outcome of this expedition, which would involve UNESCO.

Then, in 1995, Peruvian jets bombed an Ecuadorian military base and the project had its first setback.

In 1997, Hall used a major anthropology conference to promote the idea of his expedition. Six anthropologists came to meet him, interested in what he was trying to accomplish. But that same year, Ecuador's political regime changed (in Hall's opinion, for the worse); Hall felt that his family could not live in the new political reality, so he moved back to Scotland with them. Nevertheless, planning for the expedition continued. But in 1998, the expedition had a major setback: Hall received by telephone the sad news from the mother of Petronio Jaramillo that he had been assassinated. Was he murdered because of the plans that were in motion? Life in South America is cheap, as anyone who has visited or lived there knows, and that day Jaramillo was carrying a large amount of money on him. He was killed in a street robbery, close to his home. Random violence stopped one of the world's biggest discoveries dead in its tracks.

Now, Moricz and Jaramillo had both died, and Hall was in his 60s. Would he go it alone and claim the Metal Library for himself? Hall wasn't a treasure-seeker, but he knew that the region was a veritable El Dorado, with gold everywhere; the roads are quite literally paved with it. It's possible that the library books are made out of gold—though Jaramillo never spoke of gold but of "metal" (in fact, it seems copper was an ingredient, as Jaramillo had seen a green color on the books)—but in any case there is more gold outside the library than inside. In fact, the reason Moricz was in the region in the first place was because he held extensive gold concessions; his interest in the library was not for its monetary value but for its historic importance.

Though Moricz was not one of them, various treasure hunters did try to open the cave throughout the years. One of them, Count Pino Turolla, made contact with Jaramillo in the 1960s through the same channels that later brought Moricz to him. Turolla was obsessed with Edgar Cayce's theory of a Hall of Records, which the American prophet claimed resided under the Sphinx at Giza. He claimed there were other such halls, each containing evidence of the existence of Atlantis, elsewhere in the world. For Turolla, the Metal Library would be absolute proof of Cayce's prophecies. But Turolla's attitude prevented he and Jaramillo from getting along. Turolla pressed Jaramillo for details that the latter was simply unwilling to offer, so Turolla opted to search around the Cueva de los Tayos and came up empty-handed.

One active Indiana Jones–type today is Stan Grist, who knew Juan Moricz as well as his confidante, Zoltan Czellar, also a good friend of Hall. In 2005, Grist wrote: "As I write these words, I am in negotiations with the native Shuars who live near the Cueva de los Tayos, whose permission is necessary to enter and explore the area of the caves. I plan to mount an expedition in the coming months to search for the secret entrance to the cave from which the alleged metallic library can be accessed. Many people have entered the cave by the well-known, vertical entrance near the top of the mountain. However, I calculate that it is nearly impossible or is impossible to reach the metallic library through this well-known entrance. The secret entrance is only accessed from underwater!"[8] When I confronted Hall with Grist's opinion, he said, "Jaramillo always said that the entrance was under the river. But that river is not near the Tayos Cave. That river is the Pastaza River."

Though Hall never learned the location from Petronio Jaramillo himself, after Jaramillo's death in May 1998, Hall organized a trip with Mario Petronio, Jaramillo's son, in which they combined their knowledge about the site. The trip had to be abandoned before "point zero" could be reached. In May 2000, Hall returned. He said, "When we were preparing the expedition in the 1990s, whenever diving equipment was discussed as a necessity Petronio would say that even though [the entrance to the cave] was under the river, it did not mean we would get wet." Hall showed me aerial maps, pointing out a bend in the river that meets a fault line, which is known to open up into a cave system that runs for several miles. His suggestion is that the fault line opened up the underground network, which someone at some stage in the distant past then discovered and used as a place to install the Metal Library. Hall had visited this location and deduced that it fit Jaramillo's description perfectly.

So, what happened next? When Hall was 68, he decided that he more than likely would not see this story come to its conclusion. So, on January 17, 2005, Hall informed the Ecuadorian government of the location of a cave that fits Jaramillo's description, and that he hopes will one day become the focus of an expedition. That location is at 77° 47' 34" west and 1° 56' 00" south. GoogleEarth brings you very close and can satisfy any initial curiosity—but knowing the location doesn't mean it will be easy to find! Hall thinks it will take decades or a paradigm shift before people can work together in a manner that will result in a successful expedition. He argues that the 1976 expedition only succeeded because a military regime was in power; "a democratic bureaucracy will swamp the expedition before it crosses any swampy river," he said. What is required, Hall felt, is a sense of cooperation and openness. Stan died in September 2008.

⬧ ⬧ ⬧

Is the Metal Library or the "treasure of the Aztecs" as revealed to White Tiger evidence of alien beings, on par with what Indiana Jones discovers in *Indiana Jones and the Kingdom of the Crystal Skull*? No. But it is evidence that the civilization of the New World was far more complex than we think or even can imagine. It is evidence that there is so much left to discover, if only we are willing to *believe* that history isn't a closed book. What the New World does prove is that it is very much like the Old World. There are pyramids. There was building on a massive scale. Some of these buildings were constructed using massive stones. There are stories of gods apparently coming out of nowhere, who taught the people civilization. The ensuing civilization ever since has contained evidence of that encounter with the divine, for those who are willing to recognize the artifacts for what they are.

All of this is clearly evidence that our history is not as simple as what we read in standard reference works. There is a large body of evidence, on various continents, that shows that someone in our past was far more advanced than we assume, possessing technology and/or knowledge that today is not part of our society, which is precisely why we cannot truly explain these archaeological sites and artifacts. But they do not *prove* that we were not alone. Fortunately, however, they are not the best evidence available in our efforts to answer the Ancient Alien Question.

Chapter 6

The Best Evidence

What would constitute the "best evidence" to convince a jury that ET dropped by, maybe as early as many millennia ago? First, we need to assume that ET will have left physical traces of his presence, and further that these traces have withstood the test of time. This is not a given. A spaceship landing off the shores of some country, followed by ET walking onto the beach and speaking with the local inhabitants, will have left no physical traces—except, perhaps, an oral or written tradition of "some ancestor" conversing with "a mysterious being" on the shore "a long time ago." We could hope that this being left a gift with our ancestors, who in turn carefully preserved it, and that this gift can be proved to be of alien origin. But this is once again not a given.

The "best evidence" therefore needs to be a clear, long-lasting sign that contact was made. There have been a number of "oop-arts" (out-of-place artifacts) that have been looked upon as furthering the cause of the Ancient Alien Theory, but they are not evidence of an advanced extraterrestrial civilization—only evidence that some of our ancestors, or entire civilizations, were (and sometimes are) far more clever than academics are willing to concede.

Dr. Vladimir Rubtsov thinks that "the search for ancient 'extraterrestrial artifacts' (ETAs) is one of the most important and worthwhile directions of investigation in paleovisitology."[1] His focus has been on trying to identify artifacts on planet Earth that might be of extraterrestrial origin, and he believes he has found a few candidates for that extraordinary distinction.

Rubtsov has identified a metal object found in 1976 near the Vashka River, a river in the Komi Republic and Arkhangelsk Oblast in Russia, as a possible alien artifact. The object is a cylinder, about 4 feet in diameter. When it was subjected to coercion, or rubbing, the object sparkled. The object was cut into several pieces and studied in various Soviet laboratories, including the All-Union Institute of Nuclear Geophysics and Geochemistry, the S.I. Valiov Institute of Physical Problems, and the V.I. Vernadsky Institute of Steel and Alloys. Dr. Vladimir Fomenko coordinated the research, and published its findings in 1985, noting that the object consisted of an alloy of the following rare earths: cerium (67.2 percent), lanthanum (10.9 percent), and neodymium (8.78 percent). There were also small amounts of uranium and molybdenum (less than 0.04 percent). The alloy clearly had artificial origins, but, as it contained no traces of calcium or sodium, it was noted that it was impossible to create such an artifact on planet Earth with the current technologies. The fragment appeared to be made of a mixture of powders with various crystalline structures. The finest particles of the powder each consisted of several hundreds of atoms only.

Unfortunately, as the discovery and announcement of the artifact was made during the Cold War, Western science as a whole is largely unaware of it, and uninterested in it. In the eyes of the

The Best Evidence

people who studied the object it is a candidate for best evidence, but it is definitely not the best-known evidence.

One famous example of an oop-art is the so-called Baghdad Battery. It was found in 1936, when the Directorate General of Antiquities carried out excavations in the mounds east of Baghdad, known as Khuit Rabboua. The finds date back to the Parthenian Period (227–126 BCE), though the excavations were not well recorded and the style of the pottery is actually Sassanid, which is 224–640 CE.

The finds included a pottery jar that measured 5 inches and contained a copper cylinder with an iron bar fixed in its center that extended a little out of its opening. The cylinder was covered by a layer of bitumen (tar) and its copper base was also covered with bitumen, as was the jar itself.

In 1940, Wilhelm König, the German director of the National Museum of Iraq, published a paper speculating that the objects might have been galvanic cells, perhaps used for electroplating gold onto silver objects. If he's correct, the Baghdad Battery would predate Alessandro Volta's 1800 invention of the electrochemical cell by more than a millennium. In 1973, the battery was displayed in the Baghdad Museum and was regarded as the oldest kind of dry battery ever discovered. Around that time, German Egyptologist Arne Eggebrecht built a replica of the battery and filled it with freshly pressed grape juice. He generated 0.87 volt of current, which he then used to electroplate a silver statuette with gold.

Another oop-art is the Antikythera Device. In 1900, a Greek sponge diver named Elias Stadiatos, working off the small Greek island of Antikythera, found the remains of a Greek ship at the bottom of the sea. In early 1902, Valerio Stais was sorting through the recovered material, all donated to the Museum of Athens, when he noticed a calcified lump of bronze that did not fit anywhere, and that looked like a big watch. He guessed it was an astronomical clock and wrote a paper on the artifact. But

The Antikythera Device was found in 1900 in a shipwreck. It was 50 years before anyone realized the device was a mechanism that incorporated accurate workings for various bodies of our solar system. It is now often considered to be the first computer. © Marsyas via Wikipedia.

when it was published, he was ridiculed for even daring to suggest such a thing. His critics argued that sundials were used to tell time. A Greek dial mechanism was unknown to the archaeological community, even though it was described on what must therefore have been a purely theoretical basis. The status quo was that "many of the Greek scientific devices known to us from written descriptions show much mathematical ingenuity, but in all cases the purely mechanical part of the design seems relatively crude. Gearing was clearly known to the Greeks, but it was used only in relatively simple applications."[2] And therefore, because scientific dogma had said so, the Antikythera Device could not be. It was physical evidence, but deemed to be impossible, and therefore ridiculed and debated away.

In 1958, Yale science historian Derek J. de Solla Price stumbled upon the object and decided to make it the subject of a scientific study, which was published the following year in *Scientific American*. This marked the revival of interest in the Antikythera Device, more than half a century after its discovery. Part of the problem, Price felt, was the device's uniqueness. He stated: "Nothing like this instrument is preserved elsewhere. Nothing comparable to it is known from any ancient scientific text or literary allusion. On the contrary, from all that we know of science and technology in the Hellenistic Age we should have felt that such a device could not exist."[3] He likened the discovery to finding a jet plane in Tutankhamen's tomb, and at first believed the machine was made in 1575—a first-century BCE creation date remained hard to accept, let alone defend.

Ever since, the Antikythera Device has been subjected to some of the most innovative scientific studies. They have shown that the Greeks were extremely advanced when it came to applying their astronomical knowledge. Today, the Antikythera Device is worshipped by many as the first calculator—the first computer. Price labeled it "In a way, the venerable progenitor of all our present plethora of scientific hardware."[4]

It took more than a century from the discovery of the Antikythera Device until we had some understanding of its technical complexity, as well as a general consensus that it is indeed a highly technical artifact. Part of the problem was that the find was unique; if ET in fact only gave us one present, then it appears it's not good enough proof.

Ancient Aliens

Palenque's Ancient Astronaut Slab

The lid of Lord Pacal's tomb in Palenque is among the most often quoted evidence for the Ancient Alien Theory. The discovery of this tomb occurred once Alberto Ruz Lhuillier was appointed director of archaeological exploration of the Mayan ruins of Palenque in 1949. Though the site had been known since 1750, it was only in 1925 that the first archaeological work was carried out. Ruz Lhuillier began by clearing the ruins of earth and rubble, and in 1952 he penetrated deep inside the so-called Temple of Inscriptions, where he discovered a sarcophagus belonging to Hanab-Pacal, the ruler of Palenque, who died in 683 CE at the age of 80, after an impressive 68-year reign.

It was highly unusual to find an intact tomb, and it was a minor miracle that when Ruz Lhuillier lifted up the lid of the coffin, it did not break. Inside was a mummy, its head covered by a mask made up of 200 pieces of jade. Very quickly one magazine ran a story on the "Palenque giant," claiming Lord Pacal was 12 feet tall. In reality, he was 5.9 feet, which was still remarkably taller than the average height of his subjects.

If Pacal had been a giant, that would have received widespread interest, but instead, it was the slab of the sarcophagus, which weighs 4.5 tons, that took the limelight, as it depicted one of the most intricate and baffling reliefs found anywhere in the world. The carvings are about 1 inch deep and depict a human being in an unusual pose. That's about the only thing everyone agrees on. The first explanation offered was that this was a Native American on a sacrificial altar, about to have his heart ceremonially removed. Ancient astronaut proponents thought differently: In *Chariots of the Gods* von Däniken compared the pose to that of the 1960s Project Mercury astronauts. The relief has since attracted decades of intense speculation by other Ancient Alien enthusiasts, who believe that the relief should be turned 90 degrees, at which angle it depicts Lord Pacal riding a technical

The Pacal tomb is one of the best-known billboards for the traditional Ancient Alien Theory. When flipped 90 degrees, it appears as if Pacal is riding a type of flying scooter. Only when confronted with this challenge did archaeologists finally begin to look more carefully into the potential meaning of this tomb slab. © Madman2001 via Wikipedia.

device resembling a low-flying scooter. Engineer Laszlo Toth has done a series of technical drawings that detail the workings of the machine on which Pacal supposedly rides. He claims to have identified a mask on Pacal's nose, his hands manipulating controls, the heel of his left foot on a pedal, and a little flame issuing from the machine's exhaust.

Archaeologists strongly disagree. To their credit, they no longer argue that the image is of a brutal human sacrifice, but instead interpret the lid depicting Pacal descending into Xibalba, the Mayan Underworld. They support their conclusion by showing that below Pacal is the Mayan water lord, the guardian of the underworld, and the "device" is in fact the world tree. As he falls, he travels down the tree, which was identified with the Milky Way, or *Sak Beh*. Along the edge of the sarcophagus are a series of inscriptions, which lists the death sequence of the eight generations of kings before Pacal. One of the best detailed explanations of the lid is offered by Linda Schele and Peter Mathews, who in *The Code of Kings* conclude that "Pacal falls in death, but his very position also signals birth—his birth into the Otherworld."

There are numerous other examples of this imagery depicted on various Mayan sculptures, some dating to the Olmec period. The difference between Pacal's tomb and the other depictions is that Pacal's rendition of this descent is highly stylized, and the end result, when tilted 90 degrees, is indeed suggestive of a space-bike-riding king. Given that this image is on Pacal's tomb, depictions of the Underworld and the world tree are definitely more apt than a vehicle.

Pacal's tomb is evidence that treating objects in isolation can sometimes mean that the answer is no. As with the Nazca lines, though, posing the Ancient Alien Question did mean that science was pushed to come up with the correct answer.

One of the dangers of any theory, of course, is interpretation. For example, the statues at Tula, in Mexico, have enigmatic ears—largely rectangular, which some Ancient Alien theorists have proposed could be interpreted as hearing protection. A more logical explanation is that the ears are either overly stylized or protected by a rectangular part of a headdress. Though the statue indeed holds an object in its right hand that *could* be interpreted as a type of laser, it could just as well be a wooden or metal object. What it is—or should be—is largely determined by the perspective of the observer. And when one has only a simple depiction for evidence, that depiction, or any analysis of it, will never be proof of an alien presence.

The Goldflyer

Looking at the archaeological record and finding anomalies is precisely how major advances in the alien debate have progressed. In *Chariots of the Gods*, Erich von Däniken remarked that, in his opinion, a particular artifact recovered from Colombia was nothing short of a prehistoric airplane. His statement was controversial, as archaeologists had catalogued the small artifact as an insect. The artifact in question is currently on display in the Smithsonian Institution in Washington, D.C. Its explanation states: "Gold artifact, a stylized insect, from the Quimbaya culture, Antioquia province, Colombia, ca. 1000–1500 AD." At one point, replicas of the piece could be bought from the Smithsonian gift shop.

There are a number of other such "insects," five in the collection of the Gold Museum at the Bank of the Republic in Bogota. The "Bogota aircraft" was first publicized by Ivan T. Sanderson, who thought the artifact represented a high-speed aircraft. He sought the opinion of a number of aircraft engineers, who supported his idea. Another stylized "goldflyer" is in the possession of the Museum of Primitive Art in New York City, where it is identified as a "winged crocodile." Dr. Stuart W. Greenwood has tracked down 18 of these artifacts in museums and private collections, but in all instances, archaeological officialdom labeled them insects or something similar.

Ancient Aliens

The Goldflyer is one of a series of scale models produced by a team of German enthusiasts who demonstrated that the "bees" found in the gold collections of many museums were actually planes, as von Däniken alleged.

The standoff between archaeologists and Ancient Alien researchers did not break until 1994, when three Germans, Algund Eenboom, Peter Belting, and Conrad Lübbers, decided to create a scale model of the Colombian "airplane." They wanted to experiment with its flight capabilities. At the same time, they began to draw parallels between the features of this artifact and similar artifacts, which were indeed likely to be bees and insects.

A key point in the debate is that all insects have their wings on the tops of their bodies. However, there were some golden artifacts, like the one from Colombia, that had the wings underneath the body—anatomically incorrect, but valid for an airplane, as we can see on any airport runway, where Boeings and Airbuses all have under-fuselage wings.

The German trio soon realized that the people of South America were able to depict insects and other flying animals anatomically correctly, so if this gold artifact was indeed an insect, then it was an anomaly, and a serious mistake at that. Eenboom, Beltung, and Lübbers therefore concluded that it could not be an insect. Their drawings showed that the design of the artifact corresponded perfectly with the design of a modern jet-engine aircraft—such as the space shuttle and the supersonic Concorde.

In 1996, they were allowed to photograph all of the "golden airplane" specimens on display at the Bremen Overseas Museum in Germany. They were also allowed to measure them and even make impressions of the originals. That same year, Peter Belting created his first scale model—an area he was well-versed in. In fact, it was his interest in the field of scale models that had led to his decision to study the Colombian artifact in the first place. The scale model was baptized "Goldflyer I." Built at a scale of 16:1, the plane measured 35 inches long, with a wingspan of approximately 3 feet. It weighed 1.5 pounds. A propeller was added to the nose of the plane and the wings were equipped with the necessary flaps and rolls, so that it could take off and land. Early test flights were a success: The plane had a stable flight path and was able to make accurate and comfortable landings. In short, the artifact behaved as a plane was meant to behave, and this was the first demonstrable evidence that the "bee" was a plane.

Next in the development line was the Goldflyer II. This model had the same dimensions as the first, but was equipped with landing gear and a jet engine. The engine itself was a "Fun jet," able to make 20,000 rotations per minute. The modification from a propeller to a jet engine was made because the original gold artifact did not have a propeller. (If it had, it would have been quite a task for established scientists to have labeled the artifact an insect!)

The problem to overcome was where the jet engine should be placed. On modern airplanes, the jet engines are on the wings (as on modern Boeings and Airbuses) or at the back of the fuselage (as on the Fokker); the space shuttle has them at the very back of the craft, but its takeoff and flight are vastly different from traditional airplanes, as its flight is aided by booster rockets. In the end, Goldflyer II's jet engine was positioned at the back of the aircraft, in an unusual position when it comes to what we know from modern aviation, but it was the only position the original gold artifact allowed for such an engine. The insertion of the jet engine in that position was not only a novelty, but also a risk: The air flow into the engine would be different from the accepted standards as used in the airline industry. Subsequent test flights revealed that the plane continued to behave impeccably: Takeoffs and landings were perfect, and its flight path was stable. In short, the insertion of an engine at the back of a plane could be perfectly achieved in modern aviation—the team had just shown modern aviation a novel approach, based on ancient technology!

During the Ancient Astronaut Society World Conference in Orlando, Florida, in August 1997, Belting and Eenboom gave a demonstration of the object in flight. I was a speaker at this conference, which was interrupted at one point so that attendees could go outside and watch the takeoff of the space shuttle from Cape Canaveral, which could be seen on the horizon. But going out to watch the Goldflyer II in action that afternoon was truly one of the most memorable events of my life. I saw how Goldflyer II behaved impeccably during takeoff and flying, and its landing was a thing of beauty.

In 1998, Belting and Eenboom presented at the annual conference of the Deutsche Gesellschaft für Luft and Raumfahrt, where the majority of scientists displayed a positive and open-minded attitude toward their ideas. The notion that the bee was an aircraft was beginning to be accepted, for Belting and Eenboom, along with Lübbers, had already demonstrated that the object could fly. Professor Apel of the Technical University of Bremen, Germany, even concluded, "Anyone who understands even a little bit about aerodynamics will be able to make one single prognostication: those approximately 1,500-year-old amulets from the pre-Columbian region have such perfect aerodynamic characteristics that they simply have to fly, and very well at that."[5]

It is impressive to see enthusiasts take this approach and demonstrate their case; no one can argue with the flight capabilities of the "insect" as it is. This is what the model looks like, and this is how it flies. In my opinion, Belting, Eenboom, and Lübbers have been able to demonstrate that the artifact is not an insect. At the moment, they have only been able to prove it is an anomaly, an "item" that has all the characteristics of an airplane. But is it an airplane? Or is it something else? Only new evidence, or comparisons with other findings of a similar nature, might give us the final answer.

The Piri Reis Map

Apart from tangible artifacts, knowledge can also be considered best evidence—Robert Temple argued as such in *The Sirius Mystery*, where he tried to demonstrate that the Dogon of Mali possessed knowledge that they simply could not have had. (Alas, in the final analysis, the evidence to support his claim is lacking.)

Most people can accept the idea that any advanced civilization would have a detailed understanding of geography and would also have detailed maps of their region. This knowledge leads us to the well-known Piri Reis map, a medieval map designed in 1513 by the Turkish admiral Piri Reis. It was discovered in 1929 in the old imperial Topkapi palace in Istanbul by German theologian Gustav Adolf Deissmann while cataloguing the Topkapi Sarayi library's non-Islamic items. At the time, it was the only known 16th-century map that showed South America in its proper longitudinal position in relation to Africa. One of the maps it was based on belonged to Christopher Columbus on his voyage to discover America. From the 1960s onward, largely due to the work of Charles H. Hapgood, who published *Maps of the Ancient Sea Kings* in 1966, the Piri Reis map has been seen as incorporating information that could likely only have been gathered through satellite photography. Thus, as our ancestors clearly are not credited with satellite technology, the map could constitute convincing evidence of an alien presence.

Though dating from 1513, the Piri Reis map is known to have been based on numerous older maps, most now lost. Researchers came to this conclusion because the "center" of the map is the intersection of the Meridian of Alexandria at 30 degrees East and the Tropic of Cancer at 23 degrees North—the old bailiwick of Ancient Egypt. But the part of the map most relevant for Ancient Alien proponents is the manner in which the coastline of Antarctica is depicted: It conforms to pre-glacial conditions of about 12,000 years ago, which suggests that the mapmaker either had a very accurate imagination or had maps at his disposal that dated back thousands of years, allowing him to map a continent that was officially not even known to the Ancient Egyptians—Antarctica was only discovered in 1819 by the American seal hunter Nathaniel Palmer.

There are even more interesting aspects to the Piri Reis map. For example, it shows a large inland lake in Brittany, as well as a large lake present in the Sahara. As mentioned, it is also the first map that showed the correct longitudinal position of Brazil in comparison to Africa—not an easy feat for anyone in 1513! The "other side" of the argument has maintained that more accurate maps of the world *were* created in the 16th century, including the Ribero maps of the 1520s and 1530s, the Ortelius map of 1570, and the Wright-Molyneux map of 1599. However, the idea that there were later, better maps is fine, but the real topic of intrigue with the Piri Reis map is precisely that it was the earliest, and had information on Brazil that was apparently only discovered in 1500.

The Best Evidence

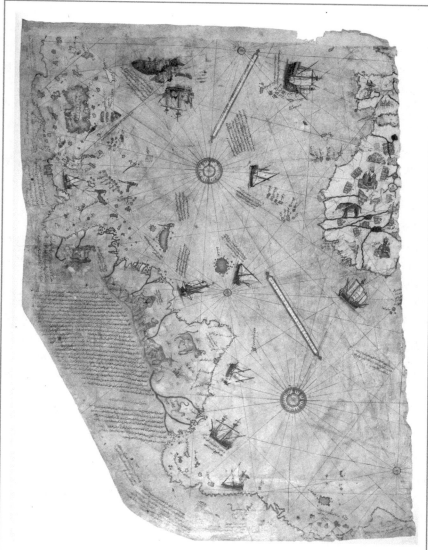

The Piri Reis map is an early 16th-century map known to have been constructed by synthesizing several other maps. It shows correct longitudes for the Brazilian coastline, and some researchers even suggest that it shows the correct, pre-glacial coastline of Antarctica, a continent that would only be discovered three centuries later.

What about the coastline of Antarctica? Peter Kames and Nick Thorpe in *Ancient Mysteries* write that this mystery was "so shocking that professional archaeologists and historians could not bring themselves to discuss it." Eventually, historian of cartography Gregory McIntosh did. He feels that the resemblance of the map's Antarctican coastline to the actual coast of Antarctica is tenuous. He states that cartographers had depicted a massive landmass at the bottom of their maps for centuries before the actual discovery of Antarctica, and that Piri Reis merely followed in this tradition. He also believes that it is possible that the map's "Antarctic coast" is actually the eastern coastline of South America, skewed to align east-west, for as simple a reason as getting it to fit on the page! There are even more solid concerns, such as the fact that if the landmass pictured is Antarctica, then 2,000 miles of South American coastline are missing from the map. So the map loses all of its accuracy when it comes to the southern half of South America, but picks up its accuracy in its display of Antarctica? Also, Hapgood relied on a seismic survey carried out in 1949 to argue his case for the pre-glacial coastline of Antarctica being depicted, but more recent scientific studies of the continent have revealed that the coastline of Antarctica looks radically different from the results of the 1949 survey.

Either way, it is interesting to note the manner in which science has held the Piri Reis map debate: To explain away the anomalies of the Piri Reis map, traditional scientists have done precisely what the Ancient Alien proponents have done with the Pacal tomb slab, which is to take everything in isolation. When you only look at Antarctica, the similarities could be a coincidence, but if you look at the entire map as a whole, a vastly different picture emerges: It has correct longitude differences, at a time when calculating longitude was practically impossible. It also employed a projection that was more appropriate to ancient Egypt than the Turkish Piri Reis. Hapgood therefore felt confident to conclude that the Piri Reis map was evidence of one possibility: "It appears that accurate information has been passed down from people to people. It appears that the charts must have originated with a people unknown and they were passed on."[6] Those people possessed knowledge of our world with which we do not credit our ancient civilizations.

But is it evidence of an alien presence? No. Graham Hancock has argued that the Piri Reis map is evidence of a *lost* civilization, but there is indeed no evidence that this lost civilization had any *alien* influences. So the quest for the best evidence continues.

World Ages

December 21, 2012, is the end date of a Mayan calendar round. For the Mayans, it is the end of the Fourth Age, which began on August 11, 3114 BCE—roughly 5,000 years earlier, when the gods convened in Teotihuacán. This means that the First Age of the Mayan Calendar—the First Creation—was believed to have begun 15,000 or 20,000 years earlier—tens of thousands of years before archaeology accredits humankind's presence in Middle America, let alone the existence of a Mayan civilization. However inconvenient this Mayan belief is for scientists—who dismiss it as fantasy—this time period does push us back to before the last ice age, and could in theory explain why someone knew the correct coastline of Antarctica in preglacial conditions.

Today, archaeologists are often reported as stating that the Mayans left us very little writings, and how hard it therefore is to draw any definitive conclusions about them. Compare this to what Father Diego de Landa, who accompanied the Conquistadors, boasted about: "We found great number of books...but as they contained nothing but superstitions and falsehoods of the devil we burned them all, which the natives took most grievously, and which gave them great pain."[7] It is therefore not so much the

Mayans who left us with little, but we who destroyed what we had taken from the Mayans by force, thus creating a blank canvas on which we could rewrite the history of the Mayan world and pretend that they were poor pagan idiots.

After the conquest of the Aztec Empire by Spain, after they committed most of the Aztecs' books to the fire, in the late 17th century Don Carlos de Sigüenza y Góngora studied some of the few remaining Aztec manuscripts and learned that the Aztecs possessed a calendar lasting 52 years. The calendar was a combination of a "regular" solar year, lasting 365 days (known as *haab*), and a calendar that was 260 days long (known as *tzolkin*). The former consisted of 18 months of 20 days, to which the Aztecs added five days to make it coincide with the solar year. The latter is normally linked with the duration of a fetus's gestation inside the womb—the time from conception to birth. The tzolkin is known to have been used as early as 600 BCE, and though it was found in Aztec material, it is Mayan in origin. Today, several Mayan people, specifically those living in the highlands of Guatemala, continue to use and cherish the calendar. "New Agers" in the West are beginning to embrace the calendar as well.

De Sigüenza's discovery was the first of many Mayan calendars that were found to have been used either throughout or for long periods of Mayan history. The most famous calendar today is the so-called Mayan Long Count Calendar, a calendar that was used for almost one millennium; it has been found on hundreds of monuments, dating from approximately 36 BCE to 909 CE, and it is the calendar that mentions the famous date of December 21, 2012 CE.

In the Mayan Long Count, the date December 21, 2012 is rendered as 13.0.0.0.0. This date should be read as 13 Baktun, 0 Katun, 0 Tun, 0 Unial, and 0 Kin, and illustrates the basic building blocks of the Mayan calendar:

The Best Evidence

📖 1 Kin equals 1 day.

📖 1 Unial equals 20 days.

📖 1 Tun equals 360 days.

📖 1 Katun equals 7,200 days, or 20 tuns.

📖 1 Baktun equals 144,000 days, or 20 katuns.

This sequence shows the wheels within wheels of the Mayan calendar—its cyclical nature. The date marks the end of a cycle, which is equivalent to 13 times 144,000 days, or a period of 5,125 years. The Long Count therefore began on August 11, 3114 BCE, annotated as 0.0.0.0.0—the beginning of the Fourth World, said to end on December 21, 2012 CE.

As mentioned, we can use this Long Count Calendar to work our way back to circa 18500 BCE, when the First Age was said to have begun. But did you know that the Mayans had calendars that were 34,020,000,000 days, or more than 90 million years long? The Mayans were not alone in this. A Babylonian clay tablet in the Library of Nineveh gives to the Assyrian king Ashurbanipal (685 BCE–ca. 627 BCE) a calendar that is 195,955,200,000,000 days long—a period that is many, many, many, *many* times the few billion years our planet has existed! It has therefore been suggested that the number does not represent days, but seconds, which would still make it 2,268,000,000 days, or a period that is more than six million years!

As incredible as it may be, Dutch author Willem Zitman has been able to show that these two periods, one from Central America and one from the Middle East, are actually related: The Babylonian period is 15 times smaller than the Mayan period! This is not a coincidence, and shows that the two cultures either worked out extremely long cycles of time, based upon astronomical events, on their own, or that both cultures have a common heritage: a knowledge of astronomy that was somehow shared by two cultures that lived on two ends of the world at a time when standard history states there was no exchange of culture at all!

195

Among the many questions this idea raises, one important one is why the Babylonians and Mayans were obsessed with such incredibly long cycles of time. The only light that Zitman can shed on this is that if we assume the Babylonians thought that the cycle of precession (a change in the orientation of the Earth's axis resulting in changes to the position of the stars in the sky) lasted 25,872 years, then the Babylonian unit expresses 240 Precessional Cycles. As to why this would be important, again, no one has an answer, if only because science does not address the issue. But seeing as two ancient civilizations that were experts in astronomy highlighted the cycle, I would suggest that astronomy in future years is likely to uncover a very interesting significance for this period of time.

Massive cycles of time are not only typical of the Mayans or Babylonians, but also of the Egyptians. In the 1970s, a French Egyptologist claimed to have discovered an inscription in the Temple of Isis in Denderah that represented a period of time of 36,159,177,600 years, or a staggering 13,207,139,618,400 days. Of what use is a period of time of 36 billion years? We do not know, but the Ancient Egyptians clearly felt it was important.

Whatever these cycles represent, it is clear that our ancestors held these calendars to be important. It is equally clear that it had to have been a nonhuman intelligence that told our ancestors that a cycle of 90 million years was somehow important, for 90 million years ago there were no humans on this planet! Not even a lost civilization like Atlantis can bridge that divide. Therefore, whatever intelligence knew of this cycle was either millions of years old or had knowledge—if not technology—at its disposal that had calculated a period of 90 million years and had revealed its importance. That intelligence must somehow have made contact with humankind and given our ancestors this knowledge.

The Best Evidence

Oannes

In the third century BCE, the Babylonian Berossus, head of the temple organization between 258 and 253 BCE, reported on the existence of a mythical being called Oannes who had taught humankind wisdom. The name *Oannes* was a Greek rendering of the Babylonian *Uanna*, a name used by the god Adapa, a son of Ea. In mythology, he was indeed the god of wisdom and the one who brought civilization to the city of Eridu—the cradle of Sumerian civilization, and for some the word from which the name for our planet, Earth, originates from. Though Ea gave Adapa knowledge, particularly of the arts and civilization, eternal life was not bestowed upon him.

What was remarkable about Oannes was not only that he taught people how to create temples, compile laws, and use geometry, but that he rose out of the Persian Gulf at daytime and returned to this watery abode at night. He had the body of a fish, but underneath the figure of a man—he was, by all accounts, nonhuman.

The first century BCE scholar Alexander Polyhistor summarized Berossus's *Babyloniaca* and left us the following account of Oannes:

> At Babylon there was (in these times) a great resort of people of various nations, who inhabited Chaldæa, and lived in a lawless manner like the beasts of the field. In the first year there appeared, from that part of the Erythraean sea which borders upon Babylonia, an animal destitute of reason, by name Oannes, whose whole body (according to the account of Apollodorus) was that of a fish; that under the fish's head he had another head, with feet also below, similar to those of a man, subjoined to the fish's tail. His voice too, and language, was articulate and human; and a representation of him is preserved even to this day.

This being was accustomed to pass the day among men; but took no food at that season; and he gave them an insight into letters and sciences, and arts of every kind. He taught them to construct cities, to found temples, to compile laws, and explained to them the principles of geometrical knowledge. He made them distinguish the seeds of the earth, and shewed them how to collect the fruits; in short, he instructed them in every thing which could tend to soften manners and humanize their lives. From that time, nothing material has been added by way of improvement to his instructions. And when the sun had set, this being, Oannes, retired again into the sea, and passed the night in the deep; for he was amphibious.[8]

Oannes was the first of the Apkallu, seven Sumerian demigods who gave civilization to humankind. They served as priests of Enki and as advisors or sages to the earliest "kings" or rulers of Sumer, before the flood. Gustav Guterbrock in his study of the Apkallu concluded that they were the "bird men" visible in many Sumerian depictions. The Greeks would label the Apkallu "heroes": They were not immortal, but they were more than mere men. At the same time, they were religious educators and seem to have formed the blueprint of the priest class. In primitive civilizations, these priest classes were termed "shamans" and they were specifically identified with totem animals, most often with birds. This was because the shaman was said to fly and enter the Otherworld to seek advice from the ancestors.

The story of Oannes was picked up by Carl Sagan in his book *Intelligent Life in the Universe*, where he commented, "I support the contention that a major cultural change did take place with the advent of the Oannes." Elsewhere he noted: "These beings were interested in instructing mankind. Each knew the mission and accomplishments of his predecessors. When a great inundation threatens the survival of this knowledge, steps are taken to insure its preservation."⁹ Sagan was therefore convinced that the series of nonhuman civilizers were part of a larger plan, as each one knew of its predecessor's mission.

He also believed that of all ancient accounts, the story of Oannes was the best evidence for the possibility that an alien had interacted with our ancestors, presenting a gift—the gift of civilization—which would enable major cultural change for those who received Oannes' information.

Babylonia was not the only culture that credited a nonhuman intelligence with the gift of civilization; in fact, most civilizations on all continents relate that their dawn of civilization came about through contact with mythical creatures—sometimes human, sometimes less so, as in the case of Oannes. In Egypt, author R.T. Rundle Clark noted a wall painting in the tomb of Ramses IV as depicting Osiris with seven fish-like genii, beings from the "Abyss of the waters." In the case of the Inca, we know their civilizing deity was the god Viracocha, and though we have so far not identified how he came about, we do know he appeared around Lake Titicaca and went down the Sacred Valley, bringing civilization to the people. In Ancient Egypt, wisdom was linked with the god Thoth, the scribe of the Gods, who was said to have been physically present—as were the other gods—in Egypt, many millennia ago.

Civilization, in short, was a gift from an unknown group of beings, all of whom were labeled "gods," who seemed to have a clear mission: to visit the various continents and emerging cultures of the world and educate them, not just with the basic means of making fire and basic commands like "Do not kill," but also with detailed information having to do with geometry, mathematics, astronomy, and the like. Indeed, this "central command" as the source of all knowledge might explain why, across the world, all ancient civilizations divided the sky in the same constellations—a remarkable feat, seeing as our ancestors had thousands of stars to pick from!

Going back to Christianity, Byzantine Chronicler George Syncellus specifically linked the "Seven Sages" with the Egregori, or Watchers, "who had descended to earth in the cosmic year 1000, held converse with men, and taught them that the orbits of the two luminaries, being marked by the twelve signs of the Zodiac, are composed of 360 parts."[10] In short, the Watchers had taught astronomy. And the Watchers, of course, were those beings who somehow had fallen from the sky to mate with women....

Atomic Warfare in India

Another candidate for best evidence is the conquest of the atom—nuclear warfare, which, according to Zecharia Sitchin, is precisely what occurred in the Middle East in the third millennium BCE. In support of this conclusion, Sitchin consistently pointed to photographs of the Sinai Peninsula, taken from space. They purportedly showed an immense cavity and crack in the peninsula's surface, revealing where a nuclear explosion had taken place. He explained that the area was strewn with crushed, burnt, and blackened rocks, which contained a highly unusual ratio of the isotope uranium-235, "indicating in expert opinions exposure to sudden immense heat of nuclear origin," to quote Sitchin.[11] Alas, he provided no further details as to who these experts were, or where they had expressed such opinions, thus weakening his case despite what would otherwise be very good evidence.

In recent publications, Sitchin has also argued that the article "Climate Change and the Collapse of the Akkadian Empire: Evidence from the Deep Sea," which was published in the April 2000 issue of *Geology*, is confirmation of his claim. The essay argues that an unusual climate change occurred in the areas adjoining the Dead Sea, which gave rise to dust storms, and that the dust—an unusual "atmospheric mineral dust"—was carried by the prevailing winds over the Persian Gulf. According to Sitchin, this was due to an "uncommon dramatic event that occurred near 4,025 years before the present," or about 2025 BCE.[12] He added that the water level of the Dead Sea fell abruptly by 100 meters at the time, further indicating that something truly catastrophic did happen.

Alas, consultation of the article itself reveals that Sitchin has been more than selective in his summary of it. Though the article states a catastrophe did occur, it also clearly reveals that the likely cause of this climate change was a volcanic eruption—not a nuclear explosion. The article is unable to identify which volcano was responsible for this sudden climate shift, but clearly correlates the presence of volcanic ash with the ensuing disasters. And volcanic ash is very distinct from nuclear fallout. In short, the quoted report is not evidence of a nuclear explosion at all; it is evidence of a so-far unidentified volcanic eruption. As there are specific references to volcanic ash in the abstract and summary of the report, the question should once again be asked why Sitchin failed to see or report this.

Despite decades of searching, Sitchin seems to have been unable to find supporting evidence that the Sinai Peninsula is indeed strewn with nuclear debris. This does not invalidate his theory as such, but has stopped him—and the Ancient Alien cause in general—to advance. Indeed, his often-maligned unscientific methodology of writing has been seen by some as hindering, more than advancing, that cause.

Another possible site of a long-ago nuclear explosion is the Indus River Valley, where towns such as Harappa and Mohenjo Daro flourished. Some believe that these ancient cities might have been irradiated by an atomic blast. If true, it would be impossible to ignore the conclusion that some ancient civilizations possessed high technology.

All work in Harappa and Mohenjo Daro in recent years—and so many other sites across the world—has been about preservation, not exploration. This scientific attitude makes it very hard to find new information to settle *any* controversy, let alone the Ancient Alien Question. We do know that a layer of radioactive ash was found in Rajasthan, India, after a very high rate of birth defects and that cancer was discovered in that area. It covered a 3-square-mile area, 10 miles west of Jodhpur. The levels of radiation registered so high on investigators' gauges that the Indian government cordoned off the region. Scientists then apparently unearthed an ancient city where they found evidence of an atomic blast dating back thousands of years: from 8,000 to 12,000 years ago. The blast was said to have destroyed most of the buildings and probably a half-million people. So far, this story seems to have all the necessary credentials—but can it be proven?

Archaeologist Francis Taylor stated that etchings he translated in some nearby temples suggested that the local population prayed to be spared from the great light that was coming to lay ruin to the city. "It's so mind-boggling to imagine that some civilization had nuclear technology before we did. The radioactive ash adds credibility to the ancient Indian records that describe atomic warfare."[13]

Another curious sign of ancient nuclear war in India is a giant crater near Mumbai (formerly Bombay). The nearly circular Lonar crater has a diameter of 7,064 feet, is located 250 miles northeast of Mumbai, and is dated at around 50,000 years old. No trace of any meteoric material or the like has been found at the site or in its vicinity, and this is the world's only known "impact" crater in basalt. Indications of great shock (from pressure exceeding 600,000 atmospheres) and intense, abrupt heat (indicated by basalt glass spherules) can be ascertained from the site.

The Best Evidence

Whereas the story of the Mahabharata is indirect evidence, the archaeological and geological discoveries in India pose serious problems for those trying to deny the possibility of ancient atomic warfare. What makes it all the more remarkable is that these indications were found in a corner of the earth where accounts say that just such horrible warfare had occurred! Indeed, when confronted with these findings, one skeptic stated, "I am sick and tired of hearing this [the possibility of an atomic explosion in India], and I cannot find any debunks of this either. [Is there] anyone who can debunk this, or is this really true?"[14] That is indeed the question—and it is an important one. The stakes are high, as one would expect when facing the best evidence for the Ancient Alien Question.

Let us further examine this best evidence in India. The first question is whether the named archaeologist Francis Taylor existed. Alas, no one has ever been able to identify him. There was a Francis Taylor, an American museum director, who died in 1957; he was, however, not an archaeologist. There is also a "Franciscio Taylor," but he is not the quoted Francis Taylor either.

Not a good start. Skeptics have also wondered whether this ancient atomic warfare theory is meant to deflect attention away from a serious issue: modern atomic contamination. In 1998, it was reported that some Indian power stations had major problems, including an incident in which 2,000 workers became exposed to excess radiation, 300 of whom had to be hospitalized. Surendra Gadekar investigated the conditions of the villagers at Rawatbhatta in Rajasthan and confirmed that there were indeed gross radiation-related deformities. Rawatbhatta is in the same region as the "ancient warfare" site. Gadekar did not find evidence of ancient warfare, but he did find evidence of modern negligence: Wood that had been used in the power plant had then somehow made its way into the local community, where it was subsequently used as wood for fires. This in itself was a minor incident, but could there have been more serious incidents, whereby a decision was made to create an "ancient enigma" to cover up a modern disaster? This is a possibility, but there is no evidence to back up this conclusion at present.

Regrettably, no newspapers carried the story of the discovery of radioactive material in Rajasthan. The Indian archaeological authorities are not aware of it. And as there is a government laboratory in Jodhpur, Rajasthan, the question is whether something might have gone wrong there. With these objections, the case has become more controversial than straightforward. Still, it is clear that the counterarguments have not demolished the potential of this evidence.

Until the subject is seriously tackled, the bodies of Harappa and Mohenjo Daro remain a mystery. Whether or not the Indian radioactive site turns out to be modern or ancient, it is, at least, an uncontested fact that the site was radioactive. The anomalous crater adds power to the ancient-nuclear-warfare possibility, as does other circumstantial evidence, such as the Mahabharata. Finally, the fact that all these enigmas are within the same general region (as opposed to scattered across the world) adds even further weight to the case.

The Chief Fetish

Mitchell-Hedges never came across extraterrestrial beings, but he did come upon what experts told him was a unique human being—which looks just as strange as an alien being. This bizarre "mummy" is the so-called Chief Fetish of a tribe known as the Chucunaque, which Mitchell-Hedges and his frequent travel companion, Lady Brown, discovered in Panama. When the two arrived among the Chucunaque, the tribe decided to kill the white intruders, as it was a tribal custom that death should be dispensed to anyone violating their territory.

Mitchell-Hedges's intelligence and knowledge was put to the test when he realized that the best way to deal with this lethal danger was to pretend he and his companion were gods. To that end they put on a spectacle: He had brought some flares and Lady Richmond Brown's Queen of Sheba costume, resulting in a performance that convinced the Chucunaque that Mitchell-Hedges and Lady Richmond Brown were indeed gods sent to cure their ills!

During their subsequent stay with the tribe, a huge number of fascinating exhibits were collected. Among these was the Chief Fetish of the Chucunaque tribe, used to treat males on the point of death. The artifact itself was assumed to be a male human fetus preserved by an unknown means. But when Professor Arthur Keith, FRS, regarded by Mitchell-Hedges as one of the greatest anthropologists of his day, examined the fetish, he declared it had a skull formation "hitherto entirely unknown."[15] The unique specimen was presented to the British Museum

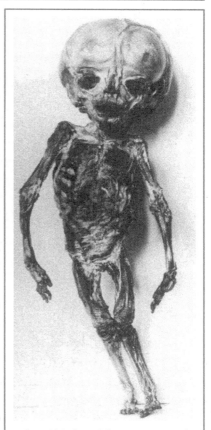

The Chief Fetish appears to be a human male fetus, given to Mitchell-Hedges by a native tribe in Panama. But expert analysis revealed the formation of the skull to be a true anomaly, involving the eyelashes, the bones, and more. It currently resides in the British Museum, and no research has been done at all toward exploring the mysteries of this object.

along with hundreds of others—and nothing else has since ever come of it; this anomaly has never been explained.

To quote from Mitchell-Hedges's *Danger My Ally*:

> This chief fetish was used only as a last resort, when an Indian was at the point of death. As far as we could discover only males were privileged to undergo the treatment, and if the sufferer subsequently recovered it was considered that a miracle had occurred. But to us the significance was in the fetish itself which proved to be unique, for it was found upon examination to be a human male fetus.

> Professor Sir Arthur Keith, FRS...gives it as his opinion that its age was from five to six months when it was removed from the womb of the mother. It had been preserved perfect in every single detail, even the fine skin; and under a microscope one can see the beginning of the eyebrows. This preservation of an embryonic child shows a scientific knowledge of the highest order in contradistinction to their habits and conditions of living. All anthropologists who have seen it are unanimous in their opinion that it has neither been smoked, sun-dried nor cured by any process known today, neither has it been treated with spirit; yet it is as perfect as when first removed from the mother.

> Subsequent close examination disclosed that the fetus had a skull formation hitherto entirely unknown.

> When we were told by experts that it was probably the only specimen of its kind in the world, we felt its proper place was The British Museum, to which we gladly presented it.

The Best Evidence

The Chief Fetish currently remains in storage at the British Museum, where two friends of Anna Mitchell-Hedges, Jon Rolls and Cris Winter, viewed it in 2005. Jon says that it "was the most amazing object I have ever seen—and I have visited many museums. It had incredible detail and looked like it was sleeping; it was so lifelike I expected its eyes to open any second. As I examined it, a number of questions sprung to mind which remain unanswered to this day."[16] These questions involve the method of preservation, as well as various anomalies with the fetus, for example in its eyelashes, its bone structure, and the absence of any scar from an umbilical cord. As of yet, these questions remain unanswered. The object is about 4 inches high—making it too small to be a four- to six-month-old fetus. Those who have seen it also mention that the eyes and head are too big for a fetus of that age.

Apart from the extraordinary find, it is interesting to note that impersonating a visiting deity saved Mitchell-Hedges's life. And though it is assumed that the fetish was given to him in gratitude for the extraordinary medical care he gave the tribe, one can also wonder whether, from the perspective of the tribe, maybe something that they felt or knew was from the gods was given back to the gods? Though little analysis has gone into the object, the expert opinion from one of the leaders in the field declared it to be a total anomaly!

The Dropa

Just before the outbreak of the Second World War, Chinese archaeologists stumbled upon a cave containing small skeletal remains. Alongside the bodies they found stone discs that, when deciphered 20 years later, seemed to tell of an extraterrestrial craft that had crash-landed in the mountain range of Baian-Kara-Ula 12,000 years ago.

The so-called Dropa disks were rumored to contain information about a crashed alien spaceship in the Chinese mountain range of Baian-Kara-Ula. They are among the most controversial evidence that extraterrestrial beings once visited our planet.

When the story of this craft reached the Western media, they treated the news with the usual attitude of "It's Communist propaganda—don't believe a word of it." In the mid-1990s, German author and tour guide Hartwig Hausdorf reignited the debate as to whether aliens had crash-landed their craft in the remote mountainous region of Baian-Kara-Ula, in China's Qinhai Province, and it became popularly known as "The Chinese Roswell" (after the Roswell, New Mexico incident of 1947, where it is popularly assumed an alien spacecraft crash-landed).

At the core of the story is this: In 1937–38, an expedition led by Chi Pu Tei, an archaeologist with the Chinese Academy of Sciences in Peking (Beijing), was trying to find shelter in the Kunlun-Kette mountain chain. The team members entered a cave and found inscriptions on the walls. At the back of the cave they found several tombs, aligned in a row, containing strange-looking skeletons, each measuring about 45 to 50 inches in length and having an abnormally large skull. Buried with the skeletons were unusual stone discs, 716 in all, each about 15 inches wide and half an inch deep with a hole in the center, each bearing strange hieroglyphs.

Few images of the Dropa tribe exist, but the few that do show that the facial features of these people are quite extraordinary. Scientists have made various attempts to explain these features away, but could it be that they look the way they do because their ancestors interbred with the survivors of a crashed spaceship, as the Dropa themselves believe?

Closer inspection revealed that each disc was a book, but, upon their discovery in 1938, nobody possessed the dictionary for this language so no one was able to read the books. All the discs were collected and stored along with the other findings from the area. There was no reason to consider these stone discs special or important; perhaps just odd.

The discs were kept in Peking, where, for the next 20 years, a line of experts tried to decipher the writing. Nobody succeeded. In 1962, Professor Tsum Um Nui did succeed, and learned of the astonishing message the discs contained. He announced his findings to a small group of friends and colleagues, but the public remained unaware of his discovery. The authorities felt it wise not to announce the professor's findings; the Peking Academy of Prehistory forbade the professor from publishing anything about the discs.

After two years of what must have been utter frustration, the professor and four of his colleagues were finally allowed to publish the conclusions of their research. They decided to call it "The cartelled script relating to the spaceship that, as is written on the discs, descended on Earth 12,000 years ago." The discs told the story of inhabitants of another world stuck in the mountains of Baian-Kara-Ula. The peaceful intentions of these people had not been comprehended by the local population, and many extraterrestrials had been chased and killed by members of the Han tribe who lived in nearby caves.

Professor Tsum Um Nui offered a few lines of his translation: "The Dropa came out of the clouds in their aeroplanes. Before sunrise, our men, women and children hid in the caves ten times. When they finally understood the sign language of the Dropa, they realized the newcomers had peaceful intentions."[17] Another part of the text stated the Han tribe regretted that the Dropa had crashed in this remote area, and that they were unable to build a new spaceship so the Dropa could return to their home planet.

Since the discs' discovery more than 25 years before, other archaeologists had learned more about the history of the area. That newly acquired knowledge indicated that the story, as it appeared in Tsum Um Nui's translation, could be correct. Legends circulating even at that time spoke of short, skinny, yellow men that "had come out of the clouds a very long time ago."[18] These people had big, knobby heads and small bodies and were a terrible sight to see, according to the locals who had chased these people away on horseback. The description of these people is identical to the bodies Professor Chi Pu Tei had recovered in 1938.

Mural paintings were also found inside the cave. They depicted sunrise, the moon, unidentified stars, and the Earth—all connected with dotted lines. The discs and the cave's contents were dated to about 10000 BCE. In the 20th century, some of the caves were still inhabited by two tribes, calling themselves the Han and the Dropa—the latter people of strange expression. Barely 4 feet tall, they were neither Chinese nor Tibetan. Even the experts of Professor Tsum's team could not indicate their racial background.

Next, enquiries came from the Soviet Union, with scientists requesting some of the discs to be sent to them for study, which the Chinese did. The Soviets removed pieces of "dirt" and made various chemical analyses. The Soviet scientists were surprised to learn that the discs contained fairly high amounts of cobalt and other metals. Dr. Viatcheslav Saizev reported in the Soviet magazine *Sputnik* that he had put the discs on a special machine that was somewhat like a gramophone. When turned on, the discs "vibrated" or "hummed" as if some kind of special electric charge had been pushed through the discs in a particular rhythm; or, as one scientist stated, "as if they formed a part of an electric circuit."[19] Somehow, at one time they had been exposed to high electric charges.

Such findings, however, had little to do with the other discs that stayed behind in China. Shortly after Tsum Um Nui's decoding, the Cultural Revolution of the late 1960s swept over China, and there was no public concern for the discs' fate or their message. In 1974, an Austrian engineer, Ernst Wegerer, stumbled upon two discs in the Banpo Museum at Xian and photographed them. Erich von Däniken learned of the discs and Wegerer's photographs, and wrote about the discs in one of his books. But in March 1994, Hausdorf and Peter Krassa, a friend of von Däniken, left for China and visited Xian and the Banpo Museum, searching for the discs that Wegerer had photographed two decades earlier. Nowhere could they find any trace of the discs. Had Wegerer made up the entire story? That seemed unlikely. They asked their guides and Professor Wang

Zhijun, the director of the museum. At first, they denied the discs even existed! Within an hour of having been shown the photographs, Zhijun stated that one of his predecessors had indeed given Wegerer permission to photograph the discs, and that the discs did indeed exist or had at least existed. Shortly after having given Wegerer permission to photograph the discs, that director was asked to resign.

Director Zhijun showed Hausdorf and Krassa a book on archaeology in which photographs of the discs could be seen. Afterward, he took them to the location where the museum's artifacts were cleaned and catalogued. On one chair stood an enlarged copy of a stone disc. Zhijun hinted that, a few years ago, word had come down from above—from his superiors—that all traces of the discs had to be wiped out, and that he was to go on record as saying everything was one big lie. Had Hausdorf and Krassa been less obstinate, they might have classed Wegerer as a hoaxer.

In their efforts to find the truth about the Dropa saga, Krassa and Hausdorf also came across the story of an Englishman, Dr. Karyl Robin-Evans, who had traveled to China in 1947. Before his arrival, a Professor Lolladorff had shown him a stone disc that he believed to have been found in northern India. The object appeared to have belonged to a tribe, the "Dzopa," who had used the discs during religious ceremonies. Dr. Robin-Evans stated the discs had a radius of about 5 inches and were about 2 inches thick.

The professor put the disc on a balance and connected the balance to a typewriter. He illustrated how the disc, throughout a period of three and a half hours, apparently gained and lost weight. After one day, this change in weight created a printed line on the paper in the typewriter. The change in weight had allowed the typewriter to print, leaving characters on the paper. The discs could (sort of) type! Though it was easy to explain what had happened, how it had occurred was basically impossible.

The Best Evidence

How could a stone disc change weight? (Apparently Dr. Robin-Evans was unwilling to lose face over the stunning weight experiment: Though his report had been written in 1947, it was not published until 1978, four years after his death.)

After his meeting with Professor Lolladorff, Dr. Robin-Evans set course for the Chinese mountains in search of the Dzopa tribe. First, he passed through Lhasa, Tibet, where he was welcomed by the 14th Dalai Lama, who was 12 years old at the time. In 1947, Tibet was still independent. Only in 1950, when the Dalai Lama fled to northern India, did the Chinese take possession of the country. Once in the high mountains, Robin-Evans's Tibetan carriers decided to stay behind. They were afraid. Dr. Robin-Evans managed to reach his destination and gain the confidence of the Dzopa people. He was provided with a language instructor who taught him the basics of the Dzopa language. Then, Lurgan-La, the religious leader of the Dzopa, told him the history of the tribe. He stated that their home planet was in the Sirius system. Lurgan-La explained that two expeditions had been sent to our Earth: the first, more than 20,000 years ago; the second in 1014 CE. During the 1014 visit, a few spaceships had crashed; the survivors were unable to leave Earth. The Dzopa were the direct descendants of those people.

Among the estate of Robin-Evans was a most remarkable photograph: the royal couple Hueypah-La and Veez-La. They measured 47 and 42 inches! Not only was their height small; their entire appearance could only be described as strange.

The important question was whether the "Dropa" and the "Dzopa" tribes were one and the same. But Robin-Evans had apparently been aware of some controversy regarding that subject. Though "Dropa" was the correct spelling, "Dzopa," or, rather, "Tsopa," was closer to the correct pronunciation of the word. He felt it would be better to write "Dzopa," as that was closer to the correct pronunciation.

There were only two remaining problems: The date on the stone discs, 12,000 years ago, did not coincide with the statements of the religious leader (20,000 years ago and 1014 CE). Furthermore, the discs appeared to contain statements by non-Dropa tribesmen describing the Dropa, but were supposedly written *by* the Dropa. Did some locals intermingle with the Dropa? Or was the information somewhat garbled?

Were there still descendents of the Dropa? Hausdorf looked into the latest, 1982 list of recognized national minorities in China and learned that the Dzopa are not recognized as a minority in their home province, Qinghai. Might they therefore no longer exist? The list does specify that 880,000 people making up 25 tribes are not recognized as ethnic minorities. So, the Dzopa might not be recognized, or they might be listed under a different name, as the Hanyu-Pinyin transcription "translated" certain names completely differently from what they were before.

Another mystery with which Hausdorf battled was the name of Tsum Um Nei, a name that wasn't Chinese. This fact had led to rumors that the man had never existed and was a figment of someone's imagination. But an Asian friend of Hausdorf told him that "Tsum Um Nei" was a mixture of Chinese and Japanese; the Japanese pronunciation of the name had been written down in Chinese, the way a German named "Schmidt" would be named "Smith" in America. "Obviously the guy was Japanese," Hausdorf realized, which also explained why the professor decided to move to Japan after the stone disc controversy—he returned home to retire.[20]

There are several aspects to this story: the strange skeletons; the discovery of a little-known tribe of dwarf-like beings; the nature and whereabouts of the discs; and the decipherment of the inscriptions. What is the truth?

As for the discs, it has been pointed out that stone discs are a known ingredient of Chinese culture and are called "Bi" discs.

The Best Evidence

Although their origin is unknown, these Bi discs have been dated to as far back as 10000 BCE—thus largely coinciding with the time-frame of the alleged crash. Bi discs were normally made from jade or other precious materials and were regarded as status symbols: In the aftermath of war, the losers were required to hand over their discs as a sign of submission. Furthermore, it is known that the discs were used in burials: In aristocratic burials, the discs were normally placed above the head, below the feet, and on the chest of the deceased. Interestingly, Bi discs were often called "the Ear of Heaven," and sometimes the hole in the disc was placed in front of the mouth so that the dead could speak to their ancestors.

The story that stone discs with hieroglyphs were found in a tomb is therefore not only plausible but likely—considering, too, that Bi discs often carried inscriptions.

This begs the question of whether the discs that Wegerer photographed in 1974 and the disks seen by Hausdorf, which are similar in description to those reportedly discovered in Baian-Kara-Ula, were just Bi discs or actual examples of the ones found in the mountain cave during the 1937–38 expedition.

Many people incorrectly believe that the story of the Dropa tribe was first aired in a 1978 book titled *Sungods in Exile*, edited by David Agamon. This book details the 1947 expedition of the English scientist Dr. Karyl Robin-Evans. It is now known that the book was largely science fiction dressed up as nonfiction, but many people had already decided that the Dropa story was bogus—especially those who erroneously argue that the book was the first to mention the "ridiculous" story. It would seem that *Sungods in Exile* either was meant to cash in on stories about the Dropa that were in circulation for a few years before it was published, or—if you like a conspiratorial explanation—was meant to discredit the story. Why? Perhaps it was merely because China was a Communist nation and any interest in things Chinese was officially discouraged at the time by Western governments.

However, it was definitely not a hoax—at least not one executed in 1978. The Berlin-based historian Dr. Jörg Dendl has been able to trace the first mention of the Dropa story to 1962, when a monthly magazine for vegetarians, *Das vegetarische Universum* (*The Vegetarian Universe*), published an article titled "UFOs in Prehistory?" in its July edition. Dr. Dendl has so far not been able to find the original Chinese or Japanese source, but it is clear that the story is much older than 1978, as skeptics claim.

Furthermore, the story reported in *Sungods in Exile* of an expedition coming across dwarfish people in the Baian-Kara-Ula region has nonfictional counterparts. Dr. Dendl found a 1933 clipping about a Chinese confrontation with dwarflike beings. Though some might argue that the location was in Tibet, at that time Baian-Kara-Ula was indeed mistakenly labeled as being part of Tibet. The article relates how a woman, only 4 feet tall, was seen being escorted by Chinese soldiers and that she and her group were being held as slaves. There was also a statement that they were cannibals, but this might merely have been an excuse to cover for their inhumane treatment.

Most importantly, the existence of the Dropa—or a tribe like them—has been confirmed. In November 1995, the Associated Press (AP) stated that some 120 "dwarfish beings" had been discovered in Sichuan Province, in a so-called Village of the Dwarfs. Some skeptics cast doubt on the AP account, though it is easily verifiable. In fact, on November 9, 1995, the German publication *Bild* ran a report titled "Das Dorf der Zwerge—Umweltgifte schuld?" ("The Village of the Dwarfs—Environmental pollution to blame?") about the discovery. The tallest adult in this village was 3 feet 10 inches tall; the smallest was 2 feet 1 inch.

The location of the village is only a few hundred miles from the Baian-Kara-Ula mountain range. However, despite China's becoming more open, this entire area, including the village, remains off-limits to foreigners. Hartwig Hausdorf ponders whether in recent years the Dropa's descendants might have

The Best Evidence

abandoned the mountains and settled in the nearby lowlands—where they were "discovered" in 1995.

According to a report in *Bild* on January 27, 1997, a Chinese ethnologist claimed that the tribe's dwarfism was due to a high concentration of mercury in the soil, which had poisoned their drinking water for several generations. The claim did not go unchallenged. Dr. Norbert Felgenhauer of the Munich Institute for Toxicology argued that this theory is nonsense. He stated that such poisoning would result in immediate death, not stunted growth, and introduced as evidence the case of the Japanese town of Minamata, where in the 1960s many inhabitants died from mercury poisoning. He also noted that mercury was unable to change human DNA and hence could not be held responsible for causing a hereditary trait—which was clearly apparent in this tribe.

So, we know that the existence of stone discs is possible, if not likely, and that, if the 1933 report is correct, there were dwarfish people living in that region. The question, then, is this: Is the decipherment of the script correct? If it is, then it does not necessarily prove that alien beings crash-landed in China, but at the very least it shows that these genetically bizarre beings believed they were descendants of aliens.

There is no verification of the 1962 successful translation of the discs as such, though it should be pointed out that neither is there any evidence to suggest that the 1962 story and the translation are invented. So far, the best the detractors have been able to argue is that the story is improbable (of course!) and that no one has ever been able to decipher a stand-alone language, let alone an extraterrestrial language. That is true. But nowhere does the account say, and no one has ever argued, that this was a unique language. The only claim in this connection is that in 1937–38, when the discs were discovered, their inscriptions could not be read immediately. Only in 1962 did a team of specialists succeed in this task. For all we know, the language in which the script was written had not yet been deciphered in 1937, or no one had paid sufficient attention to the inscriptions, or only in 1962 was someone able to identify the language in which the inscriptions were written.

But note the year: 1962. This is the year that the earliest known reference to the story appeared—found by Dr. Dendl in a German magazine—and it would suggest that something happened in 1962 that made a Chinese or Japanese source report on it. The translation of the discs might be precisely such an event: Professor Um Nui publishes his translation, and the media picks it up and creates a controversy; he decides to retire and return to Japan, while the media outside of China also reports on it, where it ends up in the German magazine *The Vegetarian Universe*. If the story was invented, it means that it was invented (or misreported) in 1962.

The 1962 article also discusses some technical details of the discs, underlining the potential factual nature of the story. It notes that the discs were composed of cobalt, iron, and nickel—the only metals to produce a magnetic field. Nickel is found largely in Canada and Central Africa, but in recent years it has been found in China, in the general area where the discs were located. For Hausdorf, this is a further indication that the story is factual, for this find post-dates the discovery of the discs—and the 1962 article. In short, what in 1962 was unlikely and improbable has now been confirmed.

The story of the Dropa is the story of an accident—an alien accident; how an alien spacecraft crash-landed on planet Earth. Its survivors had to make the most of it, and their presence was recorded in legends, as well as showing up in the genetic make-up of their descendents. The story of the Dropa, however, also brings to the forefront another issue, which is how incredibly divided the world of science is. However much we can pretend that "scientific evidence" is easy to collect, the world is divided into political factions that have had great influence on scientific communities. The story of the Dropa for a long period of time was not deemed to be credible—because it originated in China. And then it was quickly labeled a hoax as scientists had "shown" that it all originated from a science-fiction novel.

There is a general unwillingness from the scientific community to go out and find or analyze evidence of an alien presence on planet Earth, and the question as to whether there is any best evidence for the Ancient Alien Question should maybe be reworded, asking instead whether science is willing to explore and will ever accept *any* evidence in favor of the Ancient Alien Question.

Scientists are likely to push what they deem to be credible proof for the Ancient Alien Question into the realm of the absurd. There might never be a satisfactory answer, for the only thing we have to show are mute archaeological objects. It might indeed take an extraterrestrial being to land on the lawn of the White House before we accept the presence of a non-human intelligence. But even that will not prove the Ancient Alien Question. For that, after having landed on the White House lawn, ET needs to tell us whether his people ever visited us in the past, or whether he knows of other races that have come here in the past. It is quite likely that ET does not know the answer to that question!

However, if we look at all the archaeological and legendary evidence available, it is clear that the question of whether ancient aliens were here in the past is not a spurious question to ask. Scores of scientists, including Carl Sagan, studied the available evidence and came away with the conviction that contact had indeed been established in the distant past. There is best evidence, loads of it, but it depends on where your threshold of

Ancient Aliens

belief lies. What it takes to convince someone is a purely personal experience. For some, it takes too little; for others, a lot; for still others, nothing is satisfactory. There should be a consensus parameter, a problem our judicial system has resolved by installing trial by jury, in which a group of people need to arrive at a consensus view—what they accept to be credible evidence, and therefore what likely happened, and what we believe to be the truth. Science, however, is not a democracy. I leave it to the jury, though, to draw its own conclusion.

Chapter 7

Alien DNA, Earthly Life

On February 17, 1600, the Dominican friar Giordano Bruno was burned at the stake after the Roman Inquisition found him guilty of heresy. Bruno believed that God and the Universe were identical, which was considered to be heresy. When he was turned over to the state, he was condemned to death. Though it is commonly believed that Bruno was convicted because of his belief that the Earth orbited the sun and not vice versa, this was really but one component in a much larger vision Bruno shared and that caused his downfall. Bruno argued for an infinite number of planets, stars, and even galaxies. Most important, he proclaimed that life-forms, including intelligent beings, existed on a number of worlds throughout the infinite universe.

The belief that life exists elsewhere in the universe is referred to as *cosmic pluralism*, *the plurality of worlds*, or simply *pluralism*. The belief can be traced back at least as far as Thales of Miletus in 600 BCE, and to several of the founding fathers of the United States, specifically Benjamin Franklin and John Adams. Thales was—in my opinion, unfortunately—also the man who tried to explain everything without incorporating mythology. Bertrand Russell described him as the father of Western philosophy, but he should also be seen as the man who lay at the origins of our modern attitude of scorning myths and legends and treat them as unimportant. From Thales onward, we have removed thousands of years of our history, because it was based on or incorporated mythology.

In Greece, the greatest proponents of pluralism were the atomists, who believed that the world was made up of two parts: atoms and nothingness, the empty void—specifically Leucippus, Democritus, and Epicurus. The reason why these philosophers are largely unknown is because Plato and Aristotle, their opponents, argued for the uniqueness of the Earth. The two now-famous philosophers argued that the Earth was unique, and, as a consequence, there could be no other worlds. Plato and Aristotle won the popular debate, but have now been proven to be at least partially wrong, though more than two millennia later it is clear that their skepticism continues in the scientific community. Even though we have not yet found definitive proof of extraterrestrial life, exobiologists (scientists who search for life beyond Earth and study the effects of extraterrestrial environments on organisms) have shown that there are numerous planets and moons that have all the necessary conditions and ingredients to harbor life. As humankind has downsized its space program in recent decades, it is an unfortunate fact that we may not soon find proof of extraterrestrial life, and may need to contend ourselves with mere indications.

In the 1960s, the situation was completely different. The world was caught up in a frenzy as the two world superpowers, the United States and the Soviet Union, made space the final frontier of showing the world their superiority. Most of this ambition was concentrated on militarizing space and equipping it with a series of information-gathering satellites, if not weapons. But for general consumption, this true aim was dressed in far nobler terms. The Soviet Union took the first trophy when Yuri Gagarin became the first human being to travel into space, on April 12, 1961. The next, if not bigger trophy was handed out on July 21, 1969, when American Neil Armstrong became the first man to walk on the surface of the moon. Since then, apart from depositing a number of robots on Mars, humankind has not physically reached farther into the depths of the solar system, let alone the universe. "Boldly going where no one has gone before" has, at least for the moment, been consigned to the realm of Hollywood and its spectacular use of CGI.

In 1960 American astronomer and astrophysicist Frank Drake conducted the first search for radio signals from extraterrestrial civilizations at the National Radio Astronomy Observatory in Green Bank, West Virginia. The Search for Extra-Terrestrial Intelligence (SETI) had just begun. Shortly afterward, Drake created the "Green Bank formula," a mathematical formula that could calculate the likelihood of life elsewhere in the universe. The Green Bank formula tried to identify the number of planets similar to Earth in the Milky Way galaxy, as earthly conditions were deemed to be required for life to develop anywhere else.

Ever since, the Drake Equation—as it became popularly known—has been a beloved instrument in the quest for alien life, though it has never been properly able to provide a good indication of how universal—or not—life is. Some exobiologists find that the equation is too limited, as it only focuses on planets where life originated, rather than where life was seeded; as people move from country to country, so life might have moved from planet to planet. Specifically, in the event that life on Earth itself was seeded from elsewhere, even Earth's life would not be included in the results of the Drake Equation! Most scientists, however, will point out that all the factors in the equation are unknowns and therefore nothing but guesses, meaning that the possibility of life in the universe, if based on the Drake Equation, can be anywhere from zero to billions of billions, depending on the predisposition of the person feeding the Drake Equation with these values. The Drake Equation is a nice gimmick, and judging from the manner in which Drake created it, it seems to have been designed that way.

Another scientific tool linked with the Drake Equation is the Fermi Paradox, created by Enrico Fermi in 1950, which argues that there is an apparent contradiction between the high estimates of the probability of the existence of extraterrestrial civilizations and the lack of evidence for, or contact with, such civilizations. Of course, as science refuses to look for, or validate evidence of potential contact with extraterrestrial civilizations, the existence of this paradox is something of a paradox in itself.

Adrian Kent of the Perimeter Institute in Waterloo, Ontario, Canada, argues that there might be a very good reason why ET has not made its presence known to us through radio astronomy. He believes that it is possible that there is competition for resources not just on planet Earth, but throughout the universe. Advanced species might therefore want to exploit other planets for their own purposes, which is precisely the theory that Zecharia Sitchin put forward. If this were the case, then Star Wars would not simply be a thing of science fiction, but pretty much what we would find in galaxies far, far away. Within this type of interstellar economy, evolution might favor the inconspicuous, Kent believes.

Both the equation and the paradox are great tools armchair researchers and skeptics use to deride the entire field. To help resolve this problem, NASA set up the Kepler space telescope, which was designed to search for planets that transit or cross in front of their stars, as seen from Earth. The telescope has been reporting back to NASA since its launch in March 2009. As of

Alien DNA, Earthly Life

February 2011, Kepler has confirmed 15 new planets and found an additional 1,235 planet candidates, including the smallest planet yet spied outside our solar system. In March 2011, it was announced that our Milky Way galaxy might be home to at least two billion Earth-like planets, or 2.7 percent of all sun-like stars. If we extrapolate that to other galaxies—and there are approximately 50 billion in the known universe!—the likelihood is that there are 100 billion Earth-like planets out there. At least! The odds are clearly stacked in favor of other life being out there somewhere, so the odds that we have been contacted in the past are looking up.

Panspermia

But what if alien life did not contact us; what if we *are* alien life? What if we—all life on planet Earth—come from elsewhere? The idea that life did not originate on this planet is old. One of the first known proponents of panspermia—as this idea is scientifically labeled—was the Greek philosopher Anaxagoras, Socrates' teacher. Anaxagoras claimed that the universe consisted of an infinite number of spermata, or seeds. He believed these seeds gave rise to life-forms when they reached Earth. He coined the term *panspermia*, meaning literally "seeds everywhere."

In 1864, Louis Pasteur revived the idea of extraterrestrial origins of life and found support for his experimental thinking from British physicist Lord Kelvin and German physicist Hermann von Helmholtz in the 1870s. In the early 1900s, Swedish chemist and Nobel laureate Svante Arrhenius postulated that bacterial spores propelled through space were the seeds of life on planet Earth. British astrophysicist Fred Hoyle and his Sri Lankan student and, afterward longstanding collaborator, Chandra Wickramasinghe, revived the idea in the 1970s. Following Hoyle's death in 2001, Wickramasinghe has remained the most vociferous proponent of the idea.

225

Panspermia is directly opposed to the widely held assumption that life originated and evolved on Earth, without any outside interference, known as Darwinism, which is the thinking that has invaded all sciences. This is precisely why the notion of ancient aliens is such a scientifically controversial subject.

However, the theory of evolution has one major shortcoming, which is its very starting point. Darwin proposed that life began in a "warm little pond" somewhere, almost like a geological stove, where some ingredients were haphazardly thrown together, accidently creating the soup of life. In 1857, Louis Pasteur showed that microorganisms are always derived from preexisting microbes, and so life as we know it here on Earth is *always* derived from life that existed before. In short, Darwin was wrong, but this did not stop the Darwinian perspective on the origins of life from continuing to dominate the Western scientific mindset. The standoff between Pasteur and Darwin is therefore interesting for the very fact that Darwin's model was a theory, and Pasteur's conclusions were based on scientific, experimental research. Yet for more than a century, Western science has preferred to believe in and promote a disproven theory!

The key to panspermia is DNA, for without DNA, there would be no life. Still, it was only in 1953 that Dr. James D. Watson and Francis Crick discovered the structure of the DNA molecule, for which they were awarded the 1962 Nobel Prize for Physiology or Medicine. The discovery showed how incredibly complex DNA was. Crick has labeled it the best photocopying machine ever. Whereas we are continuously amazed at how many terabytes of information we can store on what is basically sand inside our computers, the amount of information stored in the DNA of our cells is still far more ingenious and complex!

Though the discovery of the DNA structure—a double helix—was a tremendous feat, the immediate reaction from Crick was amazement: DNA was so complex and so perfect that he concluded that it could not have been formed in the primordial ooze that ruled the Earth four billion years ago. "At a molecular level life even in its primitive form is so incredibly complex that any prospect of transforming an inorganic system into biology must be considered awesomely difficult to say the least," Wickramasinghe notes in *Cosmic Dragons*. On top of that, there simply had not been sufficient time on planet Earth for a complex system like DNA to form here. So where did it come from? Interestingly, the origins of life on Earth coincided with the last phase of the accumulation of material coming from comets that were passing through our solar system. Coincidence? Crick didn't think so, and therefore concluded that DNA had come from elsewhere in the universe, thus subscribing to the theory of panspermia. So in the opinion of the man who had discovered the structure of life—DNA—life itself was alien.

Crick proposed that DNA had ridden on the tail of one or more meteors and comets, landing on Earth from somewhere else in the cosmos. Where precisely DNA had originated from Crick did not postulate. The implication of his theory was that, because DNA was extraterrestrial, there was a high probability of coming across DNA-based life elsewhere in the universe that greatly resembled our own earth-bound life.

Since Crick postulated this theory, other scientists have gone even further down this line of thinking. NASA astrobiologist Louis Allamandola has discovered that RNA—very similar to DNA—spontaneously forms in interstellar space. This means that any object, whether a comet or a meteor, traveling through interstellar space, would pick up this RNA and bring it back to a planet. Scientists have always objected to the notion that life could travel on a meteor or comet, arguing that it would be subjected to intense radiation and would therefore not survive the ride. But physicist Paul Davies has shown that if the microbe is inside the meteor, it would be shielded from such radiation.

An even larger implication of Allamandola's finding is that the universe spontaneously creates RNA, which suggests that our universe was somehow *designed* to create RNA/DNA-based life—not just on Earth or in our part of the galaxy, but throughout the entire universe! Life is therefore a universal imperative. This would mean that the entire universe could be teeming with DNA-based life. It would mean that life, as it exists on Earth, is not as unique as we believe, and other planets would contain similar life-forms. Indeed, the idea that DNA was created elsewhere in the universe and arrived ready-made on our planet is now extremely likely. These findings have extraordinary implications for the Ancient Alien Question.

Though this is a tremendous scientific discovery, the scientific community is largely unwilling to accept it. Until recently, scientists' consensus view was that there *could* be extraterrestrial life, but if there was, it would be too distant for us to have active contact with it. In short, the answer to the Alien Question is *no*. They argued that the fabric of the universe—space-time—hindered beings from traveling over such vast interstellar distances. The problem is one of food, the human life span, fuel, and other rather mundane subjects that are nevertheless key ingredients. And with these objections, they feel that they can uphold their consensus view that We Are Alone.

We Are the Martians

Life on Earth is often found in the most unexpected places, from the deepest crevices of the oceans to the hottest walls of active volcanoes. Finding life in what we would consider to be an inhospitable environment, such as inside a meteor crashing to Earth, would therefore seem unlikely, but not impossible. Finding evidence of life inside a meteor would prove that life exists elsewhere in our solar system, thereby destroying scientific consensus that life is all about our Earth.

Alien DNA, Earthly Life

Richard Hoover, an astrobiologist at NASA's Marshall Space Flight Center in Alabama, has argued that filaments and other structures in rare meteorites appear to be microscopic fossils of extraterrestrial life that resemble algae known as cyanobacteria. He discovered these features after inspecting the freshly cleaved surfaces of three meteorites that are among the oldest in the solar system, one of which is the Orgueil meteorite, which crashed on May 14, 1864, near the French town of Peillerot. Some of the bacteria Hoover identified resemble bacteria found on Earth, though others looked less familiar. His findings suggest that some of the bacteria found here on Earth have extraterrestrial origins.

The best candidate for life in our solar system outside of Earth has always been Mars. In the early phases of our solar system, conditions on Mars and Earth were pretty similar, and it was only later on that Mars became the inhospitable place it is now. Though we have never been to Mars, Mars has come to us. We know that an estimated one billion tons of rock have traveled from Mars to Earth. We know that microbes have been shown to be capable of surviving traveling the distance between the two planets and the shock of an impact on our planet. If there was life on Mars, it certainly could have traveled to our planet riding on a meteorite.

Allan Hills 84001 (commonly abbreviated ALH 84001) is a meteorite that was found in Allan Hills, Antarctica, on December 27, 1984, and that in 1996 was made famous when Bill Clinton entered the White House Press Room to broke with business-as-usual and announced to the world that NASA had found evidence of life on Mars. The announcement came about as NASA scientist David McKay believed he had found microscopic fossils of Martian bacteria based on carbonate globules inside the meteorite. Since 1996, the issue of whether or not this particular meteorite contains evidence of extraterrestrial life remains, to say it modestly, controversial, largely due to diverging scientific camps, showing once again that exobiology does not seem to be an exact science.

There are 34 meteorites on our planet currently catalogued as likely originating from Mars. Among these, two have been put forward as being on par with ALH 84001 when it comes to indications of Martian life. One of them, the Shergotty meteorite, fell to Earth at Shergotty, India, on August 25, 1865. Its interior is said to indicate the remnants of biofilm, and therefore could be evidence of the existence of microbial communities. The other candidate, the Nakhla meteorite, fell to Earth on June 28, 1911, near Alexandria, Egypt. Many people witnessed its explosion in the upper atmosphere before it fell to Earth in about 40 pieces. When analyzed, the Nakhla meteorite turned out to be the first Martian meteorite to show signs of aqueous processes. The meteorite contained carbonates and hydrous minerals, which are the result of chemical reactions in water. Scientists also learned that the rock had definitely been exposed to water, which proved that there was once water on Mars. There is further evidence of carbon inside some of its fragments, but the presence of carbon is insufficient to convince all scientists that bacteria once lived on Mars.

In recent years, the Mars orbiter and rover missions have shown that the Red Planet indeed once had abundant water. Though the surface of Mars today is too cold and dry to support known life-forms, there is evidence that liquid water may exist not far beneath the surface.

The odds are—once again—in favor of Mars once having had basic microbial life. But that is—unsurprisingly—not the scientific consensus. In order to settle the debate, a team of researchers at MIT and Harvard in 2011 developed an instrument that they hoped could provide the proof that life on Mars did once exist, and may have been responsible for life on planet Earth. The team of Christopher Carr and postdoctoral associate Clarissa Lui, working together with Maria Zuber, head of MIT's Department of Earth, Atmospheric and Planetary Sciences (EAPS), and Gary Ruvkun, a molecular biologist at the Massachusetts General Hospital and Harvard University, have created an instrument that should allow them to discover evidence of DNA or RNA. They have labeled their quest the Search for Extra-Terrestrial Genomes (SETG). Their instrument could take a sample of Martian soil from below the surface and process it to separate out any possible organisms and amplify their DNA or RNA, as well as use biochemical markers to search for signs of particular genetic sequences that are nearly universal among all known life-forms. Their hope is that, when it's finished, their device will find a ride on a future exploration to the Red Planet.

If the device lifts off, it will become one of a very short list of instruments that have been sent to Mars to search for life. The first was launched in 1976 with the *Viking* Landers and produced ambiguous results. The most commonly accepted version of the 1976 tests is that they revealed no signs of life. But Gilbert Levin, the principal investigator of this project, felt that the conclusion was too quickly reached. In 1986, he reexamined the results and concluded that *Viking* may well have found evidence of microbial life on Mars.

One image from the *Viking 2* Lander showed early morning frost at the landing site, offering further support that the planet once had water. But most importantly, one of the experiments was to detect metabolizing microorganisms. When the experiment was conducted on both the *Viking* Landers, it gave positive results! Yet despite the straightforward, positive result, the conclusions were debated away! Does anything more need to be said?

When probes landed on Mars, early experiments apparently showed that there was no life on the Red Planet. But since then, those results have been questioned. Together with evidence from meteorites, images like these, which show frost on the Martian surface in the morning, indicate Mars once was home to living organisms.

Alien Probes

Professor Chandra Wickramasinghe argues that after 1982, evidence for cosmic life and panspermia acquired a status close to irrefutable, but publication avenues that were hitherto readily available to its proponents became suddenly closed. He has gone on the record with his opinion that, after 1982, attitudes hardened to a point that panspermia and related issues were decreed taboo by all respectable journals and institutions. Nothing that challenged the scientific dogma of how life had originated on planet Earth could be published, in spite of the vast amount of scientific data showing that life did not originate here.

He adds, "Even though the general public reveled in ideas of extraterrestrial life, science was expected to shun this subject

Alien DNA, Earthly Life

no matter how strong the evidence, albeit through a conspiracy of silence. It was an unwritten doctrine of science that extraterrestrial life could not exist in our immediate vicinity, or, that if such life did exist, it could not have a connection with Earth."[1] Wickramasinghe became evidence of this "conspiracy of silence" himself when in March 2010 he was dismissed from his post at Cardiff University's Centre for Astrobiology, as funding was withdrawn from his department.

Wickramasinghe has gone far beyond the idea that life was seeded here on planet Earth; he argues that every day, alien life-forms enter our planet, in the form of flu viruses. He has found that outbreaks of the flu are often found to coincide with major meteor showers that sprinkle the Earth's atmosphere with what is literally extraterrestrial material. Specifically, he believes that diseases such as the Spanish Flu virus actually rode to Earth from space on meteors, before it caused widespread death in 1918–20. Between 50 and 100 million people, or 8 to 16 percent of the world's population, died from the Spanish Flu, making it one of the deadliest natural disasters in human history: some 550 million people, or 32 percent, were infected. Worst affected was Western Samoa, where 90 percent of the population was infected, and one-third of adult men, one-fifth of adult women, and one tenth of all children were killed.

The lethal second wave covered almost the entire world in a very short period of time, suggesting that the speed at which it traveled was beyond a human carrier, and that the virus was literally seeded from space. Lau Weinstein observed that "Although person-to-person spread occurred in local areas, the disease appeared on the same day in widely separated parts of the world on the one hand, but, on the other, took days to weeks to spread relatively short distances."[2] The best evidence for its extraterrestrial delivery mechanism was that in the winter of 1918, the disease suddenly appeared in Alaska, in villages that had been isolated for several months.

Wickramasinghe also points to the Plague of Athens and the Plague of Justinian as two further examples of plagues that might have had alien origins. The Plague of Athens was a devastating epidemic that hit the Greek capital during the second year of the Peloponnesian War (430 BCE). The cause of the plague remains unknown. The Plague of Justinian afflicted the Byzantine Empire, including its capital Constantinople, in the years 541–542 CE. It was one of the greatest plagues in history. Wickramasinghe includes the more recent SARS (Severe Acute Respiratory Syndrome) outbreak as having potential extraterrestrial components. SARS created a near pandemic, between November 2002 and July 2003, with 8,422 known infected cases and 916 confirmed human deaths. Within a matter of weeks, SARS had spread from the Hong Kong province of China to 37 countries around the world. Microbes have been identified in the upper atmosphere, and though it is known that storms, monsoons, and volcanic activity can transport them to these regions, the mesosphere is also the first region where meteors begin to fragment.

The evidence accumulated so far suggests that the worst flu epidemics coincide with peaks in the 11-year cycle of sunspot activity, and this was once again the case in 2000. Removing Wickramasinghe from his position has not helped him find more evidence for this possibility. He points out that as much as a ton of bacterial material might fall to Earth from space daily, which translates into some 1,019 bacteria, or 20,000 bacteria per square meter of the Earth's surface. This is an astonishing amount of material. Most of it simply adds to the unculturable or uncultured microbial flora present on Earth. But in some cases, this bacterial material turns against nature, and leads to death and destruction. Just as life came from elsewhere, death, too, is sometimes an alien invader.

Wickramasinghe also argues that our ancestors drew the same conclusions he has drawn. Ancient Chinese astronomers chronicled numerous episodes when the apparition of comets preceded plague and disaster. The Mawangdui Silk, compiled in 300 BCE, details 29 different cometary forms and the various disasters associated with them, dating as far back as 1500 BC. Wickramasinghe concludes, "All ancient civilizations, without exception, have looked upon comets with a sense of trepidation and awe. Comets were considered to be harbingers of doom, disease, and death, infecting men with a blood lust to war, contaminating crops, and dispersing disease and plague.... The views of ancient civilizations—the Chinese, Egyptians and Indians—that laid the foundations of philosophy and science, including astronomy, should not be so easily dismissed."[3] And so we have almost come full circle, for it was with the original proponent of panspermia that we saw the drive to remove mythology from "the scientific approach." The current billboard of the theory of panspermia is suggesting we once again allow legends, myths, and ancient accounts to be included in the debate.

The big question, of course, is whether life is a cosmic imperative, which would mean that the Bible and so many other religious texts are likely true when they say that God created life. And even though the Universe created life, was God helped by "gods"—extraterrestrial beings—who assisted the Creator by sending life throughout the universe, making this not only a scientific, but a religious mission, to help create life everywhere?

The debate as to whether such alien probes were ever sent out normally focuses on the so-called von Neumann probes, named after Hungarian physicist John von Neumann, who wrote about self-replicating machines. In the realm of space exploration, such probes would use the raw material of the galaxy they're exploring to make copies of themselves, which would then head off elsewhere into space to collect more data. (The monolith of Stanley Kubrick's epic film *2001: A Space Odyssey* was actually a von Neumann probe. The film was meant to start with scientists explaining how von Neumann probes were the most efficient method of space exploration, but Kubrick cut the opening segment from his film.) Many people believe that such self-replicating—or von Neumann—probes would be the most efficient means of space exploration.

We have sent a number of manned missions into space, but we know that our efforts could best be described as a cumbersome exercise. With our very basic space-traveling technology, we know that in order to go farther, we can, at the moment, only rely on robots, which are easier to send across longer distance. Still, robots are extremely limited when it comes to deep-space exploration. For that, what is required are machines that are able to make copies of themselves, as they progress on their voyage of discovery—in other words, seeding. The smaller the self-replicating machines, the easier they would be to deliver. As it happens, the best piece of "nanotechnology" that we have on planet Earth is DNA.

The Case for Mars

Was there ever life on Mars? NASA communications expert Maurice Chatelain was one of several people who believe that the pyramids that grace so many ancient monuments are an extraterrestrial legacy. From the late 1970s onwards, their camp has focused on finding clear evidence of artificial constructions elsewhere in the solar system, as this would seriously strengthen their argument.

The best candidate for housing an ancient civilization is Mars. The expression "little green men from Mars" is part of our daily vocabulary. In 1974, the magazine *Icarus* ran a short article by Mack Gipson, Jr., and Victor K. Ablordeppy, which reported that "triangular and pyramid-like structures have been observed on the Martian surface." The discovery was made in the Elysium Quadrangle of the Red Planet. The authors noted that these structures cast triangular and polygonal shadows, suggesting a pyramidal structure. Still, the authors seemed to favor a natural explanation, as "steep-sided volcanic cones and impact craters occur only a few kilometers away." The four pyramids were paired, facing each other across a plain.

Leading American astronomer Carl Sagan decided to comment on these structures in 1977, initially innocently writing that "the largest are three kilometers across at the base and one kilometer high." He made a comparison to artificial structures on Earth: "...much larger than the pyramids of Sumer, Egypt or Mexico on Earth. They seem to be eroded and ancient and are, perhaps, only small mountains, sandblasted for ages. But they warrant, I think, a careful look."[4] That was all that was needed to create controversy and generate speculation. In 1996, Robert Bauval and Graham Hancock abandoned their usual exploration of the Egyptian and Mexican pyramids and devoted an entire book to the Martian anomalies. They wondered, "Could they be the first sign, as many independent researchers claim, that Mars is marked by the 'fingerprints' of an ancient extraterrestrial civilization?"[5]

The shape of this Martian debate transformed when an area of the Martian Cydonia region was photographed by the *Viking 1* space probe, on July 25, 1976. When the photographs were later analyzed by NASA, people saw an area approximately 2 miles long and 1 mile across that seemed to resemble a human face. NASA—for some reason that, in retrospect, should be classified as unwise—decided to announce this "quirk of nature" in a press release six days later. Despite the humoristic tone that NASA tried but perhaps failed to convey in the news release, some people wondered whether it could indeed represent an artificial monument.

In July 1976, the Viking space probe photographed something the camera suggested to be a face. For many years to come, until NASA sent another space probe to Mars and re-imaged that region, this image led to enormous speculation that a Martian civilization had been discovered.

The most notable advocate of this theory became the American journalist Richard Hoagland. In his 1987 book, *The Monuments of Mars: A City on the Edge of Forever*, Hoagland interpreted other nearby surface features as remnants of a ruined city and artificially constructed pyramids. In short, he argued for the artificiality of the so-called Face on Mars by arguing that other nearby structures could likely be artificial, too. Bauval and Hancock's *The Mars Mystery* was largely a repetition of Hoagland's theory, but brought it to a wider audience, riding high on both authors' recent best-sellers. Hoagland, Hancock, and Bauval each drew a parallel between the Martian structures and the pyramids of Earth—specifically the Great Pyramid—thus convincing many that there was a connection between the two structures; namely, that there was an alien component to the Great Pyramid.

As quickly as the Martian Face became popular, it disappeared. The Mars Global Surveyor probe in 1998 and 2001, and the Mars *Odyssey* probe in 2002 photographed the "Face" under completely different lighting than the *Viking* probe had in 1976, and at much higher resolution. The new photographs made the structure now look very little like a face, although for some observers, this was "clear proof" either that the images had been doctored, or that, in fact, Earth's powers (the United States of America?) had bombed the Martian surface somewhere between 1976 and 1998 to destroy evidence of the extraterrestrial civilization.

The obliteration of the Face on Mars also killed the interest in Martian pyramids, even though they continue to rule certain conspiracy-loving corners of the Internet. So what to make of the Martian pyramids? We only have—and perhaps only ever will have—photographic evidence at our disposal. These are the same photographs that convinced some that there was a face. Even skeptics saw the face; they just felt it was a natural anomaly, a trick of light, or a photographic illusion—or a combination of all three. When it comes to seeing the pyramids, many observe that, unlike the Face, these structures do not seem to have withstood the test of time. Those claiming that there is clear evidence of a pyramid on the Martian surface argue that the pyramids are partially destroyed—which makes them, in my opinion, extremely difficult to maintain as "clear evidence," for a heap of rubble or a natural hill are difficult enough to distinguish when you are in front of them, let alone when seeing them from miles up in the sky.

Hoagland and a Russian author, Vladimir Avinsky, both wrote about pyramidal hills in the Cydonia region, but what for one was a clear pyramid was not seen as such by the other. Of all contenders for the honor of being named a Martian pyramid,

Ancient Aliens

the most famous is the so-called D&M Pyramid, which actually looks nothing like a pyramid, if only because it has a pentagram as its ground plan. (Not a single pentagram-based pyramid has ever been discovered on Earth.) The name of this pyramid derived from its discoverers, Vincent DiPietro and Gregory Molenaar, computer scientists working at the Goddard Space Flight Center near Washington, D.C. Adding to the pyramid's fame was its relative proximity to the Face (10 miles) and the fact that it was almost aligned perfectly north–south, like the Great Pyramid of Egypt. The pyramid was massive: almost 1 mile on its shortest side and 2 miles on its long axis, and half a mile high—roughly five times the height of the Great Pyramid. This seems to be not a structure built by hands, but with elaborate machines—as our extraterrestrial neighbors would have had. But if these pyramids were indeed built by the same people who built pyramids on Earth (as most of these authors, Hoagland foremost, argued), why do we not see such gigantic pyramids on Earth? I would find it grossly unfair that alien visitors build gigantic pyramids on Mars, but only big pyramids on Earth...

Anyway, no one was debating whether there was *something* there, but was it (a) five-sided, (b) a pyramid, and (c) artificial? Neglecting these questions, Hoagland and others felt that pointing out other anomalies or regular shapes on the photographs strengthened their case. They then draw lines between the various structures and concluded that, together, they proved the presence of a city. Hoagland even identified a city square in this complex.

In the final analysis, it is impossible to argue that there are no pyramids on Mars—it's impossible to prove a negative. But it is equally clear that any analysis purely based on aerial photography, as has been proven both on Earth and in the case of the Face on Mars, is highly tenuous. As to the D&M Pyramid, it is most likely a natural hill, seeing as it doesn't really look like a pentagram when you look at it without Hoagland's white-line pentagram drawn on top. But the debate of Martian pyramids will only ever be answered when humans mount an archaeological expedition to the Red Planet, and so it may linger for many decades to come.

Before returning back to Earth, let us quickly note that the moon also has had its fair share of extraterrestrial pyramid fever. A pyramidal structure was seen in the Sea of Tranquility by Soviet space engineer Alexander Abramov, who claimed that it was positioned exactly like the pyramids at Giza. The area was the very region the astronauts of *Apollo 11* landed in on the first trip to the moon in July 1969. In my humble opinion, the article may have been solely intended to create controversy—a piece of Soviet propaganda to argue that perhaps the Americans were hiding a major discovery from humankind. Several Americans have added to this speculation, including Fred Steckling, whom we single out for arguing that his photographic analysis had revealed possible pyramids in various craters; one image had been shot by the *Apollo 8* mission, the other during the *Apollo 16* mission. These are indeed *all* anomalies on photographs, but they are at best indications of anomalies on the ground, and nothing more, until we go back to the moon and do an on-site inspection.

These photographs, whether taken on the moon or Mars, are all interesting, and *could* point out evidence of extraterrestrial structures, and they *should* be analyzed and discussed. However, extraordinarily complex theories have been proposed that so far remain unsupported by evidence. These photos are not proof of anything. They cannot prove that we were not alone, but it *is* clear that in recent decades, an enormous amount of discoveries have been made that show that life is a cosmic imperative. Even though life on Mars might not have evolved to the stage where it built superstructures, Mars definitely once had microorganisms, some of which have been found on Earth. And all indications are that life on Earth itself was alien in origin. We *are* the aliens.

Chapter 8

Evidence of Nonphysical Contact

The Gate of the Gods

Twenty miles outside the city of Puno, on the borders of Lake Titicaca, is the Puerta de Hayu Marca, or Gate of the Gods. The "gate"—sometimes nicknamed "stargate"—is in truth a carving in natural rock, measuring 23 feet in height and width, with a smaller alcove in the center at the base, just under 6 feet in height. Ancient traditional names for the site are Wilka Uta, meaning House of Divinity, and Altarani, the Place With the Altar. The name the Spanish used for it was the Devil's Doorway.

In appearance, it is identical to the many false doors that are found in and around Egyptian tombs, through which the spirit was said to pass to the Otherworld. At Lake Titicaca, the Gate of the

Gods is said to be a gateway to the lands of the Gods. In times long past, heroes went through it to join their gods, to a life of immortality. However, the door was said to swing in two directions, for it was known that those men, as well as the gods, came back from that realm into ours, though only for small periods of time.

The Gate of the Gods is located in the very region where the god Viracocha is said to have appeared on planet Earth, and his cult center is nearby, at Tiahuanaco. History has no answer as to where the builders of Tiahuanaco came from. Pablo Chalon was certain that the ancestors of the local Aymara had nothing to do with Tiahuanaco: "We must suppose that the builders arrived suddenly in that place from some region that was already civilized by the influence of the Old World, only to disappear after a short residence without leaving descendants and without having transmitted [to] their successors the secret of their prodigious capabilities."[1] The idea that people of the Old World who were responsible were Tiahuanaco was inspired by the notion that Viracocha was said to have been white. But Viracocha could not have been European, for in Europe there was no one with the technical capability to create the intricacy of Puma Punku.

The obvious question to ask is whether Viracocha, a god, emanated from this gateway, the Gate of the Gods. There is, of course, no actual door. There is only solid rock. So this stargate is perhaps purely symbolic, is reliant on some form of technology that can turn rock into something else, or is something non-physical. The skeptics and traditional scientists will endorse the symbolic nature, while the traditional Ancient Alien theorists will quickly adopt the technological perspective. But the likeliest scenario might be that the Ancient Alien Answer is found in the non-physical realm.

Evidence of Nonphysical Contact

Coral Castle

South of Orlando, Florida, and Cape Canaveral is Homestead, home to one of America's most enigmatic constructions: Coral Castle. Coral Castle is a stone complex comprising numerous megalithic stones, each weighing several tons, and mostly made of limestone formed from coral—thus its name. The complex is the brainchild of Edward Leedskalnin, a Latvian amateur sculptor who only received a fourth-grade education. At the age of 26, he was engaged to Agness Scuff, but when she broke off their engagement he decided to immigrate to the United States, finding work in lumber camps. When he contracted tuberculosis, he moved to the warmer climate of Florida, around 1919.

In the first half of the 20th century, Edward Leedskalnin, a Latvian immigrant with no formal education, built an elaborate stone complex in Homestead, Florida. He used no heavy equipment or machinery, and teenagers sneaking into the complex said they saw the stones float as if they were balloons. © Christina Rutz via Wikipedia.

Leedskalnin proclaimed, "I know the secrets of how the pyramids of Egypt were built!"[2] If he had not built Coral Castle, this would have been just another big claim. But the way in which Coral Castle was built is evidence that he might have known what he was talking about. In fact, the things he knew may have surpassed the knowledge possessed by the builders of the Great Pyramid. For example, the average block used in the construction of Coral Castle is larger than those used in the Great Pyramid. There is one 30-ton rock, a 9-ton gate, a 22-ton obelisk, a moon block, and a coral rocking chair weighing in at 3 tons. He labored for 28 years, alone, using a total of 1,100 tons of rocks, using no cranes or other heavy machinery. He worked in utter secrecy, almost exclusively at night, to make sure that no one saw what he was doing. A few teenagers claimed to have seen him work, saying that he moved the blocks as if they were hydrogen balloons.

Leedskalnin originally built his oeuvre in Florida City, but moved it to Homestead in 1936, necessitating transporting several large rocks 10 miles north by truck. When preparing to place a 20-ton obelisk on the truck, Leedskalnin asked the truck driver to leave him alone. After a few minutes, the driver heard a loud crash, which he felt was ominous, only to realize that it was merely the sound of Leedskalnin somehow placing that obelisk on the flatbed of the truck. In Homestead, the driver was asked to leave the flatbed overnight; in the morning the stone was in position in its new home.

The U.S. government visited Leedskalnin, in the hopes of finding answers as to how he accomplished this construction, but he refused to cooperate. In 1952, Leedskalnin checked himself into a hospital, and shortly afterward passed away from stomach cancer, taking his secret with him.

Leedskalnin did not seem to possess any type of technology, though some suggest he did, largely in the effort to explain away the mystery of Leedskalnin's building methodology: He had to have machines, right? But how did he *really* do it? Leedskalnin stated that modern science had totally misunderstood nature. All matter, in his opinion, consisted of individual magnets. It was the movement of these magnets within materials and through space that created magnetism and electricity. It seems that Leedskalnin somehow understood and applied magnets in ways no one else could. And from all accounts, including the teenagers who witnessed it with their own eyes, the end result was that the stones somehow floated into position, "as if they were balloons."

Coral Castle was made in the first half of the 20th century, but it sits in the same company as the ancient monuments that defy explanation: The stones at Coral Castle were fastened without mortar; simply placed on top of each other. The stones are fitted so precisely that no light passes through the joints. Most remarkably, when category-5 Hurricane Andrew hit on August 24, 1992, it leveled everything in the area, but nothing in Coral Castle even shifted.

It is unlikely that we will ever know where Leedskalnin acquired this knowledge. It is said that he healed himself from tuberculosis by using magnets, which suggests that he learned the importance of magnetism early on. Maybe it was handed down to him in his family, or maybe it was somehow given to him, not by a visiting alien being in a spaceship in a forest, but in a flash of "inspiration"—an insight?

Channeling The Nine

Thousands of people claim to be able to "channel" extraterrestrial intelligences. Channeling is an ability that entails inviting nonphysical entities into your consciousness and allowing them to speak through you. Some channelers are better known than others, and it is unfortunately quite often the more extreme and bizarre cases that have received public notoriety. One of the most intriguing cases is the well-documented but little-known saga of "The Nine," otherworldly intelligences that claim to be the deities of Ancient Egypt. They also claim that they have guided humankind throughout civilization.

From the 1950s onward, such contact was established from quite mundane living rooms in houses in the United States. The man responsible for this contact was Andrija Puharich, and though he is not a household name, he is regarded as the father of the American New Age movement. Puharich was born in 1918 in Chicago, of Yugoslavian parents. He graduated from medical school at Northwestern University in 1947, and his interest was immediately captured by the paranormal. He was particularly interested in the possibility of enhancing, in some way or another, the innate psychic abilities that many—if not all—of us seemed to possess.

The experiments to contact The Nine began in 1952 and involved a group of nine individuals, mostly friends and acquaintances of Dr. Puharich. It would be a few years later, in the late 1950s, that he wrote and published two books: *The Sacred Mushroom* and *Beyond Telepathy*. He then disappeared into the background and apparently worked for a number of years on his favorite topic, parapsychology, for a secret project of the U.S. government. In the early 1970s, with the full consent of the U.S. government and as part of a psychic experiment—most popularly known as "remote viewing"—Puharich traveled to Israel and returned with Uri Geller, the spoon-bending psychic who would create so much controversy and to this day is an international celebrity.

That Geller arrived in the United States as part of a secret CIA project was only officially confirmed in 1994 when the CIA declassified its series of remote-viewing projects, one of which was named STARGATE. These projects came about when the CIA learned that the Soviets were experimenting with psychically gifted people in the hope that they could learn secret, classified information on the United States and its military capabilities. The United States felt it could not be left behind in this endeavor and turned at first to Puharich, and later to Stanford Research International and two physicists, Russell Targ and Hal Puthoff, to help them create a series of projects that would explore whether psychic intelligence-gathering could work. Eventually, a protocol was developed in which a series of coordinates were given to these psychics—all of them would eventually be employed by the Department of Defense—in the hope that they could locate information on the target, which included the locations of nuclear submarines, rockets, and whatever information the CIA and other intelligence agencies could not gather through technological means. Where technology failed, the psychics were meant to provide the answers that were needed. What is also now declassified, but still little known, is that the Israeli intelligence agency Mossad allowed the CIA to test Geller in return for a series of satellite images that allowed Israel to strike back at strategic locations during the 1973 Yom Kippur War.

Because of the controversy that would erupt over Geller from the 1970s onward, Puharich's *The Sacred Mushroom* has received little attention, but it is a most important book for anyone trying to answer the Ancient Alien Question. In fact, its subtitle carried the intriguing word *doorway*: "Doorway to Eternity"—or, as we would tend to call it these days, a stargate. The book tackles seemingly random events occurring during the time when Puharich was doing psychic experiments as a "private initiative with government support" with two psychics, one of whom, identified as Harry Stone, frequently went into a spontaneous trance during which he spoke in riddles and performed motions that seemed to be rituals. In 1954, Puharich received a transcript from one of Harry Stone's trances, some of which was in English, some in Egyptian. "The first time this occurred, Harry had been at Mrs. Davenport's apartment in New York. When admiring a gold pendant, in the form of a cartouche, he had suddenly started to tremble all over, got a crazy staring look in his eyes, staggered around the room, and then fell into a chair."[3]

From this no doubt bizarre-looking spectacle, Puharich was able to deduce that Stone was "remembering" a previous incarnation, when he was a high priest in Egypt, at the time of the building of the pyramids. Stone was stressing to Puharich the importance of a cult of a mushroom, the use of which the ancient Egyptians had ritualized, allowing its users to access another dimension where they could communicate with the gods. Puharich stated that a specific chemical in mushrooms, as was known at that time, was a hallucinogenic substance that allowed this connection between humankind and the gods—in this instance, the gods of ancient Egypt.

What fascinated Puharich the most was the trance description that Stone had given of a plant that could separate consciousness from the physical body. Stone's drawings of the plant looked like mushrooms, and the description he gave was that of the fly agaric, or amanita muscaria. Puharich realized that Stone had given him the answer to his problem: This mushroom could enhance extrasensory perception in human beings. He knew that the ancient Greeks and the shamans in Siberia had an ancient tradition in which men partook of a plant that could detach the soul from the body, allowing it to travel far, and then return with knowledge that was otherwise inaccessible to the human mind. In this way, more than a decade before von Däniken would popularize the Ancient Alien Question, Puharich, working for U.S. intelligence, had likely come up with the answer to how alien intelligences were able to contact humankind, as well as how we had been able to acquire information and knowledge from the gods. That the answer is not as well-known as it should be is because it originated from the darkest corners of the intelligence community and involved "psychic abilities," some made apparent through the use of hallucinogenic substances—both of which are controversial subjects.

Evidence of Nonphysical Contact

From late 1955 onwards, Puharich tested 35 "psychically ungifted" people with the standard tests of the time, such as showing them the blank side of a card and asking what was on its other side, but none reported anything out of the ordinary. But in the case of Harry Stone, during a visit by the famous English writer Aldous Huxley, Stone asked to have the mushroom administered. Rather than chewing it, Stone applied the mushroom to his tongue and the top of his head, in a ritualistic manner he said he had been taught. Five minutes later he began to stagger around as though he were heavily intoxicated with alcohol. At that point, Puharich wanted to test whether Stone's psychic abilities had enhanced. The results were positive. In fact, they were not just positive, but perfect: He scored 10 out of 10.

This was a major revelation for Puharich, and the experiments were detailed in his book, *The Sacred Mushroom*. But Puharich was not the only one to write about it. Aldous Huxley stated, "I spent some days, earlier this month, at Glen Cove, in the strange household assembled by Puharich.... Harry, the Dutch sculptor, who goes into trances in the Faraday Cage and produces automatic scripts in Egyptian hieroglyphics...whatever may be said against Puharich, he is certainly very intelligent, extremely well read and highly enterprising. His aim is to reproduce by modern pharmacological, electronic and physical methods the conditions used by the Shamans for getting into a state of traveling clairvoyance. At Glen Cove they now have found eight specimens of the amanita muscaria. This is very remarkable as the literature of the mycological society of New England records only one previous instance of the discovery of an amanita in Maine. The effects, when a piece as big as a pin's head is rubbed for a few seconds into the skin of the scalp, are quite alarmingly powerful, and it will obviously take a lot of very cautious experimentation to determine the right psi-enhancing dose of the mushroom."[4]

In 1955, Puharich also heard from Gordon Wasson that a ritualistic mushroom cult wasn't only a thing from ancient Egypt, but still existed in Mexico. It had existed there for hundreds of years, and was still practiced in some remote parts of the country. Wasson wrote his own book on mushrooms in 1957, which is considered to be a landmark publication. Two years later, Puharich's own book on "magic mushrooms" was published. Shortly after its publication, in June 1960, Puharich set out for the village of Juquila in the state of Oaxaca, 200 miles south of Mexico City. Four weeks later, one team member returned saying all the others were ill, but Puharich was apparently crazy, as he had gone on alone. The escapade was not appreciated by Puharich's second wife, as he was literally risking his life, at a time when he had a pregnant wife and four children at home. Upon his return, Puharich found a university and television company willing to sponsor a second expedition. In the end, ABC screened *One Step Beyond*, documenting the expedition locating the mushroom cult in Mexico, and the ESP tests before and after eating the mushroom, at Puharich's home.

Of most importance to the Ancient Alien Question is that Puharich concluded that the intelligence he contacted was an extraterrestrial intelligence known as "The Nine." He identified The Nine with the Nine Principles, which the ancient Egyptians saw as the ordering principles that controlled the universe. They were directly linked with their creator deity, Atum. In Ancient Egypt, control over these Nine Principles was deemed to be instrumental in the successful rule of a pharaoh: Proper control over them meant that balance (linked with the deity Ma'at) was maintained and all was well with Egypt, the world, and the universe. In Ancient Egypt, it was the pharaoh's task to liaise with The Nine, meaning that—if Puharich was correct—contact with ancient aliens was the bailiwick of every pharaoh. As we shall see, it was part of his job description!

Evidence of Nonphysical Contact

Puharich believed that The Nine were an alien intelligence: not necessarily physical, but definitely not terrestrial in the most literal sense. The nine participants in the ritual that summoned them each channeled one entity, which communicated through them as a collective. Puharich claimed that Geller was the exception to the rule and that he could channel all nine together.

As Geller's fame rose, Puharich decided to write a biography of the exploits of this remarkable psychic. In the book, Puharich mentioned The Nine, but for reasons that will forever remain obscure, he largely ridiculed them, even though for several decades before and after he would remain obsessed with them. Geller himself has always remained silent on what transpired with The Nine, as he was unconscious throughout the channeling. To this day, in some of the private conversations I have had with Uri, it is clear that he has tremendous respect for Puharich, who at some point became something of a father figure to him, but that he himself is somewhat unclear as to what really happened in those days and what it all means.

We therefore only have Puharich's word for it, and whereas that might not mean much to anyone who doesn't know him, for the U.S. government, at one point, Puharich's word meant an awful lot. According to Puharich, when in contact with The Nine, they summoned him to UFO fly-pasts and more. Puharich claimed that he made tape recordings of these sessions, but none have ever been made public, so it truly is a case of Puharich's word against the world. Supposedly Puharich asked The Nine, "Are you behind the UFO sightings that started in the United States when Kenneth Arnold saw nine flying saucers on June 24, 1947?" They answered, "Yes."

According to Puharich, The Nine stated they were from a world called Hoova, though on occasion, they called themselves Rhombus 4D. They contacted Puharich and Geller because they had been chosen to prevent war, as well as help steer the Earth's fate into a specific direction, which The Nine said was indeed to their benefit, though it was also for the benefit of humankind. The Nine also claimed that they were responsible for Geller's powers, and that the way in which humankind used Geller would determine whether The Nine's "program for Planet Earth" would continue or not. What is apparent from these communications is that The Nine, whoever they were, were clearly akin to the Nine Principles of ancient Egypt, in the sense that they were primarily all about directing the fate of humankind.

Other psychics, such as Phyllis Schlemmer, have since claimed to have contacted The Nine, too. Schlemmer claims to have spoken to "Tom"—a modern rendition of the name *Atum*—who claimed to be the spokesperson for The Nine. Her story made it into Stuart Holroyd's *Prelude to the Landing on Planet Earth* and the later *The Only Planet of Choice*. Other Nine contactees are Don Elkins and Carla Rueckert, who channeled "Ra," a member of The Nine who declared that it was he who had built the Great Pyramid. In sessions with Puharich, "Tom" said the Sphinx was built and named after him.

I would not go as far as to argue that everyone who has channeled The Nine should be treated with the same respect as Puharich. I have done extensive research into The Nine for more than a decade, and they are, quite simply, a complex issue that defies easy categorization. But what can be definitively said about them is this: It is clear that each culture, whether Mayan, Egyptian, or 20th-century Western society, was and is in contact with an alien intelligence, which each time relates messages that are identical in context. And in the case of the Mayan civilization, there is even archaeological evidence that shows that the story of The Nine is directly relevant to the Ancient Alien Question: The Nine are mentioned in an inscription on Monument 6 of the Mayan site Tortuguero, in the Mexican state of Tabasco. The monument was erected in 669 CE and is one of the very few pre-Conquest sources that mention the infamous date of December 21, 2012 CE. Various translations or partial translations of the Tortuguero inscription exist; this is the most common:

> At the next creation [i.e. December 21, 2012], the
> Bolon Yokte Ku, or Nine Support Gods, will return.

However, the actual word *return*, sometimes translated as *descent*, is not intact on the monument. Still, it is a safe conclusion to make that the missing word is *return*. Why? Because other Mayan sources reference the return of these deities at the ending of each baktun.

There is no doubt whatsoever that the returning deities are the Bolon Yokte Ku—The Nine. But who are they within a Mayan context? They have variously been translated as the God of Nine Strides, the Nine-Footed God, Jaguar-Foot-Tree and Nine-Dog-Tree. They were seen as living in the Underworld and were generally described as god(s) of conflict and warfare, and are thus linked with dangerous transition times, social unrest, eclipses, and natural disasters like earthquakes. It is said that at the end of a baktun, the end of a cycle, they would abandon their Underworld realm and rise to the Earth's surface, where they would do battle with the 13 deities of Heaven.

To further identify what The Nine Support Gods are supposed to be, we need to consult other sources—in this case, anthropological ones. Such evidence makes it clear that The Nine Gods were said to have appeared during ceremonies that were held at the end of each baktun, the last of which occurred in 1618 CE, shortly after the Conquest of Mexico by Spanish troops.

The ceremony of the baktun is described in Chapter 29 of *The Book of Chilam Balam de Chumayel*, a Mayan chronicle composed after the Spanish Conquest and therefore sometimes treated as less interesting by archaeologists, who have little interest in anthropological material. The book nevertheless provides a detailed description of the ceremonies that were performed in

Merida in 1618 CE, at the end of 12.0.0.0.0. In total, there are 20 acts, each representing one of the 20 katuns that make up a baktun cycle. After some initial preparations, in Act 2, the bee god ties the masks of the 13 gods of Heaven to those people who were going to perform in the ceremonies. The actual baktun cycle's end was described in Act 3, whereby The Nine Gods fought, conquered, and sacrificed these 13 gods; night had conquered day.

The subsequent acts involved rituals to do with the election of the new officials for the new period, and in Act 12, The Nine Gods sacrifice the Seven Pacers and count the mats, which is an initial lineup of the candidates for investiture for the coming era, as a new leader for the Mayan people had to be chosen; that ruler's task was to rule and maintain an active "up and downlink" with the gods. Most importantly, in Act 15, The Nine Gods announce the fate of the new era. This fate was largely the will of the gods, which the community had to achieve during the new era, and it reflects what The Nine said in communications with Puharich.

In short, the baktun ceremony was a series of rituals, focusing on the Nine Gods and their emanation and rulings. For the Mayans, the ceremonies were extraordinarily elaborate and were performed within the sacred precincts of temple complexes, such as Chichen Itza and Teotihuacán. It was, after all, at Teotihuacán that the first council of these deities had occurred in 3114 BCE, and the temple complex was a three-dimensional rendering of the Creation Act, for—as in ancient Egypt—the deities that were contacted were linked with the creator deity. For Puharich, the rituals were performed in the privacy of a mundane living room, but the end result was nevertheless contact with nonhuman intelligences that claimed they were the gods that had brought us civilization—and were responsible for the pyramids.

The Pyramid Purpose

The idea that the pyramid was a place of initiation, rather than a gigantic mausoleum, was very much in vogue a century ago, mainly among people who adhered to a Masonic ideology. The "pyramid as temple of initiation" debate was revived in 1982 by the Egyptologist Edward Wente and has been principally discussed by British author Jeremy Naydler, most prominently in his book *Shamanic Wisdom in the Pyramid Texts.* Naydler stated that "While scholars generally accept that this 'voluntary death' was one of the central aims of the Greek and Hellenistic mystery cults, Egyptology has resisted the idea that any such initiatory rites or experiences existed in Egypt." This would make Egypt unique among all ancient civilizations—by the absence of such practices. It would mean that Egypt, of all ancient cultures, did not have a religion that allowed for the spiritual development of the soul—which would be extremely odd, because all accounts, including several from Ancient Greece, written down by men who went to Egypt and often were taught in the Egyptian temples, argue that Egypt was the world's authority on such practices.

It is precisely this attitude from the Egyptologist—making Egypt into something that it was not—that has contributed to so many people asking the Ancient Alien Question. By making ancient Egypt into something that it never was, the Egyptologists created a fertile soil for outlandish theories, many of which do not involve extraterrestrial beings, but which are nevertheless extremely unlikely. To properly answer the Ancient Alien Question, we therefore need to render Egypt back to what it was.

The answer to the Ancient Alien Question can be found in the Book of the Dead and the earlier Pyramid Texts. These texts have been overlooked as the obvious solution because they became a victim of their own child, the Corpus Hermeticum, a concise and clear synopsis of the religious framework of ancient

Egypt, codified in the third century BCE, following the Greek conquest of Egypt. The texts inspired the alchemists of the Middle Ages, lay at the foundation of the Italian Renaissance, may be a key to explaining the symbolism in paintings by Leonardo da Vinci and Sandro Botticelli, and even contain the earliest reference to the Grail. But above all, the Pyramid Texts were believed to contain the true—native—message of ancient Egypt, unlike the Corpus Hermeticum, which was written for a Greek audience.

At the time of their discovery, it was felt that the decipherment of the hieroglyphic language of the Pyramid Texts—which the ancient Egyptians used as a sacred language, as it was deemed to be the language of the gods themselves—would soon reveal ancient Egypt's true doctrine. But when Gaston Maspero, the first to publish the Pyramid Texts in translation, summed up his effort to translate these texts, he confessed that despite trying, he was unable to discover any profound wisdom in ancient Egypt's religious doctrine.

The disappointment came because the Pyramid Texts did not contain the doctrine of the ancient Egyptians, but "only" the rituals, the manuals used in that religion, through which contact with the gods was established. To put this in today's terms, a manual of your television set does not reveal what programs it shows or what you watch on it, nor what the experience of "television watching" really is or feels like. The manual will never reveal the joy you experienced when Goran Ivanisevich finally won Wimbledon, but only how to increase the volume on your set during those agonizing last few minutes of his final against Australian Pat Rafter. The Pyramid Texts were just such a manual, for in ancient Egypt (as elsewhere), the doctrine itself was apparently never put to print. But in Ptolemaic times, when the Greeks ruled over Egypt and when most scholars now accept the Corpus Hermeticum was written, there was a need for Jews and Greeks to learn the religious doctrine of the Egyptians, to

Evidence of Nonphysical Contact

understand the religious life of their neighbors and compatriots. The doctrine was therefore finally written down, though the Greeks and the Jews had no need for the rituals themselves, and hence the Pyramid Texts were not incorporated into the Corpus Hermeticum. Millennia later, when the mystique of the hieroglyph had lifted, the disappointment of not seeing the true breadth of the Egyptian doctrine hung over Egyptology as a black cloud—which is only slowly drifting away.

Though the Pyramid Texts are ancient Egypt's most extraordinary document, the fact that they contain rituals on how to contact the gods is not well-liked by Egyptologists, who would prefer that they contain anything but. Egyptologists have argued that the Pyramid Texts are the rituals that were said during the funeral of the deceased pharaoh—a logical conclusion, seeing as they were originally written down in the pyramids, which Egyptologists believed to be the tombs of the pharaohs, and later on the coffins of the deceased, thus clearly showing there is a funerary aspect to these rituals.

But Naydler has shown that the Pyramid Texts in no single instance actually imply that the king is dead. Naydler has seen phrases in the Pyramid Texts that suggest that the king is very much alive—physically alive—at the time when that section of the texts is supposed to be read out. Though it is therefore without doubt that the Pyramid Texts focus on the king, Naydler argues that they focus mainly on his role as an active ruler—not as deceased head of state. The Texts thus become records of the rituals that the king performed, at key times of his rule, which Naydler has identified as his coronation and the Heb Sed festivals, which was a renewal of his kingship that occurred at 30-year (or shorter) intervals. These rites specifically confirmed the power of the king over this world and the Otherworld, symbolized by his ability to control the Nine Principles, as well as the union of Egypt and the Otherworld by the king, through which he established his divine rule over the land.

In Naydler's interpretation, the pyramid was built as a temple, and the inscriptions on its wall were not meant to be read by the funeral cortege, or by the deceased soul of the pharaoh, but by the living pharaoh, as he performed these rituals in the interior of the pyramid during key ceremonies. This would mean that the pyramids of ancient Egypt were—indeed—communication devices, helping the pharaoh establish contact with the gods, through a series of rituals.

Though in ancient Egypt maintaining contact with the gods was seen as the pharaoh's daily occupation, there were certain occasions, one might say on par with the baktun-ending ceremonies of the Mayan calendar, that stood out more. One of these festivals was the Heb Sed festival, and it is this ceremony that Stone channeled in 1954. As were the baktun-ending festivals, the Heb Sed festivals were held in temple complexes and involved both public and private displays and rituals.

The Heb Sed festival is named after the short kilt with a bull's tail that the king wore for the culminating rites of the festival. The festival lasted five days in total and took place immediately after the annual Osiris rites, at the time when the Nile's flooding retreated, at the moment of the rebirth of the land, mimicking the creation of the world—a new age. For the five days preceding the Heb Sed festival, a fire ceremony called "lighting the flame" served to purify the festival precincts. But though much of the ceremony was public in nature, the most sacred parts of the Heb Sed rite occurred in a secret chamber—and the question is where precisely this chamber was located. From the reliefs of Niuserre, the Sixth ruler of the Fifth Dynasty, we know that this chamber contained a bed (a couch?), though other depictions show that in certain cases a sarcophagus was used. Naydler has suggested that this secret chamber was inside the pyramid and that the pharaohs in fact built their pyramids because they were specifically linked with their Heb Sed festivals.

Evidence of Nonphysical Contact

The main purpose of the Heb Sed festival was to confirm that the pharaoh was still fit to rule; that he was still able to maintain his link with the Otherworld. Naydler points out that upon a pharaoh's death, he was meant to join the gods permanently in the Otherworld, where he would help guide his successors and Egypt as a whole from the other side. Thus the Heb Sed rituals were closely linked with the king's preparedness to make a successful voyage after death; they were a test run for his ascension to the Otherworld. This may explain the confusion about why pyramids were seen as tombs and why the Pyramid Texts were seen as evidence supporting this conclusion.

The fit state of mind that the pharaoh had to be in, both in life and in death, was known as "akh." Intriguingly, the pharaoh accomplished this state in a place known as the "akhet," which is often translated as "horizon," but which should be interpreted as a place of spiritual illumination, which historian Mircea Eliade labeled an awakening as well as ascension. Egyptologist Mark Lehner has suggested that this "akhet" is the Giza Plateau, further supporting the conclusion that the pyramids were linked with this ceremony.

Naydler titled one of the chapters of his book "The Pyramids as the Locus of Secret Rites," where he argues that the Heb Sed festivals were performed in the pyramids. He notes that there is an obvious contradiction in the fact that the construction of a pyramid was often abandoned as soon as a pharaoh died. So, when he was most in need of a tomb, all work on that tomb was stopped? Let us also note that several pharaohs who did not live long had no pyramids whatsoever. Djedefra, Khufu's son, did not live very long, and his pyramid was never completed— though he clearly died the son of a dynasty of pyramid-builders extraordinaire who could surely have spared some men to build at least a small or minuscule tomb for their king. This scenario makes little sense. Surely the pharaoh's successor—often his beloved son—on occasion would desire to have his father's tomb completed, so that his father could be buried inside before work commenced on his own pyramid? If the successor was in his early 20s when he ascended to the throne, there was more than enough time left before he had to wonder about his own death, as the life expectancy of an Egyptian pharaoh was not too different from most of us. But each time a pharaoh dies, construction work on his pyramid is stopped, as if the pyramid is no longer required now that the pharaoh is dead. In the "pyramid = tomb" equation, that practice does not make sense.

But the Heb Sed festival is the key to unlocking the true purpose of the pyramids. The Heb Sed festival was normally to be held for the 30th year of the king's rule. Is it a coincidence, therefore, that Khufu was said to have taken 10 years to plan his pyramid, which included diverting the river Nile, and that it took a further 20 years of work to actually build his pyramid? According to archaeologist Rainer Stadelman, two of the three pyramids of Sneferu were built between the 14th and 30th years of his reign. Coincidence, or evidence of a link with the Heb Sed festival?

In summary, Naydler has found evidence for the practice of this festival in most pyramids (including the intact pyramid of Third Dynasty Pharaoh Sekhemkhet), but he focuses on the Zoser complex, if only because it is perhaps the best remaining evidence—and was, after all, Egypt's original pyramid, built by Imhotep. For one thing, the walls of the Zoser pyramid complex are not blank as they are at Giza. Of all the possible scenes they could display, the texts and depictions show various stages of a Heb Sed festival. If they were tombs, why not show scenes from the afterlife? To use Naydler's own words, "As these are the only reliefs inside the pyramid, there could be no stronger evidence to demonstrate that the interior of the pyramid was as much associated with the Heb Sed festival as were the buildings and architectural spaces in its vicinity."[5] Let us add that the causeway of the Great Pyramid also has scenes of Khufu's Heb Sed festival.

Evidence of Nonphysical Contact

The Zoser pyramid is the oldest pyramid built in ancient Egypt. The entire complex, both in layout and inscriptions, reveals the true purpose of the pyramids. They speak of a festival in which the pharaoh was said to become one with the gods, so that his power and character as a proper ruler was proven in the eyes of the country.

There is also the famous Heb Sed dance, in which the king circumambulated the courtyard, which represented the country of Egypt—such large courtyards stand in front of the Pyramid of Zoser, and are also present at the Giza pyramids of Khufu and his successor Khafre. In the Heb Sed ceremony, the pharaoh would arrive by boat and moor at the Valley Temple. From there, the procession would make its way up the causeway, which at the time was actually a covered walkway, with only a slit in the roof to allow daylight to penetrate. The next stop would be at the Pyramid Temple, from which entrance to the pyramid would be the logical—and only available—next step. The "tomb chamber" inside the pyramid would thus be the secret chamber, with the sarcophagus being the site where the secret ceremony of the Heb Sed would occur.

What was this ceremony? Details are sketchy, but it was described as the king unifying the two dimensions: the divine realm of the gods, and Earth. In mythology, this occurred at a

"Mound of Creation," and the pyramid was considered to be just that: a place where heaven and earth met, where the pharaoh communicated with the gods, where he ascended to heaven, and/or where the gods came down to earth. That the pyramids were therefore landing places for the gods is literally true, but should not be interpreted physically, in the sense that their spaceship landed there.

Other aspects of the pyramids confirm that the Heb Sed festival was their purpose. For example, the Zoser complex incorporated chapels for statues of visiting gods of the regions of Egypt who attended the ceremony. This fits with archaeologist Gilles Dormion's observation that the gallery leading into the Queen's Chamber originally had niches for statues; other pyramids have similar niched corridors, all of which have been found to be empty, and were therefore interpreted as evidence that tomb robbers had penetrated into the structure. But, if used for the Heb Sed festival, the niches would only ever have contained a statue during the festival; afterward the statues returned to their temples elsewhere in Egypt.

With this interpretation, we have explained the pyramids of Egypt within the emerging framework that is slowly replacing the outdated Egyptological dogma. Remarkably, it appears that the rituals and symbols of the Egyptian pyramids are similar and sometimes identical to their colleagues across the world, such as the baktun-ending rituals of the Maya. But there is more....

The New Fire Ceremony

A series of rituals was also performed at Teotihuacán. They were written down by Martin Matz of the Mazatec Indians, who had transmitted them for several centuries within his community before finally committing them to paper. His text is known as the Codex Matz-Ayauhtla, or "the Pyramid of Fire,"

Evidence of Nonphysical Contact

and describes a series of legends, from the Creation Myth to the New Fire ceremony. The latter is the finale of the initiatory spiritual journey that is encoded in the codex. The text underlines the essence of the Maya's religious experience, namely that life is a spiritual journey to ascension—a return to God, the One who created the universe. The text states how the supreme deity, Tloque Nahauque, manifested itself as three forces: a duality functioning against a neutral background, from which the four prime elements—earth, water, wind, and fire—were created.

Matz only wrote the texts after he had made the journey himself; he visited an initiatory site with his shamanic guide, where he took a hallucinogenic substance (in his case, mushrooms), entered a cave at a specific moment in the calendar year, and consequently had visions of a landscape of pyramids, including one that was dedicated to the moon. The initiate was then taught about the World Ages and how ascension and World Ages were connected via the New Fire ceremony, as well as how they were performed every 52 years. The American author John Major Jenkins has described this as "the ultimate self-sacrifice that is the ritual death attending the mystic initiation into divine life...in order to merge with Quetzalcoatl," who is seen as the intermediary deity that connects the living with the Creator God Tloque Nahauque.[6]

This New Fire festival was performed at the temple complex of Teotihuacán. The complex was physically laid out in the pyramid landscape the initiate saw in his vision. Similar to the secret rite of the Heb Sed festival inside the pyramids of Egypt, the Pyramid of the Sun contains a cave, and it is known that this cave was specifically aligned to certain stellar phenomena. The cave is 7 feet high, runs eastward for more than 300 feet, until it reaches a point close to the pyramid's geometrical center. Here it leads into a second cave, which was artificially enlarged into a shape very similar to that of a four-leaf clover. Each "leaf" was a chamber, about 60 feet in circumference, containing a variety of artifacts such as slate discs and mirrors. There is also a complex drainage system of interlocking segments of carved rock pipes. This is strange, as there is no known source of water within the pyramid, and leads researchers to believe that certain rituals were performed inside this sanctuary.

When astronomer Gerald Hawkins investigated Teotihuacán, he discovered that the streets were laid out on a grid system, intersecting at angles of 89 degrees, rather than the 90 degrees you would expect to find. He thought this could simply be a design flaw, until he realized that the grid was not aligned to the four points of the compass, but was instead twisted sideways so that the Avenue of the Dead ran north–northeast, pointing to the setting of the Pleiades. On May 17, circa 150 CE, the Pleiades rose just before the sun in the predawn skies. This synchronization, known as the heliacal rising of the Pleiades, only lasted a century. It is now suggested that it was this event that was at the origin of Teotihuacán and marked its foundation. It is no coincidence that the cave opening points directly to the setting sun on that important day.

Teotihuacán was a place of pilgrimage in Aztec times; the Aztecs identified it with the myth of Tollan, the place where the sun was created, which had occurred in 3114 BCE. Yet another legend stated that the complex was built to transform men into gods. But how was man transformed? Technology, if anything, tends to ensure a more methodical approach to a process, guaranteeing a better success of the desired outcome. If a technology was used to aide this transformation, there may be an explanation for the strange sheets of mica that have been found between two of the upper levels of the Pyramid of the Sun.

In summary, it has been shown that the Teotihuacán complex was linked with a series of rituals that enabled contact with the gods. These rituals were definitely held at key dates of the calendar, which is why most temple complexes were aligned to certain stars and constellations. It seems that contact with the divine—at least in some cultures—was established at specific moments in time. And it is clear that this contact was nonphysical in nature, often aided by hallucinogenic substances.

Does that mean that our ancestors' gods were nothing more than hallucinations? That the gods are not real? The answer to that question is actually also the answer to the Ancient Alien Question. And to find that answer, we need to leave civilization and all the best evidence for the Ancient Alien Question far behind and travel to the depths of the Amazonian jungle.

The Cosmic Serpent

In July 1995, I was one of the few attendees at a nevertheless wonderfully organized conference in Fribourg, Switzerland. As it happened, the number of speakers outweighed the number of attendees. Titled *The Incident*, the conference explored phenomena such as UFOs, crop circles, and the wonders of the mind. The best minds in all three fields had gathered, ufology led by Budd Hopkins and Jacques Vallee, and the "mind" category presented by the controversial American writer Terence McKenna and the then almost totally unknown Swiss anthropologist Jeremy Narby.

At the conference, McKenna proclaimed his famous slogan that UFOs were not nuts and bolts, as most ufologists believed, and he implied that the methodology used by UFO researchers in trying to prove the existence of extraterrestrial beings visiting the Earth was never going to be successful, pointing to 50 years of documented UFO reports that had led to no solid conclusions. McKenna believed that UFOs were real, but were not physical machines. Instead, McKenna proposed that we had to use our minds to explore and answer the alien question.

McKenna's emphasis was on the use of hallucinogenic substances, specifically DMT, or dimethyltriptamine, which he almost single-handedly made famous. McKenna graduated from UC Berkeley, majoring in ecology, resource conservation, and shamanism; with his diploma in hand, he set off for India and later the Amazon, where he studied the native hallucinogenic drugs used in various South American shamanic traditions. The specific substance he was after was oo-koo-hé, a plant preparation containing DMT, a chemical naturally produced by the brain. It is therefore something of a misnomer to call DMT a hallucinogenic substance, as it does not create a hallucination as such, but does things to our brain that science at the time did not understand at all, and therefore hastily labeled a hallucination.

In the Amazon, at La Chorrera, at the urging of his brother Dennis, McKenna allowed himself to be the subject of a psychedelic experiment led by the local shaman, which he claimed put him in contact with a nonhuman, other-dimensional intelligence. Until his death in 2000, McKenna advocated the use of drugs, and particularly organic hallucinogens such as ayahuasca, which contained DMT, as it was his conviction that DMT opened a doorway to the Otherworld, the Realm of the Gods.

He was clear that these drugs should not be used by the masses, but only by carefully selected individuals, along the model of the Amazonian tribes and ancient civilizations, in which drug use was carefully regulated and taught, and largely restricted to a class of priests.

With the rising popularity of UFO abductions in the 1990s, McKenna began to preach that this phenomenon was linked with what he termed "hyperspace," and that the DMT experience was similar if not identical to the abduction experience, in which he believed the "machine elves of hyperspace," as he often called them, were seen as aliens in UFOs. This was merely the latest form they had taken on, he theorized, after their former manifestations as faeries, elves, or angels. Whatever we called them, they were real, and they were to all intents and purposes Ancient Aliens.

Evidence of Nonphysical Contact

In his books, including *Food of the Gods*, McKenna mapped the history of drug usage, specifically of DMT and psilocybin, arguing that both substances had been used throughout the ages in humankind's efforts to enter another dimension and speak with these otherworldly intelligences. He believed these beings had helped humankind throughout the ages, guiding them along the path of civilization. He argued that the extraordinary and anomalous wisdom that had often gone into ancient monuments might have been inspired and assisted by these intelligences. Rather than only a theory, he had a very personal experience that suggested this had been indeed the case.

From his very first experiences with DMT at La Chorrera, the denizens of hyperspace had given McKenna a mathematical formula that became known as "novelty" and "TimeWave Zero." In McKenna's opinion, the formula explained the mathematical construct and nature of time itself. It was said to be a system that showed how "new things"—novelty—would spring about in our timeline. Time itself was a fractal wave of novelty—the output from this wave. Time was thus built around a series of new ideas and paradigm shifts, and, in McKenna's opinion, this could explain why our ancestors were so ridiculously preoccupied with calendars and mapping time.

Whether or not the TimeWave has a foundation in reality remains a question. Too few people have seriously studied it, and, most problematically, modern science hardly knows anything about the nature of time. But the extraordinary importance of the TimeWave for the Ancient Alien Question is that it was definitely a gift of the gods to humankind, received through McKenna. The knowledge he received was highly complex and mathematical in nature, so much so that those who have studied it have been able to see the extraordinary mathematics—fractals—linked with the formula, even though they are still at a loss to grasp its full meaning. This phenomenon reveals that human beings are able to receive advanced mathematical models from an otherworldly source—which is what we find in the Ancient Alien controversy: that our ancestors had an extraordinary understanding of mathematics and the cycles of time, on a level exceeding our ancestors' and even our own understanding. Those two very ingredients were paramount in McKenna's otherworldly revelation of the TimeWave theory.

McKenna would argue that if cultures across the worlds had built pyramids for their gods, this was not necessarily evidence of physical contact between these civilizations or the result of a space-traveling ancient alien. He believed that the shamans of each culture had entered another dimension, where they made contact with an intelligence that had been contacted by our earliest ancestors. When asked, this intelligence had always provided our ancestors with the required information so that we could advance on our path of civilization. Various cultures, across time and space, that contacted it would always come away with the same message; this is why, for example, there was such uniformity between pyramid complexes in Egypt and Mexico. McKenna would have interpreted the invention of geopolymers by Imhotep as that priest entering in contact with this otherworldly intelligence, which subsequently gave him the chemical understanding and processes through which to create geopolymers.

Anthropologist Jeremy Narby was the other speaker at the conference who impressed me greatly, and I had the absolute pleasure and joy of having lunches and dinner sitting with both him and McKenna at one table. Narby had largely followed in McKenna's footsteps, going where McKenna had not yet gone. Narby grew up in Switzerland and Canada, studied history at Canterbury, and received his doctorate in anthropology from Stanford University. Then, he trekked into the South American jungles, and like McKenna before him, came away with an understanding that is potentially the greatest revelation in the history of modern science.

Evidence of Nonphysical Contact

In his youth, Narby had been an aspiring tennis player, but back problems prevented him from making it his profession. By the time he reached the Amazon, his back gave him so many problems that he finally succumbed to the invitations of the local shamans, who told him that they could cure him. Ever since, his back has not ailed him. It is a similar story to the one told by one of my guides, when I explored the jungles of Iquitos in 2004: My guide had been a computer programmer with a true Western mindset, until he fell seriously ill and could no longer work or provide an income for his family. Modern medicine could not help him, and as a final act of desperation, he tried—without any hope that they would offer him solace from his pain—the local shamans. When they cured him, he changed his profession, focusing on the tourism industry and telling tourists of the wonders and miracles of the Amazonian rain forest.

Narby himself left the Amazon with the knowledge that the rain forest is a veritable chemical lab, containing substances the shamans can mix in a manner that supersedes the techniques and knowledge of modern pharmaceutical companies. To demonstrate this, in 1999, Narby took three molecular biologists to the Peruvian Amazon to see whether they could obtain biomolecular information in shamanic sessions. The drug of choice was ayahuasca, which in itself is a miracle of science. Ayahuasca is a brew prepared from the Banisteriopsis vine—also known as the spirit vine—and is usually mixed with leaves of shrubs that contain dimethyltryptamine. Depending on the availability of the species of plants, the ingredients vary locally throughout South America. The potion is then brewed for more than 24 hours before it is drunk. If it is taken in any other way, the potion will have no effect at all. Ayahuasca is absorbed into the bloodstream, where it creates an inhibitor that temporarily (typically for a period of half an hour) stops the creation of certain chemicals in the brain, which creates what skeptics call a hallucination, but that is incorrect: Experiencers describe it as the entry into another dimension, where communication with an otherworldly intelligence occurs. The shamans say that ayahuasca itself is a gift of the gods, and Narby has underlined that it is simply impossible for someone to have accidentally stumbled upon how to make ayahuasca: It uses specific plants, which have to be brewed for more than a day. In short, someone told the shamans how to concoct this alchemical potion. Ayahuasca should therefore be described as technology—chemical in nature—that aids humankind in establishing contact with an alien intelligence.

Narby wrote a book titled *The Cosmic Serpent: DNA and the Origins of Knowledge*, in which he concluded that the shamanic experience induced through ayahuasca connected with an intelligence, and that this intelligence resided within our own DNA. The "Cosmic Serpent"—a name often given by the shamans to the intelligence they connect to—was in fact the double helix structure of DNA. In short, Narby stipulates that the means to contact the alien intelligence is through DNA, which, as we have as seen, is alien in origin itself.

A third explorer of Amazonian shamanism is anthropologist Michael Harner. In his studies, after he drank the ayahuasca potion, he described how "I met bird-headed people, as well as dragon-like creatures who explained that they were the true gods of this world.... I realized that anthropologists, including myself, had profoundly underestimated the importance of the drug in affecting native ideology."[7] Is it indeed just a coincidence that the ancient Egyptians depicted their deities as bird-headed people? Or have we come to the core of the problem—and the answer, which is that these otherworldly denizens were indeed seen as the Egyptian deities and that it was these otherworldly intelligences that provided the extraordinary knowledge that went into the Egyptian monuments?

One vision Harner had in 1961, which he recorded in *The Way of the Shaman*, is of great interest to the Ancient Alien Question. He was shown "planet Earth as it was eons ago, before there was any life on it. I saw an ocean, barren land, and a bright blue sky. Then black specks dropped from the sky by the hundreds and landed in front of me on the barren landscape. I could see the 'specks' were actually large, shiny, black creatures with stubby pterodactyl-like wings and huge whale-like bodies." The good bit is yet to come: "They explained to me in a kind of thought language that they were fleeing from something out in space. They had come to the planet Earth to escape their enemy. The creatures then showed me how they had created life on the planet in order to hide within the multitudinous forms and thus disguise their presence. Before me, the magnificence of plant and animal creation and speciation—hundreds of millions of years of activity—took place on a scale and with a vividness impossible to describe. I learned that the dragon-like creatures were thus inside all forms of life, including man."

In a footnote, Harner notes that this intelligence was "almost like DNA," but added that in 1963, he hardly knew anything about DNA. It would be more than three decades later that Narby realized that the intelligence was indeed present inside DNA. DNA is the single common denominator of all life on planet Earth. Narby highlights that Harner's observation actually coincides with the theory of panspermia: that DNA was of extraterrestrial origin and was somehow "seeded" on our planet. This is precisely the "vision" Harner was given in the depths of the Amazonian jungle, but it is also the conclusion reached by the most enterprising scientists in Western laboratories.

In *The Cosmic Serpent*, Narby explores the various ancient accounts and highlights what he sees as clear evidence that the double DNA helix was known to our ancestors as the other-dimensional intelligence that communicated with humankind. He identifies the ladder, which was said to connect heaven and earth in so many traditions as another non-scientific description of the double helix, stating, "In Australia, Tibet, Nepal, Ancient Egypt, Africa, and North and South America, the symbolism of the rope, like that of the ladder, necessarily implies communication between sky and earth. It is by means of a rope or a ladder... that the gods descend to earth and men go up to the sky."

Quetzalcoatl was seen by the Mexicans not only as their civilizing deity, but also as the deity enabling contact with God himself—the creator deity. *Coatl* in Aztec means both "serpent" and "twin"; the structure of DNA is very much serpentine and definitely twin-like, and thus Narby believes that the Cosmic Serpent—whether it is named Quetzalcoatl or differently—is indeed the enabler that connects with the gods. It is technology. It is DNA. Narby writes, "DNA is only 10 atoms wide and as such constitutes a sort of ultimate technology: It is organic and so miniaturized that it approaches the limits of material existence."[8] It is precisely the type of technology that conforms to the specifications of a von Neumann probe. Narby believes that DNA is technology, which is able to contain an intelligence that is now terrestrial, though at the same time other-dimensional, and once extraterrestrial. It was responsible for life on Earth, and was recognized by our ancestors as such. He feels his point is best illustrated by the ancient Egyptians, who used the image of a cosmic serpent and depicted it with the Ankh sign in front of it—the sign for life.

Star Messengers

The Anasazi, "ancient ones" in Navajo, are considered to be one of the more enigmatic of this planet's ancient civilizations. Popularly assumed to have vanished without a trace, their new "scientific" name, Ancestral Puebloans, suggests that, despite popular belief, we now know where they went: They became the Puebloans, the people who lived in the villages that the Spanish conquered when they arrived in the western parts of America. Their territory is what is now known as the Four Corners (northeast Arizona, northwest New Mexico, southwest Colorado, and southeast Utah), plus the Grand Canyon and on into southern Nevada. This area includes Native American tribes like the Navajo and the Hopi.

The Ancestral Puebloans were the first North Americans to use looms to weave cotton and to make blankets, and they even used socks made from yucca leaves, interwoven with turkey feathers, to make sandals. At the same time, and for no obvious reason, they also deliberately flattened and broadened their skulls by binding the heads of babies against cradleboards. For some, this is suggestive evidence that they were trying to make their children resemble the people who brought them their civilization: "gods."

The story of the Ancestral Puebloans lives on in the mythology of the Hopi, considered by many to be the most mysterious and mystical of all Native American tribes. It begins with the claim that their ancestors emerged from the Third World through a crack, into our Fourth World, in a place known as the Sipapu, which they locate near Desert View, 25 miles east of Grand Canyon Village, near the confluence of the Colorado and the Little Colorado rivers. Reaching it requires a seven-hour trek along the Salt Trail Canyon. The Sipapu itself is a natural salt dome, 20 to 26 feet high, topped by a permanent spring—a mineral hot spring, though some wonder whether it is a geyser. It is their Hill of Creation, though the Hopi label it a Place of Emergence.

At the beginning of the Fourth World, the Hopi were greeted by Maasaw, the caretaker deity of the land—their civilizing deity. He had also been appointed the head of the Third World, but had become a little self-important and lost his humility, and other deities had therefore made him the deity of death and the underworld. But Maasaw was given a second chance in the Fourth World. He ordered the survivors to separate out into clans and begin a series of migrations across the continent, on which the stars would guide them. Eventually, they would meet again and settle. Maasaw gave each clan one or more sacred tablets, which would guide them along their migrations. To each clan, he also gave a small water jar, which was magical, and came with instructions that included a description on how to make a new water jar, in case the old one was broken or needed to be replaced. The Hopi argue that this water jar is the missing component in making sense of the locations chosen by the Ancestral Puebloans to live: The water jar meant that they could settle miles away from rivers, as it allowed them to create springs and rivers wherever they settled. Once they abandoned their dwellings and continued their migration, they took the jar with them, rendering the site once again as dry as a bone. Thus, when archaeologists say the Ancestral Puebloans vacated their settlements because of drought, they might be missing the key element of the story. If the story of the water jar is true, it is definitely yet another sign of highly advanced technology.

The notion that these clans were on a divine migration also explains why several settlements were so often abandoned after a century, or even less, of occupation. The archaeological consensus that the cliff dwellings that typify the Ancestral Puebloans were abandoned because of drought might therefore be a complete fallacy, underlining the point once again that archaeology, without the active participation of anthropology and the myths and legends of our ancestors, is dry at best, and wrong most often.

Finally, the Hopi claim that each clan was supposed to complete four migrations, but that only a minority of the clans actually did—specifically those that kept the "door on top of their heads" (the real stargate) open and realized the purpose and meaning behind the four migrations, which was that they were purification ceremonies. Once the ceremonies were completed, these clans would return to the sacred circle, to establish the Hopi Mesas, their permanent settlement—until the advent of the Fifth World, which the Maya, with whom the Hopi are known to have interacted, place at December 21, 2012 CE.

These Hopi Mesas are three mesas, relatively near each other, roughly northeast of Flagstaff and southwest of Chinle in Arizona. They are quite literally in the middle of nowhere, while the entire Hopi Reservation itself is surrounded on all sides by the Navajo/Apache Indians. One of the reasons why the Hopi are such outsiders even within the Native American community is that they never signed any peace treaty, and thus seem to have missed out on certain benefits other Native Americans were able to receive from the U.S. government.

The Hopi Mesas, three settlements in a somewhat mountainous environment, are the homeland of the Hopi, the divine destination of the wandering tribes of the Ancestral Puebloans. The real Center of the World—their navel—is Tuuwanasavi, a few miles from the village of Oraibi, the Third Mesa. It was the Bear Clan that was the first to complete their four migrations; arriving from Mesa Verde, they settled on Second Mesa. Still, Oraibi, the settlement on the Third Mesa, is today seen as the oldest town in Northern America, as it has seen continuous inhabitation since it was first occupied.

When other clans arrived, they either settled on or near the other mesas; the Snake Clan, for example, came from Hovenweep and settled on First Mesa. With each tribe arriving "home," it was the task of the already-present tribes to welcome—or not—the new tribe. A key question that would determine whether the arriving tribe would gain access to the sacred center of the world was whether or not they had lived in accordance with the divine rules (as set out at the start of the wanderings by Maasaw) and had not abused their magical powers.

The Walpi Hopi Mesa is one of three mesas in the heartland of the Hopi Reservation in Arizona. Laid out according to Orion's Belt, it was the final goal of a series of wanderings by various Native Americans, carried out on the orders of their god Maasaw.

Today, many of the Hopi festivals are off-limits to outsiders, and photography is not allowed at any of the sacred sites. A brochure for visits to the Mesas advises, "Please do not approach any kivas, or ceremonial buildings. Do not go near or peer into Katsina resting places."

The kiva is the Hopi church, and each of the mesas centers around a plaza. They form the stage for the various Hopi festivals, which occur throughout the year and focus on their deities, known as Katsinas. In Hopi mythology, the deities are believed to live in the San Francisco Peaks, to the west of Flagstaff, within sight of the Hopi reservation. The highest peak, at 12,643 feet, is Mount Humphreys, a volcanic cone that dominates this desert altiplano. Though named in honor of Francis of Assisi, to the Hopi, they are known as Nyvatukya'ovi, and to the Navajo, Dook'o'oosliid.

Evidence of Nonphysical Contact

Archaeology has stumbled upon evidence that the migrations of the Hopi conform to astronomical cycles of time. At Hovenweep National Monument, the tall towers are considered by archaeologists to have functioned as astronomical observatories. Another clan sojourned at Chaco Canyon, which is now believed to have been home to 4,000 to 6,000 people, and it also had complex astronomical alignments built into its design. In fact, most of the sites of the Ancestral Puebloans are in canyons, and the Hopi see canyons as passageways from this world to the Underworld, with spirit migration occurring between the two worlds: Spirits emerged from the canyon, and the dead returned to reside in the Underworld. In fact, some stories go that these ghostly inhabitants rise from the abyss with glowing eyes and monstrous forms, traveling across the Painted Desert to revisit their earthly homes on the Hopi Mesas. The idea that rock faces are entrances to the Otherworld is something we also encountered at the "stargate" near Lake Titicaca and the "false doors" of the Egyptian tombs.

The Hopi migrations were the divine instructions of Maasaw, but according to author Gary A. David, they are far more interesting than most have assumed. In *The Orion Zone*, he argues that "[The constellation] Orion provided the template by which the Anasazi determined their villages' locations during a migration period lasting centuries. Spiritually mandated by a god the Hopi call [Maasaw], this 'terrestrial Orion' closely mirrors its celestial counterparts, with prehistoric 'cities' corresponding to all the major stars in the constellation. By its specific orientation the sidereal pattern projected on the Arizona high desert also encodes various sunrise and sunset points of both summer and winter solstices."

David has shown that the three Hopi Mesas overlap with the three stars of Orion's Belt; other key Ancestral Puebloan sites correspond to other stars of this constellation, as well as neighboring stars: Chaco Canyon coincides with Sirius. Orion itself comprises (among others) the Betatakin Ruin in Tsegi

Canyon and Keet Seel Ruin, representing the double star Rigel, or the left foot or knee of Orion. Homol'ovi Ruins State Park maps Betelgeuse, Wupatki Pueblo maps Bellatrix, and Canyon de Chelly represents Saiph, or the right foot or knee of Orion. Even the Sipapu in the Grand Canyon is mapped, and corresponds with the star Pi3 Orionis.

David's research has shown that, after Teotihuacán and the pyramids at the Giza Plateau, we are once again confronted with a civilization that has built its sacred sites in correspondence with the layout of Orion's Belt. Orion's Belt is indeed sacred to the Hopi and seen as the "Center of the World," but it was also very important to the Mayans, who actually saw it as the point where the Creation of the Fourth World occurred—which is no doubt why Teotihuacán's central pyramid complex was built according to its layout.

The three pyramids at Giza, just outside the Egyptian capital of Cairo, are seen as the ancient world's most enduring legacy. Their size and majesty can only be appreciated in person. They were laid out in the form of Orion's Belt, conforming to the layout of the Hopi Mesas in Arizona, as well as the pyramid complex in Teotihuacán, Mexico.

Evidence of Nonphysical Contact

Whether we are at the Hopi Mesas, the pyramid complexes at Teotihuacán, or the Great Pyramid, we are confronted with priests who made contact with Maasaw, Quetzalcoatl, or The Nine, and spoke to the gods, as these deities helped with a divine plan. Wherever we turn, we are confronted with legends of "star ancestors" or "star messengers"—otherworldly, extraterrestrial entities with which our ancestors communicated and that helped us on our path of civilization. In every culture, these entities were identified with the stars. And if someone wasn't convinced by the extraordinary discoveries made by people like

The Pyramid of the Sun in Teotihuacán has many things in common with the Great Pyramid of Egypt. Together with the Pyramid of the Moon and the Temple of Quetzalcoatl, it forms the layout of Orion's Belt, to which the pyramids at Giza have also been built. How did cultures separated by time and space nevertheless build according to the same template?

Jeremy Narby, namely that this is real, and not just some hallucination, let us underline that in whatever culture we look, the same specific constellations were used in an identical manner, showing that these intelligences communicated in a consistent manner to our ancestors, across time and space.

Whatever you call this intelligence, they are the Ancient Aliens. They are not evidence of a *physical* contact with an ancient alien, which is the quest most proponents are in search of, but they are definitive evidence that our ancestors were in contact—repeatedly—with a nonhuman, alien, extraterrestrial intelligence.

It explains why extraterrestrial contact and what we call "religion" often go hand in hand: Originally, religion was not just about *belief*; it was a *science*, in which rituals were employed to establish contact with the gods. The ancient Egyptians say they were continuously in contact with the gods; if so, then it is entirely possible that the gods gave Khufu the blueprints and all the knowledge required to build his pyramid, based on knowledge they had previously given to Imhotep. Indeed, the Great Pyramid was very much on par with the device humankind is instructed to build in the book and movie *Contact*: a device through which we could talk to the Ancient Aliens.

Whatever name we give them—"Gods," "Watchers," or "Angels"—they are nonhuman, alien intelligences. Wherever we turn, we find them as the intelligences for which the most extraordinary monuments were built—monuments in which and through which we made contact with them. So, *yes* is the answer to the Ancient Alien Question. We Were Not Alone. We never were. It seems "they" are still here.

Conclusion

In the 12th century, likely during the reign of King Stephen of England (1135–1154), during one summer's harvest, two children (a brother and sister) appeared in the village of Woolpit, in East Anglia (England). They walked out of an earthwork near the village. They had green skin, wore unusual clothing, and spoke a language no one could comprehend. After days of refusing all types of food, the only food they would eat was green beans. The boy soon died, but the girl began to lose her green skin color, while she also began to diversify her food. When she was proficient enough in English, she explained that she came from another world—a land where the sun never shone and the light was like twilight.

The incident was reported by two contemporary writers, Ralph of Coggeshall (died circa 1226) and William of Newburgh (circa

1136–1198). William's account was written in 1189, and Ralph's account, written in the 1220s, incorporated information from Richard de Calne of Wykes, who reportedly gave the children refuge in his manor 6 miles north of Woolpit. He was also responsible for the education of the sister, who eventually married a man from King's Lynn, about 40 miles from Woolpit, where Ralph said she was living shortly before he wrote his account. Based on his research into Richard de Calne's family history, British astronomer Duncan Lunan has concluded that the girl was named Agnes and that she married a royal official named Richard Barre.

In 1621, Robert Burton, in *The Anatomy of Melancholy*, suggested that the green children may have fallen "from Heaven." In short, they might be extraterrestrials. Others confronted with the story of the Green Children agree that there is clearly some type of mystery going on, but argue that rather than an extraterrestrial component, they came instead from the faery realm. They refer to Gerald of Wales, who told a similar story of a boy who encountered two pigmies who led him through an underground passage into a beautiful land with fields and rivers, but which was not lit by the full light of the sun. However, cataloguers of folk stories have said that the story of the Woolpit children is the only example of its type—it is, in short, unique.

Dozens of people have tried to explain this story away, opting for a purely symbolic interpretation, for we all know that such a story cannot be true, right? However, it is precisely because it *did* happen that it was reported in the chronicles; the contemporary historians considered it to be so extraordinary!

Just before he died, in 212 BCE, Emperor Chi Huang Ti ordered that all the books and literature relating to ancient China be destroyed. Similarly, according to Carl Sagan, there was once a book titled *The True History of Mankind Over the Last 100,000 Years* in the famed library of Alexandria, but the document was burned in a series of deliberate acts of arson meant to eradicate

Conclusion

the "pagan" knowledge contained in those buildings in the third century CE. When the Spanish Conquistadors conquered the Aztecs in the 16th century, they burnt all the Aztecs' books. Then, in the middle of the 19th century when the first European settler, a French priest named Eugene Eyraud, arrived on Easter Island, he made it his mission to burn as many of the native rongo rongo tablets as he could. Is it any wonder that "science" can't find any evidence for ancient aliens, or lost knowledge?

That the evidence for the Ancient Alien Question has to be found in the most gigantic monuments—which were simply too big and solid to be destroyed—and ancient legends is precisely because of the consistent trend throughout humankind's most recent history, on all continents, to eradicate large amounts, if not the majority, of our history—of "what came before." Though we no longer believe the world originated in 4004 BCE, what science and archaeology have done is to place the origins of civilization at that moment in time, and argue that anything before then cannot be validated by science, and hence by default is *believed* not to be true. However, truth simply *is*, whether you believe it or not.

Is there any object or written document that *proves* that ancient aliens visited planet Earth? No. But, as I have shown throughout this book, ancient buildings reveal that they were constructed with massive stones that could not have been moved without some form of advanced technology or knowledge—not necessarily through more gigantic cranes than are currently in use in modern building projects, but more likely via a form of knowledge and understanding of the laws of the universe. As a body of literature, the ancient myths and legends clearly state that gods were once present on Earth and gave the gift of civilization and various other knowledge to humankind. This is evidence.

Were these ancient aliens physically present on planet Earth? Maybe. Legends such as that of Oannes clearly speak of a nonhuman, physical intelligence that came out of the sea and educated humankind in the ways of civilization. But there are other legends that make it clear that the gods were not necessarily physically here, and may not even *be* physical as such; they could best be described as a nonhuman, otherworldly intelligence that we can contact through a number of means, many of which today would be classified under the label of paranormal, parapsychological, or—a term I prefer—metaphysical. Alas, the metaphysical realm has also been fenced off and deemed to be off-limits for scientific exploration, so finding more evidence in support of the Ancient Alien Question from that field can only come from personal accounts, such as what happened with The Nine in the investigations carried out by Andrija Puharich. And though it is not yet the consensus, what science has discovered—to its own horror, it seems—is that life itself is extraterrestrial in nature.

British astronomer Duncan Lunan has pondered the question of contact and communication with other intelligences for many decades. It is his conviction that, based on the number of stars and planets in the universe, an extraterrestrial civilization should have contacted us at least once, and—statistically speaking—a maximum of four times. This means that out of all the evidence that suggests we have been contacted, based upon what science currently knows, or rather, thinks, about life in the universe, statistically speaking, contact is a very rare thing. It means that out of the 230 questions posed by Erich von Däniken, out of all the evidence we have gone through in this book, only one to four of them should eventually be answered in the positive. In *Man and the Stars*, Duncan Lunan put forward 22 items of best evidence, which includes the story of Oannes, the ancient maps, the Chinese Roswell, the pyramids, Baalbek, the Watchers, Viracocha, Ezekiel, and many more. Some are clear evidence of contact with a nonhuman intelligence, whereas others are at least clear evidence of technology and knowledge possessed by our ancestors that exceeds our traditional historical understanding of these cultures.

Conclusion

What this book has hopefully demonstrated is that the manner in which science has tried to look toward these enigmas is not the correct, or at least not the only, approach. When we look at reality the way it is, rather than within the reduced framework in which science prefers to operate, it becomes clear that there is only one answer.

Were We Alone? No.

There are hundreds if not thousands of examples that show this throughout humankind's history. The gift of civilization was said to have been granted to us by the gods, but there is other evidence that shows we have never been alone. Modern UFO research is but the latest incarnation of a long tradition that argues for the presence of a nonhuman intelligence. Alas, in the materialistic mindset that continues to dominate our era, the notion has always been that this should be a physical extraterrestrial presence here on Earth. This is not necessarily so, and the work of Jeremy Narby and the accounts of hundreds of shamans in the Amazonian jungle make it apparent that people can access a realm where they can interface with this nonhuman intelligence, and that these "gods" give them highly technological information—the most famous of which is the chemical process of making ayahuasca, the potion that enables communication with the gods.

When molecular biologist Dr. Pia Malnoe was taken into the Amazon by Narby, she concluded that "The way shamans get their knowledge is not very different from the way scientists get their knowledge. It has the same origin, but shamans and scientists use different methods."[1]

In my opinion, most Ancient Alien Theories have failed in finding proof because their scope was too limited, and the answer they were after was erroneous. Though in a number of rare instances the gods *were* likely here in physical form, they definitely did not come to planet Earth to exploit its minerals or enslave Homo sapiens for that purpose. I would argue that, apart from Oannes, an accidental crash like "the Chinese Roswell" at Baian-Kara-Ulla, and one or two other similar incidents, such physical contact was probably sporadic at best. But when we really look at our history, it is clear that civilization was indeed guided by gods, by a nonhuman, extraterrestrial intelligence. Though today we would consider this to be the bailiwick of religion, it is not; it is about directly experiencing another reality and contacting this intelligence. The work of McKenna, Narby, Harner, and so many others has made it clear that this is real. The technology and information they have given us ranges from insights into DNA (as per Jeremy Narby), the enigmatic mathematical formula of time that Terence McKenna received, and maybe the chemical methodology to create geopolymers, given to the Egyptian priest Imhotep.

What is evidence? What is proof? There are clear parallels between what McKenna and Imhotep received. There are hundreds of passages in the sacred literature of every ancient civilization that speak of contact with nonhuman intelligences. In the case of Oannes, even the likes of Carl Sagan felt that the evidence was in—that this could only be explained as contact with a physical extraterrestrial entity. For some, these accounts will not be enough.

But we have also learned the answer goes far beyond a simple yes. In fact, life is a cosmic imperative. We *are* the aliens. Chandra Wickramasinghe in *Cosmic Dragons* writes, "Life is a truly cosmic phenomenon, the sum total of an evolutionary experience gained and accumulated in a multitude of different places, quite widely separated, and extending in time throughout the entire history of the Universe." Wickramasinghe is convinced that there is a slow but definitive move within the scientific community to accept the extraterrestrial origins of life, describing it as "a major paradigm shift comparable in importance to the Copernican revolution of the 16th century." When that happens,

Conclusion

the next challenge science will have to address is the Ancient Alien Question—a question it has consistently shied away from.

The key here is the consensus reality: what we all agree to *believe*. It is a basic human right that any individual has the freedom to believe what he or she wants. And so it is my hope—my wish—that in these pages, I have laid out the nature and complexity of the Ancient Alien Question in such a way that you have the necessary building blocks that will allow you to decide whether *you* believe. I have shown you the process as to why I *believe* the answer is yes. But what I *know* is that the Ancient Alien Question has to be asked again today, for there are millions of people out there who want an answer.

Notes

Foreword
1. Pessl, *The Chronological*.
2. Waddell, "Manetho."
3. Diodorus, *Historical Library*.
4. Ibid.

Introduction
1. Walter-Jorg Langbein, in an interview with Dr. Hermann Oberth, as reported at *langbein.alien.de/bericht13.html*, a transcript of the 24th Ancient Astronaut World Conference lecture delivered by W-J Langbein, August 4, 1997, Orlando, Fla.
2. Hirji, "Nature's."

Chapter 1
1. Kaku, "First Contact."
2. Story, *The Encyclopedia*, pp. 162–3.
3. Sagan, *Cosmos*, p. 193.

Chapter 2
1. Icke, David, Interview.
2. Bramley, *The Gods of Eden*, p. 16.
3. Ibid., p. 2.
4. Ibid., p. 225.
5. Ibid., pp. 3–4.
6. Heiser, "Open Letter."
7. Von Dechend and Santillana, *Hamlet's Mill*, p. 431.

8. Boulay, *Flying Serpents*, p. 51.

9. Story, *The Encyclopedia*, p. 635.

10. James and Thorpe, *Ancient Mysteries*, p. 107.

11. Ibid., p. 108.

12. Ibid., p. 109.

13. Villars, *The Comte*, p. 64.

Chapter 3

1. Blumrich, *The Spaceships*.

2. Story, *The Encyclopedia*, p. 182.

3. Cassuto, *A Commentary*, p. 260.

4. *Legendary Times Magazine*, *Vol. 10, nos. 1 and 2*, p. 20–21.

Chapter 4

1. Davidovits, "X-Ray."

2. Geiger, "Imhotep's."

3. Davidovits, "They Built," p. 61.

4. Nickerson, "Did the Great."

5. Nickerson, "A New Angle."

6. Ibid.

7. Ibid.

8. Neugebauer, *The Exact*, p. 91.

9. Dunn, *The Giza*, pp. 152–153.

10. Alouf, *History*, p. 92.

11. Thom, *Megalithic Sites*, p. 43.

12. Thompson, *Alien Identities*, p. 226.

Notes

Chapter 5

1. Haviland, et al, *Cultural Anthropology*, p. 232.
2. "Aztec Crystal Skull."
3. Morton and Thomas, *Tränen*, p. 124.
4. Morant, "A Morphological," p. 108.
5. Hancock, *Fingerprints*, p. 166.
6. Ibid., p. 171.
7. Ibid., p. 72.
8. Grist, "Mysteries."

Chapter 6

1. *Ancient Skies*, p. 1.
2. "Antikythera Mechanism."
3. Childress, *Technology*, p. 94. Also at *www.world-mysteries.com/sar_4.htm*.
4. "Antikythera Mechanism."
5. *Legendary Times*, p. 17.
6. Hancock, *Fingerprints*, p. 5.
7. Ibid., p. 112.
8. Lenormant and Chevallier, *A Manual*, p. 502.
9. Sagan, *Broca's Brain*, p. 67.
10. Wadell, "Manetho."
11. Sitchin, *The End*, p. 86.
12. Ibid., p. 95.
13. Noorbergen, *Secrets*, p. 73.
14. SciForums.com.
15. Mitchell-Hedges, *Danger*, p. 87.
16. Personal correspondence with Jon Rolls, April 22, 2008.

17. Hausdorf, *The Chinese*, p. 34.
18. Ibid.
19. Ibid., p. 35.
20. Ibid.

Chapter 7

1. Wickramasinghe, "Extraterrestrial."
2. Weinstein, "Influenza," pp. 1058–1060.
3. Joseph and Wickramasinghe, "Comets."
4. Sagan, *Cosmos*, p. 130.
5. Hancock and Bauvel, *The Mars*, Chapter 6.

Chapter 8

1. James and Thorpe, *Ancient Mysteries*, p. 241.
2. Radford, "The Mysterious."
3. Geller, Uri. "Dr. Vinod."
4. Ibid.
5. Naydler, *Shamanic Wisdom*, p. 166.
6. Jenkins and Matz, *Pyramid*, p. 37.
7. Harner, "The Sound."
8. Narby, *The Cosmic Serpent*. See also *www.world-mysteries.com/newgw/cosmicserpent.htm*.

Conclusion

1. Dicum, "The Cosmic."

Glossary

cartouche An ancient tablet with a design or inscription on it.

corroborate To provide evidence of a theory's truth.

diabolical Of or relating to the devil.

fractal A never-ending pattern found in nature that can be represented by complex mathematical equations.

geopolymer An artificial substance that resembles natural rock, created through a chemical process known as geopolymerization.

heliacal Related to the sun; especially used in reference to the first rising or last setting of the sun.

monolith A single enormous stone, often positioned upright.

mycological Of or related to mycology, the study of fungi.

nanotechnology The science of manipulating materials on a very small scale (such as individual atoms or molecules).

Nephilim An unknown people referred to the Bible; sometimes translated as "giants" or "fallen angels."

oop-art Out-of-place artifact; any ancient object found in a place where it was not previously known to be in use.

pluralism The belief that life exists elsewhere in the universe.

pulsar A star that is the source of radio waves that are emitted in a regular rhythm, or pulses.

SETI Search for Extraterrestrial Intelligence; a private, nonprofit organization that conducts research in hopes of contacting an extraterrestrial civilization.

terraforming "Earth-shaping," or the theoretical process of altering another planet so that it resembles Earth and could support human life.

Terra Preta Dark, fertile soil found in the Amazon Basin that was artificially engineered by an ancient pre-Columbian civilization.

vimana A temple or palace referred to in ancient Sanskrit epics; sometimes understood to be a flying machine of some sort.

zenith The highest point in the sky that a celestial body can reach.

For More Information

Ancient Aliens
Website: http://www.history.com/shows/ancient-aliens
Ancient Aliens, a popular series on the History channel that premiered in 2010, explores the theory that extraterrestrials have been visiting Earth for millions of years.

Carnac Stones
Lleu-dit le Ménec
56340 Carnac
France
Website: http://www.brittanytourism.com/discover-brittany/quintessential-brittany/carnac
Near the village of Carnac in northwestern France, thousands of standing Neolithic stones are lined up in three separate fields. Visitors can learn more about them on a guided tour or at the nearby Museum of Prehistory.

Coral Castle Museum
28655 South Dixie Highway
Miami, FL 33033
(305) 248-6345
Website: http://www.coralcastle.com
At Coral Castle Museum, visitors can tour Coral Castle, the enormous sculpture garden built by Edward Leedskalnin over the course of 28 years. To this day, no one is sure how he managed to work with such heavy stones (all together, they weigh 1,100 tons).

The Search for Extraterrestrial Intelligence Institute (SETI)
189 Bernardo Ave, Suite 100
Mountain View, CA 94043

(650) 961-6633

Website: http://www.seti.org

Founded in 1984, the SETI Institute is a private, nonprofit organization that conducts research to explore the origin and prevalence of life in the universe.

UNESCO World Heritage Centre

7, Place de Fontenoy

75352 Paris 07 SP

France

+33 (0)1 45 68 24 96

Website: http://whc.unesco.org

The United Nations Educational, Scientific and Cultural Organization has declared more than a thousand locations to be World Heritage Sites based on their historical, natural, and creative importance. Among them are Egypt's Pyramid Fields; Teotihuacan and other Mayan ruins; Cuzco, Machu Picchu, Nasca, and other Inca ruins; and Baalbek in Lebanon.

Websites

Because of the changing nature of Internet links, Rosen Publishing has developed an online list of websites related to the subject of this book. This site is updated regularly. Please use this link to access this list:

http://www.rosenlinks.com/CACU/Anci

For Further Reading

Byers, Ann. *Discovering Ancient Mesoamerican Civilizations* (Exploring Ancient Civilizations). New York: Britannica Educational Publishing, 2015.

Childress, David Hatcher. *Vimana: Flying Machines of the Ancients*. Kempton, Ill.: Adventures Unlimited Press, 2014.

Creighton, Scott, and Gary Osborn. *The Giza Prophecy: The Orion Code and the Secret Teachings of the Pyramids*. Rochester, Vt.: Bear & Company, 2012.

Coppens, Philip. *The Lost Civilization Enigma: A New Inquiry into the Existence of Ancient Cities, Cultures, and Peoples who Pre-Date Recorded History*. Pompton Plains, N.J.: Career Press, 2013.

Marrs, Jim. *Our Occulted History: Do the Global Elite Conceal Ancient Aliens?* New York: William Morrow, 2013.

Murphy, John. *Gods & Goddesses of the Inca, Maya, and Aztec Civilizations* (Gods & Goddesses of Mythology). New York: Britannica Educational Publishing, 2015.

Roberts, Scott Alan. *The Rise and Fall of the Nephilim: The Untold Story of Fallen Angels, Giants on the Earth, and Their Extraterrestrial Origins*. Pompton Plains, N.J.: Career Press, 2012.

Shea, Therese. *Investigating UFOs and Aliens* (Understanding the Paranormal). New York: Britannica Educational Publishing, 2015.

Staley, Erin. *Discovering Ancient Egypt* (Exploring Ancient Civilizations). New York: Britannica Educational Publishing, 2015.

Ancient Aliens

von Däniken, Erich. *Remnants of the Gods: A Visual Tour of Alien Influence in Egypt, Spain, France, Turkey, and Italy.* Pompton Plains, N.J.: Career Press, 2014.

Webb, Stuart. *Alien Encounters* (Paranormal Files). New York: Rosen Publishing, 2013.

Bibliography

Alford, Alan F. *The Midnight Sun: The Death and Rebirth of God in Ancient Egypt*. Walsall, Sandwell, UK: Eridu Books, 2004.

———. *The Phoenix Solution: Secrets of a Lost Civilisation*. London: Hodder & Stoughton, 1998.

———. *Pyramid of Secrets: The Architecture of the Great Pyramid Reconsidered in the Light of Creational Mythology*. Walsall, Sandwell, UK: Eridu Books, 2003.

———. *When the Gods Came Down: The Catastrophic Roots of Religion Revealed*. London: Hodder & Stoughton, 2000.

Allen, Richard Hinckley. *Star-Names and Their Meanings*. London: G.E. Stechert, 1899.

Alouf, Michel. *History of Baalbek, 25th Edition*. San Diego, Calif.: The Book Tree, 1999.

Ancient Skies, the newsletter of the Ancient Astronaut Society, Volume 16.5. Highland Park, Ill.

"Antikythera Mechanism." *The Economist*, 2002. World-Mysteries. com: *www.world-mysteries.com/sar_4.htm* (accessed July 2014).

Appleby, Nigel. *Hall of the Gods: The Quest to Discovery the Knowledge of the Ancients*. London: William Heinemann, 1998.

"Aztec Crystal Skull a Fake, Says Cardiff Professor." Questia. *www.questia.com/PM.qst?a=o&d=5008275609* (accessed July 2014).

Bauval, Robert. *The Egypt Code*. London: Century Books, 2006.

———. *Secret Chamber: The Quest for the Hall of Records*. London: Century Books, 1999.

Bauval, Robert, and Adrian Gilbert. *The Orion Mystery: Unlocking the Secrets of the Pyramids*. London: William Heinemann, 1994.

Blumrich, Josef. *The Spaceships of Ezekiel*. New York: Bantam Books, 1973.

Boulay, R.A. *Flying Serpents and Dragons: The Story of Mankind's Reptilian Past*. Clearwater, Fla.: Galaxy Books, 1990.

Bramley, William. *The Gods of Eden*. New York: Avon Books, 1993.

Budge, E.A. Wallis. *The Egyptian Heaven and Hell*. Chicago: Open Court, 1925.

———. *The Gods of the Egyptians, or Studies in Egyptian Mythology*. London: Methuen and Co., 1904.

———. *Introduction to the Book of the Dead*. New York: Dover Books.

———. *Osiris and the Egyptian Resurrection*. New York: Dover Books, 1973.

Cassuto, Umberto. *A Commentary on the Book of Genesis: From Adam to Noah*. Jerusalem: Magnes Press, 1961.

Chatelain, Maurice. *Our Cosmic Ancestors*. Sedona, Ariz.: Temple Golden Publications, 1988.

Childress, David Hatcher. *Ancient Tonga & The Lost City of Mu'a*. Kempton, Ill.: Adventures Unlimited Press, 1996.

———. *Extraterrestrial Archaeology: Incredible Proof We Are Not Alone*. Stelle, Ill.: Adventures Unlimited Press, 1994.

———. *Lost Cities of Atlantis, Ancient Europe and the Mediterranean*. Kempton, Ill.: Adventures Unlimited Press, 1996.

———. *Lost Cities of China, Central Asia & India*. Stelle, Ill.: Adventures Unlimited Press, 1985.

———. *Technology of the Gods: The Incredible Sciences of the Ancients*. Kempton, Ill.: Adventures Unlimited Press, 2000.

———. *Vimana Aircraft of Ancient India & Atlantis*. Kempton, Ill.: Adventures Unlimited Press, 1991.

Clark, R.T. Rundle. *Myth and Symbol in Ancient Egypt*. London: Thames & Hudson, 1959.

Collins, Andrew. *Gods of Eden: Egypt's Lost Legacy and the Genesis of Civilisation*. London: Headline, 1998.

Crowley, Brian, and James J. Hurtak. *The Face on Mars: The Evidence of a Lost Martian Civilization*. South Melbourne, Australia: Sun Books, 1986.

Bibliography

Cruttenden, Walter. *Lost Star of Myth and Time*. Pittsburgh, Pa.: St. Lynn's Press, 2006.

Davidovits, Joseph. *Ils ont Bâti les Pyramides*. Paris: Jean-Cyrille Godefroy, 2002.

———. *La Nouvelle Histoire des Pyramides*. Paris: Jean-Cyrille Godefroy, 2004.

———. "They Built the Pyramids." Saint-Quentin, France: Institut Géopolymère, 2008.

———. "X-Ray Analysis of Pyramids' Casing Stones and Their Limestone Quarries." Geopolymer Institute. *www.geopolymer. org/library/archaeological-papers/a-x-ray-analysis-pyramids-casing-stones-and-their-limestone-quarries* (accessed July 2014).

Delgado, Jorge Luis, with MaryAnn Male, PhD. *Andean Awakening: An Inca Guide to Mystical Peru*. San Francisco/ Tulsa, Okla.: Council Oak Books, 2006.

Dicum, Gregory. "The Cosmic Servant." *www.dicum.com/clips/ the-cosmic-servant/*, February 2003 (accessed July 2014).

Diodorus of Sicily. *Historical Library*. Stuttgart, Germany: A. Wahrmund, 1866.

Dormion, Gilles. *La chambre de Chéops: Analyse Architecturale*. Paris: Fayard, 2004.

Dunn, Christopher. *The Giza Power Plant: Technologies of Ancient Egypt*. Santa Fe, N. Mex.: Bear & Co, 1998.

Edwards, I.E.S. *The Pyramids of Egypt, Revised Edition*. London: Penguin Books, 1980.

El Mahdy, Christine. *The Pyramid Builder: Cheops, The Man Behind the Great Pyramid*. London: Headline, 2003.

Emmegger, Robert. *UFO's, Past, Present & Future*. New York: Ballantine Books, 1974.

Fowler, Raymond E. *The Watchers: The Secret Design Behind UFO Abduction*. New York: Bantam Books, 1991.

Geiger, Owen. "Imhotep's Formula to Make Limestone Blocks." Geopolymer House Blog. *geopolymerhouses.wordpress*

.com/2011/07/08/imhotep's-formula-to-make-limestone-blocks (accessed July 2014).

Geller, Uri. "Dr. Vinod—Harry Stone—Peter Hurkos." UriGeller .com. *www.urigeller.com/books/maverick/maver5.htm* (accessed July 2014).

Goswami, Amit. *Physics of the Soul: The Quantum Book of Living, Dying, Reincarnation and Immortality*. New York: Hampton Roads Publishing Company, 2001.

———. *The Self-Aware Universe: How Consciousness Creates the Material World*. New York: Jeremy P. Tarcher, 1995.

Grist, Stan. "Mysteries of the Ancient Tunnels, the Cueva de los Tayos, Juan Moricz, the Metallic Library and Much More." *www.stangrist.com/TunnelsMoricz.htm* (accessed July 2014).

Hancock, Graham. *Fingerprints of the Gods: A Quest for the Beginning and the End*. London: Heinemann, 1995.

———. *Underworld: Flooded Kingdoms of the Ice Age*. London: Michael Joseph, 2002.

Hancock, Graham, and Robert Bauval. *Keepers of Genesis: A Quest for the Hidden Legacy of Mankind*. London: Heinemann, 1996.

———. *The Mars Mystery: The Secret Connection Between Earth and the Red Planet*. New York: Three Rivers Press, 1999.

———. *Talisman: Sacred Cities, Secret Faith*. London: Michael Joseph, 2004.

Harner, Michael J. "The Sound of Rushing Water: A Hallucinogenic Drug Gives the Jivaro Shaman Entrance to the "Real" World and Gives Him the Power to Cure or Bewitch." *Natural History*, July 1968.

Hausdorf, Hartwig. *The Chinese Roswell: UFO Encounters in the Far East From Ancient Times to the Present*. Redding, Calif.: New Paradigm Books, 1998.

———. *Nicht von Dieser Welt: Dinge, die es Nicht Geben Dürfte*. Munich: Herbig, 2008.

Bibliography

————. *Die Weisse Pyramide: Ausserirdische Spuren in Ostasien*. Munich: Langen Müller, 1994.

Haviland, William A., Harald E.L. Prins, Dana Walrath, and Bunny McBride. *Cultural Anthropology: The Human Challenge, 12th Edition*. Florence, Ky.: Wadsworth Publishing, 2007.

Heiser, Michael S., PhD. "Open Letter." *www.sitchiniswrong.com/letter/letter.htm* (accessed July 2014).

Hirji, Zahra. "Nature's Incredible Cover-Up: An Ancient Amazonian Civilization." DiscoveryNews. *news.discovery.com/history/natures-incredible-cover-up-an-ancient-amazonian-civilization.html* (accessed September 2011).

Hoagland, Richard. *The Monuments of Mars: A City on the Edge of Forever*. Berkeley, Calif.: Frog Ltd, 1996.

Hope, Murry. *The Sirius Connection: Unlocking the Secrets of Ancient Egypt*. Shaftesbury, Dorset, England: Element Books, 1996.

Icke, David. Interview with Terry Wogan on *Wogan: Now & Then*. Transcribed on *public.youtranscript.com/zs/880.html* (accessed September 2011).

James, Peter, and Nick Thorpe. *Ancient Mysteries*. New York: Ballantine Books, 1999.

Jenkins, John Major. *Galactic Alignment: The Transformation of Consciousness According to Mayan, Egyptian and Vedic Traditions*. Rochester, Vt.: Bear & Company, 2002.

————. *Maya Cosmogenesis 2012: The True Meaning of the Maya Calendar End-Date*. Rochester, Vt.: Bear & Company, 1998.

Jenkins, John Major, and Martin Matz. *Pyramid of Fire: The Lost Aztec Codex*. Rochester, Vt.: Bear & Company, 2004.

Joseph, Frank. *Atlantis in Wisconsin: New Revelations About the Lost Sunken City*. St. Paul, Minn.: Galde Press, 1995.

————. *Lost Pyramids of Rock Lake: Wisconsin's Sunken Civilization*. St. Paul, Minn.: Galde Press, 1992.

Joseph, Rhawn, and Chandra Wickramasinghe. "Comets and Contagion: Evolution and Diseases From Space." *Journal of*

Cosmology 7, 2010. *journalofcosmology.com/Panspermia10.html* (accessed July 2014).

Kaku, Michio. "First Contact." Discovery Channel documentary.

Krupp, E.C. *Skywatchers, Shamans & Kings: Astronomy and the Archaeology of Power*. New York: John Wiley & Sons, 1997.

Langbein, Walter-Jorg. "Gods From Outer Space." 24th Ancient Astronaut World Conference lecture, August 4, 1997, Orlando, Fla.

LaViolette, Paul. *Beyond the Big Bang: Ancient Myth and the Science of Continuous Creation*. Rochester, Vt.: Park Street Press, 1995.

———. *Earth Under Fire: Humanity's Survival of the Apocalypse*. Alexandria, Va.: Starlane Publications, 1997.

———. *The Talk of the Galaxy: An ET Message for Us?* Alexandria, Va.: Starlane Publications, 2000.

Lawton, Ian, and Chris Ogilvie-Herald. *Gizeh: The Truth. The People, Politics & History Behind the World's Most Famous Archaeological Site*. London: Virgin Books, 1999.

Legendary Times Magazine, Vol. 10, nos. 1 & 2, pp. 20–21.

Lehner, Mark. *The Complete Pyramids*. London: Thames & Hudson, 1997.

Lenormant, François, and E. Chevallier. *A Manual of the Ancient History of the East, Volume 1*. Philadelphia, Pa.: J.B. Lippincott, 1871.

Lunan, Duncan. *Man and the Stars: Contact and Communication With Other Intelligence*. London: Corgi Books, 1978.

Lutz, Henry L.F. *Canopus: The City of the "Chest of Heaven."* Berkeley and Los Angeles: University of California Press, 1946.

McCulloch, Kenneth C. *Mankind: Citizen of the Galaxy*. The Pas, Manitoba: The Rings of Saturn Publishing, 1985.

McDaniel, Stanley V. *The McDaniel Report. On the Failure of Executive, Congressional and Scientific Responsibility in Investigating Possible Evidence of Artificial Structures on the Surface of Mars and in setting Mission Priorities for NASA's*

Bibliography

Mars Exploration Program. Berkeley, Calif.: North Atlantic Books, 1993.

Mehler, Stephen S. *The Land of Osiris: An Introduction to Khemitology*. Kempton, Ill.: Adventures Unlimited Press, 2001.

Mitchell, Edgar, with Dwight Williams. *The Way of the Explorer: An Apollo Astronaut's Journey Through the Material and Mystical Worlds*. New York: G.P. Putnam's Sons, 1996.

Mitchell-Hedges, F.A. *Danger My Ally*. Kempton, Ill.: Adventures Unlimited Press, 1995.

Morant, G.M. "A Morphological Comparison of Two Crystal Skulls." *Man*, Vol. 36, July 1936.

Morrison, Tony. *Pathways to the Gods: The Mystery of the Andes Lines*. Chicago: Academy Chicago Publishers, 1988.

Morton, Chris, and Ceri Louise Thomas. *Tränen der Götter: Die Prophezeiung der 13 Kristallschädel*. Bechtermünz, Germany: Bern, 2000.

Musaios (Charles Muses). *The Lion Path: You Can Take it With You*. Sardis, British Columbia: House of Horus, 1990.

Narby, Jeremy. *The Cosmic Serpent: DNA and the Origins of Knowledge*. New York: Jeremy P. Tarcher, 1998.

————. *Intelligence in Nature: An Inquiry Into Knowledge*. New York: Jeremy P. Tarcher, 2005.

Naydler, Jeremy. *Shamanic Wisdom in the Pyramid Texts: The Mystical Tradition of Ancient Egypt*. Rochester, Vt.: Inner Traditions, 2005.

————. *Temple of the Cosmos: The Ancient Egyptian Experience of the Sacred*. Rochester, Vt.: Inner Traditions, 1996.

Neugebauer, Otto. *The Exact Sciences in Antiquity, 2nd Edition*. New York: Dover Publications, 1969.

Neugebauer, Otto, and Richard A. Parker. *Egyptian Astronomical Texts I: The Early Decans*. Providence, R.I.: Brown University Press, 1960.

Nickerson, Colin. "A New Angle on Pyramids: Scientists Explore Whether Egyptians Used Concrete." *Boston Globe*, April 22,

2008. *www.freerepublic.com/focus/chat/2010105/posts* (accessed July 2014).

———. "Did the Great Pyramids' Builders Use Concrete?" *The New York Times*, April 23, 2008. *www.nytimes.com/2008/04/23/ world/africa/23iht-pyramid.1.12259608.html* (accessed July 2014).

Noorbergen, Rene. *Secrets of the Lost Races: New Discoveries of Advanced Technology in Ancient Civilizations*. Brushton, N.Y.: Teach Services, 2001.

Parker, Richard A. *The Calendars of Ancient Egypt*. Chicago: University of Chicago Press, 1950.

Percy, David S., David Myers, and Mary Bennett. *Two-Thirds: A History of our Galaxy*. London: Aulis Publishers, 1993.

Pessl, Henri von. *The Chronological System of Manetho*. Leipzig, Germany: J.C. Hinrichs, 1878.

Picknett, Lynn, and Clive Prince. *The Stargate Conspiracy: Revealing the Truth Behind Extraterrestrial Contact, Military Intelligence and the Mysteries of Ancient Egypt*. London: Little, Brown & Co, 1999.

Pilkington, Ark. *Mirage Men*. London: Constable & Robinson, 2010.

Pinchbeck, Daniel. *2012: The Return of Quetzalcoatl*. New York: Jeremy Tarcher, 2006.

Poe, Richard. *Black Spark, White Fire: Did African Explorers Civilize Ancient Europe?* Rocklin, Calif.: Prima Publishing, 1997.

Plutarch. *The History of Isis and Osiris*.

Radford, Benjamin. "The Mysterious Coral Castle: A Fanciful Myth." LiveScience.com, March 28, 2006. *www.livescience .com/680-mysterious-coral-castle-fanciful-myth.html* (accessed July 2014).

Rice, Michael. *Egypt's Making: The Origins of Ancient Egypt 5000–2000 BC*. London: Routledge, 1990.

Sagan, Carl. *Broca's Brain*. New York: Random House, 1979.

———. *Contact*. New York: Pocket Books, 1985.

———. *Cosmos*. New York: Random House, 1980.

Bibliography

Salazar, Fernando, and Edgar Salazar. *Cuzco and the Sacred Valley of the Incas*. Cuzco, Peru: Tanpu S.R.L., 2003.

Schele, Linda, and David Friedel. *A Forest of Kings: The Untold Story of the Ancient Maya*. New York: William Morrow, 1990.

Schele, Linda, and Peter Mathews. *The Code of Kings: The Language of Seven Sacred Maya Temples and Tombs*. New York: Scribner, 1998.

SciForums.com. Pseudoscience Archive. "Can Some Sceptics [sic] Debunk This for Me." *www.sciforums.com/Can-some-sceptics-debunk-this-for-me-t-33278.html* (accessed July 2014).

Sellers, Jane. *The Death of the Gods in Ancient Egypt: An Essay on Egyptian Religion and the Frame of Time*. London: Penguin, 1992.

Sitchin, Zecharia. *The Cosmic Code*. New York: Avon Books, 1998.

———. *Divine Encounters*. New York: Avon Books, 1995.

———. *The End of Days*. New York: William Morrow, 2007.

———. *Genesis Revisited*. New York: Avon Books, 1990.

———. *Journeys to the Mythical Past*. Rochester, Vermont: Bear & Co, 2007.

———. *The Lost Realms*. New York: Avon Books, 1990.

———. *The Stairway to Heaven*. New York: Avon Books, 1980.

———. *The 12th Planet*. New York: Avon Books, 1976.

———. *The Wars of Gods and Men*. New York: Avon Books, 1985.

———. *When Time Began*. New York: Avon Books, 1993.

Story, Ronald D., ed. *The Encyclopedia of Extraterrestrial Encounters*. New York: New American Library, 2001.

Sullivan, William. *The Secret of the Incas: Myth, Astronomy, and the War Against Time*. New York: Crown Publishers, 1996.

Temple, Robert. *The Crystal Sun: Rediscovering a Lost Technology of the Ancient World*. London: Century, 2000.

———. *Egyptian Dawn*. London: Century, 2010.

———. *The Sirius Mystery*. London: Sidgwick & Jackson, 1976.

Temple, Robert, with Olivia Temple. *The Sphinx Mystery: The Forgotten Origins of the Sanctuary of Anubis*. Rochester, Vt.: Inner Traditions, 2009.

Thom, Alexander. *Megalithic Sites in Britain*. Oxford: Clarendon Press, 1967.

Thompson, Richard L. *Alien Identities: Ancient Insights Into Modern UFO Phenomena*. San Diego, Calif.: Govardhan Hill Publishing, 1993.

———. *Vedic Cosmography and Astronomy*. Los Angeles: The Bhaktivedanta Book Trust, 1989.

Villars, Abbe de. *The Comte De Gabalis: Secrets of the Elementals*. Charleston, S.C.: Forgotten Books, 2008.

Von Dechend, Hertha, and Giorgio de Santillana. *Hamlet's Mill: An Essay Investigating the Origins of Human Knowledge and its Transmission Through Myth*. Boston: David R. Godine, 1992.

Wadell, W.G., trans. "Manetho, With an English Translation." *www.archive.org/stream/manethowithengli00maneuoft/manethowithengli00maneuoft_djvu.txt* (accessed July 2014).

Weinstein, L. "Influenza: 1918, a Revisit?" *New England Journal of Medicine* 6, 1976.

Wickramasinghe, Chandra. *Cosmic Dragons: Life and Death on our Planet*. London: Souvenir Press, 2001.

———. "Extraterrestrial Life and Censorship." Abstract for the Cardiff Centre for Astrobiology, Llwynypia Road, Cardiff, UK. *sdcc3.ucsd.edu/~ir118/Leiden2010/WickFinalApr5sml.pdf* (accessed July 2014).

Witkowski, Igor. *Axis of the World: The Search for the Oldest American Civilization*. Kempton, Ill.: Adventures Unlimited Press, 2008.

Zitman, Wim. *Kosmische Slinger der Tijden*. Hollandscheveld, Netherlands: De Ring, 1993.

———. *Sterrenbeeld van Horus: Uniek Kleitablet Brengt Bakermat van Voorouders van de Egyptische Beschaving in Kaart*. Baarn, Netherlands: Tirion, 2000.

Index

Index

Index

Index

Index

About the Author

Philip Coppens's publishing career began at the age of 23, when he edited the late Belgian historian Marcel Mestdagh's research into European megaliths for a much-anticipated sequel. That same year, he also helped edit a controversial nonfiction thriller on the theft of Jan Van Eyck's altarpiece, *The Adoration of the Lamb*, which was made into a documentary both for Flemish television and the BBC.

If there is one thing that sets Coppens apart from other writers, it is that he is often ahead of the trends. He wrote the first guide on Rosslyn Chapel in more than four decades; he was the only one to do so before *The Da Vinci Code* made that Scottish chapel world-famous in 2003. He also researched the origins of the Mitchell-Hedges Crystal Skull, before the 2008 *Indiana Jones and the Kingdom of the*

Crystal Skull movie, resulting in a series of controversial articles, which even came to the attention of *The Washington Post*.

As a journalist, Coppens's investigative research into the Kennedy assassination was submitted before a U.S. government enquiry in 1993. Two years later, he broke the story of the existence of Chinese pyramids to an international audience. Many stories from the so-called esoteric field have at one point passed through his hands, including *The Templar Revelation*, the book on which *The Da Vinci Code* was based. In 1999, Coppens was the principal researcher for Lynn Picknett and Clive Prince's *The Stargate Conspiracy*, which investigated current politicians' apparent obsession with ancient Egypt, thus combining his passion for politics and history.

Coppens is the author of *The Stone Puzzle of Rosslyn Chapel* (2002), about the enigmatic Scottish chapel and its relationship with freemasonry and the Knights Templar; *The Canopus Revelation* (2004), about the lore of the star Canopus in ancient cultures; *Land of the Gods* (2007), about the prehistory of Southern Scotland and the myth of King Arthur; *The New Pyramid Age* (2007), detailing the most recent discoveries that have changed our understanding of pyramids; and *Servants of the Grail* (2009), identifying the real people encoded into the medieval Grail legends. Most recently, he has published an e-book titled *2012: Science or Fiction?* with Digital Journeys, which aims to bring clarity as to what all the hubbub about 2012 is truly about. This e-book is also the to first incorporate video, and features an interview-style conversation with Philip.

Apart from English books, he also has one French-language bestseller to his credit: *La Quête de Saunière* (2008), co-authored with André Douzet. In 2004, he also wrote *De Da Vinci Code Ontcijferd*, a Dutch guide to *The Da Vinci Code*, which saw a reprint within three weeks of publication and was a top-ten bestseller in the Netherlands.

About the Author

Philip Coppens has also contributed to, or been acknowledged in, the following books:

- 📖 *Pre-Atlantis* (Dutch title), with Marcel Mestdagh (1994)
- 📖 *The Templar Revelation*, by Lynn Picknett & Clive Prince (1997)
- 📖 *The Stargate Conspiracy*, by Lynn Picknett & Clive Prince (1999)
- 📖 *Saunière's Model and the Secret of Rennes-le-Château*, by André Douzet (2001)
- 📖 *Egypt: Image of Heaven* (*Het Sterrenbeeld van Horus*, Dutch title), with Wim Zitman (2006; Dutch edition 2000)
- 📖 *The Dan Brown Companion*, by Simon Cox (2006)
- 📖 *Rosslyn Revealed*, by Alan Butler & John Ritchie (2006)
- 📖 *The Cygnus Mystery*, by Andrew Collins (2006)
- 📖 *An A to Z of King Arthur and the Holy Grail*, by Simon Cox & Mark Oxbrow (2007)
- 📖 *Darklore* (Volumes I, II & III), compiled and edited by Greg Taylor (2007–2009)
- 📖 *Unearthing Ancient America*, compiled and edited by Frank Joseph (2009)

Philip Coppens also devotes a lot of attention to essays and feature articles, which have appeared in magazines and anthologies on all continents. His articles have appeared in *Fortean Times*, *NEXUS*, *Hera*, *Fenix*, *Mysterien*, *New Dawn*, *Atlantis Rising*, *Ancient American*, and *Paranoia Magazine*, among other publications, and he has a large and dedicated following on the Internet. He holds the record as having most articles published in *NEXUS*, a magazine published in more than 10 languages, with newsstand distribution in Australia, Great Britain, the United States, Italy, France, and many other European countries, bringing to the world exciting new discoveries, such as the existence of pyramids in China and Bosnia; controversial articles on the state of modern archaeology and Egyptology; and also politics.

In 1995, together with Herman Hegge, he established *Frontier Magazine* (formerly *Frontier 2000*), a newsstand magazine in the Netherlands and Belgium. Since 1995, his Frontier Sciences Foundation has grown to incorporate, among others, Frontier Bookshop and Frontier Publishing, and has hosted the annual Frontier Symposium and Frontier Award. In 2008, he organized the Histories & Mysteries Conference in Edinburgh, which included the first-ever public display of the Mitchell-Hedges crystal skull.

Since 1995, he has lectured on the subject of the Ancient Alien Question in the United States, Great Britain, France, Australia, Belgium, and the Netherlands. He has been extensively interviewed for radio and television, and in 2009 he wrote and was principally featured in Reality Entertainment's *2012: Signs of the Times* (released in the United States via Warner Home), providing a unique perspective on the 2012 phenomenon. He is one of the key contributors and interviewees for The History Channel's most popular television series, *Ancient Aliens*, for the third season running.

All of these books, articles, and appearances have made him a household name in the field of alternative science, where he holds a unique position, as he is considered to be a believer by the skeptics, and a skeptic by the believers—a testament to his investigative knack.